An Ocean Without Shore

AN OCEAN WITHOUT SHORE
Ibn 'Arabî, The Book, and the Law

Michel Chodkiewicz
Translated from the French by David Streight

STATE UNIVERSITY OF NEW YORK PRESS

Production by Ruth Fisher
Marketing by Lynne Lekakis

Published by
State University of New York Press, Albany

For information, address State University of New York
Press, State University Plaza, Albany, NY 12246

Library of Congress Cataloging-in-Publication Data

Chodkiewicz, Michel.
     An ocean without shore : Ibn Arabi, the Book, and the Law / Michel
Chodkiewicz.
        p.   cm.
     Includes bibliographical references and index.
     ISBN 0–7914–1625–9 (alk. paper). — ISBN 0–7914–1626–7 (pbk. :
alk. paper)
     1. Ibn al-ʿArabî, 1165–1240—Views on the Koran. 2. Koran—
Criticism, interpretation, etc.—History.   I. Title.
BP80.12C49   1993
297'.1226'092—dc20   92–38413
                                                                                        CIP

10 9 8 7 6 5 4 3 2 1

To D. C.

Oh, my beloved! How many times I have called you without your
hearing Me!
How many times I have shown myself without your looking at Me!
How many times I have become perfume without your inhaling Me!
How many times I have become food without your tasting Me!
How is it that you do not smell Me in what you breathe?
How do you not see Me, not hear Me?
I am more delicious than anything delicious,
More desirable than anything desirable,
More perfect than anything perfect.
I am Beauty and Grace!
Love Me and love nothing else
Desire Me
Let Me be your sole concern to the exclusion of all concerns!

Ibn ʿArabî, *The Theophany of Perfection*

CONTENTS

PREFACE

I am indebted to Michel Valsân for my discovery of Ibn ʿArabî forty years ago, and it is under his guidance that I undertook my study. It is approprite that I begin this work by remembering him.

For their personal contributions to research on Ibn ʿArabî and for the assistance that several of them have been able to offer me in gaining access to difficult-to-obtain manuscripts or documents, I also extend my heartfelt gratitude to Claude Addas, Bakri Aladdin, Hamid Algar, William Chittick, Roger Deladrière, Denis Gril, Souad Hakîm, Riyâd al-Mâlih, Abdelbaki Meftah, James Morris, Mustafa Tahrali, and Osman Yahia.

Certain themes developed in the pages that follow were first outlined in a more concise manner in papers written as contributions to the following conferences: "Mystique, culture et société" (Groupe d'histoire comparée des religions, Paris-Sorbonne, 1983); "Modes de transmission de la culture religieuse en islam" (Department of Near Eastern Studies, Princeton, 1989); "The Legacy of Persian Mediaeval Sufism" (School of Oriental and African Studies, London, 1990); "L'héritage mystique d'Ibn ʿArabî" (Université d'Oran, 1990); "Congrès international pour le 750ᵉ anniversaire de la mort d'Ibn ʿArabî" (Murcia, 1990); "The Concept of Man in the Traditional Cultures of the Orient" (Institut de philosophie de l'Académie des sciences, Moscow, 1990). Without the invitations extended to me to participate in these meetings, I would have never decided to take up the pen. I am thus especially indebted to professors Michel Meslin, Avram Udovitch, H. T. Norris, L. Lewisohn, Alfonso Carmona Gonzalez, Mohammed Mahieddin, and Marietta Stepaniants.

My daughter Agnès Chodkiewicz was kind enough to decipher and transcribe the manuscript of this book. I am thus, once again, in her debt.

M. C.

TRANSCRIPTION OF ARABIC WORDS

In the interest of technical simplification and economy, emphatic consonants are written the same as the others. No distinction is made between the aspirate glottal *hâ'* and the aspirate pharyngial *ḥâ'*. The transliteration system used is thus as follows:

ء	'	ض	d
ب	b	ط	t
ت ث ة	t	ظ	z
ث	th	ع	'
ج	j	غ	gh
ح	h	ف	f
خ	kh	ق	q
د	d	ك	k
ذ	dh	ل	l
ر	r	م	m
ز	z	ن	n
س	s	ه	h
ش	sh	و	w
ص	s	ي	y

Vowels: a, â, i, î, u, û, ay, aw.
Articles: al- and l- (even when the article precedes a "sun letter").

LIST OF ABBREVIATIONS

EI   *Encyclopedia of Islam* (EI^1 = first edition; EI^2 = second edition).

Fus.   Ibn ʿArabî, *Fusûs al-hikam*, critical edition by A. A. Afîfî, Beirut, 1946.

Fut.   Ibn ʿArabî, *Al-futûhât al-makkiyya*, Bûlâq, 1329 A.H. (4 vols.). References to this edition are accompanied by references to the critical edition (in the process of being published) by Dr. Osman Yahia, marked by O.Y., and followed by the number of the volume and that of the page.

GAL   C. Brockelmann, *Geschichte der Arabischen Literatur,* Leyde, 1945–1949.

Rasâʾil   *Rasâʾil Ibnu l-Arabî*, Hyderabad, 1948.

RG   "Repertoire général des œuvres d'Ibn ʿArabî," established by O. Yahia in his *Histoire et Classification de l'oeuvre d'Ibn ʿArabî*, Damascus, 1964. RG is followed by a number corresponding to the number of the work in the order in which O. Yahia's classification considers it.

Taj.   *Kitâb al-tajalliyât*, ed. O. Yahia, published in the journal *Al-mashriq*, 1966–67. (This critical edition was published in one volume in Tehran in 1988.)

INTRODUCTION

The sixteenth-century Egyptian jurist Ibn Hajar al-Haytamî, an energetic defender of Ibn ʿArabî, was willing to excuse the latter's accusers to a certain extent. Ibn ʿArabî's writings are a "fatal poison" for most men, he said, "due to the subtlety of their meanings, the delicacy of their allusions, and the abstruseness of their structure."[1] He added that legitimate concern for protecting the faith of the ignorant leads certain doctors of the law to be guilty of excessive zeal, but that it nevertheless remains true that Ibn ʿArabî cannot be placed in the hands of just anyone.

In any case, more recent witnesses have shown that the work of the Shaykh al-Akbar does not easily surrender its secrets. A few years before World War II, Nicholson suggested that one of his Egyptian students read Ibn ʿArabî's works. The student, Abû l-Alâ ʿAfîfî—author, among other works, of *The Mystical Philosophy of Muhyid Din Ibnul ʿArabi*[2]—confessed later[3] that after several readings of the *Fusûs* and Qâshânî's commentary on it he had still not understood the text. Each word was clear in itself, but the meaning of most of the sentences had escaped him. He confessed to Nicholson: "Never before have I experienced such difficulty understanding an Arabic text."

The first orientalists to take an interest in the Shaykh al-Akbar appear to have been equally perplexed. Clément Huart does not conceal the trouble that Ibn ʿArabî's *fantaisie désordonnée*[4] caused him. Arberry deplored the "confusion" of Ibn ʿArabî's "mental outlook" and "his inconsistent technical vocabulary."[5] Rom Landau declared that "his ambiguities and contradictions may drive us wellnigh to despair," and he warns whoever might wish to study his works that only the deepest admiration could encourage one "to wrangle with the innumerable difficulties that Ibn ʿArabî found it necessary to create."[6]

The complexity of a doctrine that, in a dizzying synthesis, embraces all the domains of the traditional sciences, from jurispru-

dence to metaphysics, in wording that is often paradoxical or enigmatic, together with the immensity of a work that comprises tens of
thousands of pages, could certainly discourage the spread of Ibn
ʿArabî's teachings. But this massive corpus is not only reputed to be
obscure; in Islam it has also been regularly denounced as heretical
for more than seven centuries, and these polemics continue at present with the same vigor as they did in Ibn Taymiyya's time. Even
the sufi masters themselves frequently advise caution. Novices are
still discouraged from reading the *Fusûs* and the *Futûhât* for reasons that Ibn Hajar's remarks might have suggested. All the conditions appear to be present for limiting knowledge of Ibn ʿArabî's
ideas to a small number of scholars who are intimidated by neither
the difficulty of the work nor the condemnations of the jurists
(*fuqahâ*, sing. *faqîh*). Such is not the case, however.

Numerous researchers have pointed out the *extent* of Ibn
ʿArabî's influence in geographical space, from the Maghreb to the
Far East. But it is even more important to measure and to understand the *depth* of this influence: Ibn ʿArabî's mark was not left only
on "intellectual" sufism. It is also detected in a universe of brotherhoods that touched the most diverse social classes and levels of culture. The "knowers" (or the "gnostics": *al-ʿârifûn*) for whom Ibn
Hajar reserved the reading of Ibn ʿArabî are not always found
among the licensed holders of learning. Conversely, the "unknow-
ing" for whom the *Fusûs* or *Futûhât* would be a "mortal poison,"
were often found among the ranks of the clergy.

In the work that he dedicated to the Moroccan sufi Al-Yûsî (d.
1961),[7] in which he emphasizes the considerable debt that Al-Yûsî
owes Ibn ʿArabî,[8] J. Berque pays particular attention in this regard
to the fusion in seventeenth-century Morocco of "two currents of
popular hagiology and learned speculation": "The mysticism of the
time," he writes, "combines the most learned tradition from
Andalusia or the East with a rural thrust."[9] These remarks are
valid not only for Al-Yûsî and the Moroccans of his age; the exten-
sive circulation of fundamental ideas originating in the works of
the Shaykh al-Akbar shows that they are much more widely
spread. An exhaustive study of the ways and means of this diffusion would require several on-site inquiries and an analysis of
innumerable texts from a variety of linguistic domains. Using a
much more modest documentary base, however, it appears possible

to illustrate certain aspects of this phenomenon and to offer suggestions to those who may wish to uncover the often discrete signs of the extent of Ibn ʿArabî's influence, as well as to shed light on the way that his influence was diffused. According to the evidence, the problem is of concern not only to specialists in Ibn ʿArabî: beyond whatever considerations are of interest to the history of ideas, the question raised is also that of the distance that separates "refined" from "popular" sufism.

Researchers whose works concentrate on the Shaykh al-Akbar and his intellectual posterity have, quite naturally, paid special attention to the study of the "noble" literature: that of Qûnawî, Jîlî, Qâshânî, Jâmî, and others. Such study is not to be taken lightly, for the reasons we have mentioned: the geographical dispersion of the manuscripts of these authors and the number, date, and place of the editions of their works published are important indications of the posibilities of access to Ibn ʿArabî's doctrine at a certain time in a certain place. But it is equally essential to take into consideration more modest authors of purely local reputation or even anonymous writings or those of authors difficult to identify.

One precaution is raised at the very outset: the absence of explicit reference to Ibn ʿArabî, or even the presence of a negative reference, is not a priori significant. To illustrate the first of these two points, I will cite for the moment but one clear example. In the *tarîqa ʿalawiyya* (the branch of the Shâdhiliyya-Darqawiyya founded by Shaykh Ahmad b. ʿAliwâ from Mostaganem, d. 1934), the writings of the founder are, as much today as yesterday, read and commentated on by the *fuqarâ*, the disciples, many of whom are Algerian workers living in Europe. Among these writings is a partial commentary on the Qurʾân entitled *Al-bahr al-masjûr fî tafsîr al-qurʾân bi mahd al-nûr.* This *tafsîr*, after circulating in the form of handwritten copies, was finally printed in Mostaganem. In it, the shaykh comments most notably on verses 5–7 of sura *Al-baqara.* Initially, he commentates on it in a traditional manner in a five-part expose. He then adds what he calls an *"ishâra,"*[10] (allusion) wherein he develops an interpretation that Ibn Taymiyya, among others, had denounced in Ibn ʿArabî as an unprecedented blasphemy. Shaykh b. ʿAliwâ directly and almost literally borrows this interpretation from chapter 5 of the *Futûhât,*[11] which we will address below. Shaykh Ahmad b. Aliwâ fails to mention Ibn ʿArabî,

although he does cite other authors by name in his *tafsîr*. It might
be supposed that this silence is explained by the violence of the
polemics presented by representatives of the *islâhî* movement and
in particular by Shaykh Ben Bâdîs. Adding a reference to the
Shaykh al-Akbar in a text that was scandalous in its own right
might have presented a useless provocation. For whatever reason,
this *tafsîr*, as is the case with the majority of Shaykh b. ʿAliwâ's
works, contains a number of other uses of ideas characteristic of
Ibn ʿArabî but that are not cited as such.

If, whether deliberately or not, themes of Ibn ʿArabî's doctrine
can be presented with no mention of their source—we will see other
examples of this—then a text (or a speaker's remarks) that
denounces Ibn ʿArabî may also contain ideas and wordings that
may be recognized as specifically his. This ambiguity, whether it is
dictated by reasons of spiritual opportunity or political prudence, in
fact reflects a widespread and quite old attitude. If we can trust an
anecdote apparently related by Fîrûzabâdî,[12] the famous Shafiʿite
jurist ʿIzz al-dîn b. ʿAbd al-Salâm remained silent when Ibn ʿArabî
was claimed to be a *zindîq* in his presence. *Zindîq* is a term that initially referred to the Manicheans, but heresiologists liberally
applied it to all those who were suspected of being free thinkers or
atheists. That same evening, when asked by a disciple who had witnessed the scene, ʿIzz al-dîn b. ʿAbd al-Salâm replied that Ibn
ʿArabî was the Pole (*qutb*) of his time, that is, the head of the hierarchy of saints.

In certain brotherhoods (*turuq*, sing. *tarîqa*), most notably the
Khalwatiyya and its different branches, the Shaykh al-Akbar's
influence is admitted. In many others it is frequently the case of
mashâykh who have reservations about Ibn ʿArabî or have criticized his positions or forbidden their disciples to read his works.
These may be simple oratorical precautions for the purpose of elud-
ing the *fuqahâ*'s censure. Most commonly, however, these warnings
or proscriptions stem from a concern for avoiding the circulation of
ideas that, though intrinsically true, might be misunderstood by
disciples with inadequate spiritual qualifications, the orthodoxy of
whose faith might thus be in jeopardy. It would seem as though this
is the way that Zarrûq's position (in his *Qawâ'id al-tasawwuf*[13]), as
well as that of other masters of the Shâdhiliyya, should be understood. This same care leads Shaʿrânî to recommend that an aspi-

rant (*murîd*) know how to interpret the discreet sign that his shaykh gives him as a signal to immediately curtail his reading aloud when the uninstructed are present:[14] a simple reminder, under the circumstances, of a quite generally applied rule, as can be seen as easily by reading old texts as by observing *shuyûkh* today. In a passage from the *Rashahât 'ayn al-hayât*, one of the fundamental works on the history of the Naqshbandiyya up to the sixteenth century, the author recounts that Shaykh 'Ubaydallâh Ahrâr was in the process of commentating on the *Fusûs* when some visitors arrived. The shaykh immediately became silent and hid the book. Nevertheless, this same 'Ubaydallâh Ahrâr often cited Ibn 'Arabî, and, at the time of his famous encounter with Jâmî in Tashkent in 1469, he explained a point of doctrine that the latter had been unable to understand in the *Futûhât Makkiyya*.[15] Reservations or criticisms aimed at Ibn 'Arabî from the pens of Naqshbandi authors of different times are actually accompanied, as Friedmann has clearly demonstrated in the case of Ahmad Sirhindî, by extreme dependence on his teaching. The works of R. S. O'Fahey similarly underscore, in another great reformist sufi figure (Ahmad b. Idrîs, whose disciples founded the Sanûsiyya *tarîqa* and the Khatmiyya *tarîqa*), a fidelity to the Shaykh al-Akbar's doctrine that exposed him to vigorous Wahhâbî attacks.[16]

There is a practical consequence of the above: to discern an influence, be it unconscious, voluntarily masked, or even vigorously denied, in well-known or even obscure texts, a knowledge of Ibn 'Arabî's ideas is not sufficient. Knowledge must be combined with a thorough familiarity with his vocabulary, with the peculiarities of his style, with certain characteristic wordings whose importance can be attested to by their frequency in his writings. This familiarity with technical terms (*istilâhât*), rhetorical procedures, or motifs recurrent in the Shaykh al-Akbar's work is, moreover, indispensable if one is to differentiate, in the writings of any author, between that which stems from the common patrimony of the sufis and that which constitutes the individual contribution of Ibn 'Arabî. The latter's strong individuality should not allow us to forget, as a matter of fact, that he, too, is the inheritor and the transmitter of a rich tradition. Some similarities with his thought can consequently be explained by direct recourse to Ibn 'Arabî's own sources. But the presence in a written work of certain technical terms—*nafas rah-*

mânî, al-fayd al-aqdas, al-fayd al-muqaddas, khatm al-awliyâ, tajdîd al-khalq, and so on—is usually a clear sign: even if certain of these expressions occasionally crop up in texts previous to Ibn ʿArabî's time, it is Ibn ʿArabî's work that gave them a precise usage and granted them "citizenship" in the language of sufism. By way of example on this point, I refer the reader to what I have dealt with elsewhere on the subject of the doctrine of sainthood and, in particularly, the idea of the Seal of Sainthood (*khatm al-walâya*)—which, as is known, appeared in Hakîm Tirmidhî in the third century A.H. but for which Ibn ʿArabî was to furnish a doctrinal elaboration that would become a fundamental element of later hagiology.[17]

A deeper knowledge of the forms of Ibn ʿArabî's discourse— and not only its content—allows the reader to perceive quite revealing "echo effects," which might otherwise go unnoticed. In an unpublished poem by an eminent present-day Algerian shaykh there is a verse which goes like this: *Wa sabʾ al-mathânî haqîqatu amrî.* This immediately reminds any of Ibn ʿArabî's readers of a verse that appears in the beginning of the *Futûhât*[18] and is seen repeated on a number of occasions in other writings: *Anâ l-qurʾân wa l-sabʾ al-mathânî.* That this is a deliberate allusion can hardly be doubted; and it is thus not surprising to find out that the author of this poem and his son have long studied the work of Ibn ʿArabî and even had in their hands, during a trip to Syria, the autograph manuscript of one of his treatises considered as lost.

We have emphasized the necessity of meticulously examining what might be called "second-level literature" in order to verify the Shaykh al-Akbar's influence beyond circles of the literate and to identify their links. We refer here especially to elementary manuals composed for the use of novices, but also regional chronicles (many of which are unpublished), collections of *qasâʾid* (poems) used in the brotherhoods, the *mawâlid* (eulogies) composed in honor of local saints, *ijâza* (licenses of initiatory transmission) and *silsila* (chains of transmission) of obscure shaykhs whose fame never passed beyond the confines of their village or tribe. The spread of these texts—which are often nothing more than short brochures hastily printed and sold at low prices—explains a number of things.

Ibn ʿArabî's influence is quite noticeable, for example, in a widely distributed work in the Tijâniyya, the *Mîzâb al-rahma al-rabbâniyya fî l-tarbiyya bi l-tarîqa al-tijâniyya* of Shaykh ʿUbayda

b. Muhammad al-Saghîr al-Shinqîtî (d. 1284 A.H.). It is even more evident in a compendium of rules of the Rahmâniyya (which was undoubtedly the most popular brotherhood in Algeria) published in Tunis (1351 A.H.) by order of Muhammad b. Belkacem, the shaykh of the *zâwiya* (lodge) of Bû Sa'âda: here Ibn 'Arabî is expressly cited and defended against his adversaries. Equally clear is the *Wasiya kubrâ*, written by 'Abd al-Salam a -Asmar al-Fîtûrî (the founder of a Libyan branch of the 'Arûsiyya, which itself was a branch of the Shâdhiliyya) and published in Beirut in 1958, in which the author states (p. 60): "It is incumbent on you, my brothers, to love and venerate Muhyî l-dîn Ibn al-'Arabî" (*Ikhwânî, wa 'alaykum bi-mahabbati Muhyî l-dîn b. al-'Arabî wa ta'zîmihî*). Another case worthy of note is furnished by a thin brochure first published in Aleppo in 1351 A.H. and which is today in circulation in Syria. It is entitled *Risâlat al-sulûk al-khâdima li-jamî'i l-turuq*. This is a quite cursory treatise on the stages of the Path (of which the text outlines seven) as well as particular forms of invocation (*dhikr*) and the subtle centers (*latâ'if*) that successively correspond to them in the constitution of the human being. The authors make a point of stating that they have drawn the rules outlined in this text "from the works of the Shaykh al-Akbar" (*min mu'allafât al-Shaykh al-Akbar*). In fact, one of the two authors is Muhammad Rajab al-Tâ'î, who presents himself as a descendent of Ibn 'Arabî. All writings of this sort, it must be pointed out, stress the practice of the Path and its degrees, rather than doctrinal principles. The key words to look for are thus those that, in Ibn 'Arabî's lexicon, refer to the "initiatory voyage" (*sulûk*) and to sainthood (*walâya*), rather than those that are characteristic of his metaphysical teaching. A systematic examination of these manuals shows that the few cases mentioned above are in no way exceptional; no researcher would have difficulty discovering numerous other examples.

But a number of other kinds of writings whose role, although to a lesser degree, is considerable are also to be taken into consideration. Such is the case of the *tabaqât*, of other chronicles composed by erudite regional writers. For example, it is interesting to highlight the references clearly identifiable as being from Ibn 'Arabî in a work well known to Moroccan historians, the *Salwat al-anfâs fî man uqbira min al-'ulamâ' wa l-sulahâ' bi-Fâs* by Muhammad b. Ja'far b. Idrîs al-Kattânî (1857–1927). Both René Basset and Levi-

Provençal, among others, have used this work, which is so rich in details on the topography of Fez. But what particularly attracts our attention in the *Salwat al-anfâs* is that its author, to define the spiritual status of the *awliyâ* to whom he dedicates a section, uses Ibn ʿArabî's terminology: such and such a saint is "a Mosaic type" (*mûsawî l-maqâm*), another is "a Christic type" (*ʿîsawî l-maqâm*). The quite characteristic idea of Seal of the Saints (*khatm al-awliyâ*) is mentioned a number of times.[19] What is to be considered, under the circumstances, is less the fact—not very surprising, as shall be seen—that al-Kattânî is clearly familiar with Ibn ʿArabî's hagiology than the role of transmission that a work like this can play for readers who surely do not all have either the desire or the possibility of gaining access to the *Futûhât Makkiyya*. Through an unconscious phenomenon of impregnation, the technical vocabulary of a difficult and rather suspect author becomes, thanks to works of this genre—and they are numerous—, the *lingua franca* in which saints and sainthood are discussed.

If it is not aimed only at an intellectual elite—and they are not the only ones who read it—the *Salwat al-anfâs* evidently is not "popular" literature, either. Quite different is the case of a book belonging to a famous genre whose public has always been quite large, that of compilations of the "virtues" (*khasâ'is*) of certain suras of the Qur'ân, part of the domain that might be called "daily theurgy." We are referring in particular to the *Naʿt al-bidâyât wa tawsîf al-nihâyât*, edited a number of times (from Fez to Cairo) and quite widely known both in the Maghreb and in the Middle East. Other, analogous texts deserve the same remarks; we highlight this one only because of the personality of its author and because it was composed in modern times, thus attesting to the persistence of the diffusion of the Shaykh al-Akbar's ideas. The *Naʿt al-bidâyât* is the work of the famous Mâ' al-ʿAynayn, a highly colorful figure upon whom French colonial propaganda (wrongly) laid the blame for Xavier Coppolani's assassination.[20] In the writings of this Mauritanian "marabout"—and the same might have been true in his oral teachings—explicit references to Ibn ʿArabî and some members of his school (e.g., ʿAbd al-Razzâq Qâshânî, ʿAbd al-Wahhâb Shaʿrânî, and Ismâʿîl Haqqî[21]) abounded. What appears on first glance to be nothing more than a pious collection of recipes reveals itself, under examination, to be solidly nourished in the exegetical tradition at the roots of which Ibn ʿArabî is found. The *Naʿt al-bidâyât* gives a poor, but not at all unfaithful, version of this rich tradition.

To this same kind of popular literature belong works like the famous *Shams al-maʿârif*, written by Bûnî (who mentions Ibn ʿArabî in his chains of transmission), or the *Khazînat al-asrâr* of Muhammad al-Nâzilî (d. 1884), who frequently cites Ibn ʿArabî and reproduces a long section of his *Risâlat al-anwâr* (and not of his *Tadbîrât ilâhiyya*, as announced in the title of the chapter). Found throughout the Arab world, the *Khazînatal-asrâr* is also well known elsewhere, for example, in Indonesia, where it was recently reedited. But certain commentaries on the Qurʾân have contributed more directly to Ibn ʿArabî's fame and to the circulation of his ideas. Such is the case for Ismâʿîl Haqqî's *Rûh al-bayân*, where quotes from Ibn ʿArabî are extremely numerous. This *tafsîr* is quite widely found: a complete collection of its ten volumes was seen in a Meccan bookstore in the mid-seventies: the viligence of Wahhâbî censors was obviously lacking.

Without hesitation the same function of "link" can be assigned to one of the most widely distributed texts of the *tarîqa* Tijâniyya. We refer to ʿAlî Harâzim's *Jawâhir al-maʿânî*, the reading of which is practically *de rigueur* for all members of this brotherhood, although the text has also found a wide audience outside. Our copy of the *Jawâhir* is filled with marks indicating the countless passages where mentions of Ibn ʿArabî[22] or allusions to one theme or another from his works can be detected. In addition to the numerous (stated or not, but always recognizable) borrowings from the Shaykh al-Akbar's hagiology,[23] Ahmad Tijânî, in remarks or letters meticulously recorded by ʿAlî Harâzim, incorporates into his teaching a number of other traits of Ibn ʿArabî's doctrine, and he does so with the same terms that Ibn ʿArabî uses, such as *nafas rahmânî*,[24] the idea of the five *hadarât* "presences,"[25] *haqîqa muhammadiyya*, "Muhammadan reality,"[26] and the universality of divine mercy, which embraces even the damned.[27] It is also from Ibn ʿArabî, more specifically from chapter 8 of the *Futûhât*, that what Tijânî calls *"ard al-samsama"* comes, a symbolic name for the "imaginal world" (*âlam al-khayâl*).[28]

What is even more interesting is that after ʿAlî Harâzim, or rather after Ahmad Tijânî himself, practically all the authors of the

Tijâniyya drew from the Akbarian source and contributed to the dissemination of what they collected there. Such was the case notably for Muhammad al-Shinqîtî, in his *Bughyat al-mustafîd*,[29] and for Al-Hâjj ʿUmar, in his *Kitâb al-rimah*,[30] where repeated references to the Shaykh al-Akbar, and especially, once again, systematic usage of his doctrine of sainthood can be found.[31]

One name that comes up often in these last two works, that of Shaʿrânî (d. 1565), leads us to an important detail here. The numerous writings—in general quite recent and in any case still in circulation today—that we have chosen to point out as possible transmitters of Ibn ʿArabî's influence do, to a certain extent, constitute a kind of popularization. But on the other hand they can be suspected of being tributaries of previous popularizations. In other words, the citations, paraphrases, or summaries of Ibn ʿArabî that are identified in them do not necessarily prove that their authors have read the Shaykh al-Akbar's works. Muhammad al-Shinqîtî claims to have had the *ʿAnqâ mughrib* in his hands, but he also maintains that he did not understand much of it. Clearly his borrowings from Ibn ʿArabî have passed through a more accessible intermediary, whom he also cites: Shaʿrânî's *Al Yawâqît wa l-jawâhir*, a book presented as a "commentary" on the *Futûhât Makkiyya* but that is more of a convenient summary. All kinds of questions, the organization of which conforms roughly to the headings of a traditional "profession of faith" (*aqîda*), have responses drawn from the *Futûhât*, including the number of the chapter of their origin.[32] There are several successive editions of the *Yawâqît*, and developments in Arabic printing have obviously contributed to their diffusion. However, their popularity predates this. We know, via both Shaʿrânî himself and his biographer Malîjî, that copies of his works went out in all directions into the Muslim world, from North Africa to India, as soon as they were completed; catalogues of manuscripts confirm this dispersion.[33]

Al-Hâjj ʿUmar certainly relies often on Shaʿrânî, although he undoubtedly had direct knowledge of the *Futûhât* also. On the other hand, such is probably not the case for another author from Sub-Saharan Africa, the Senegalese Ibrâhîm Nyass (d. 1975), who founded his own brotherhood and then created the African Islamic Union, and whose debt to Ibn ʿArabî Mervyn Hiskett has pointed out.[34] A dissident from the Tijâniyya, Ibrâhîm Nyass surely could have found numerous elements originating from the Shaykh al-Akbar in the masters of this *tarîqa*. But we are led to believe that his eschatological concepts are indebted to the *Yawâqît*, rather than to diligent study of Ibn ʿArabî's works. We have the same suspicion regarding the Sudanese "Mahdî" Muhammad b. ʿAbdallâh. As is known, he had belonged to the Sammâniyya *tarîqa*, whose founder was a disciple of Shaykh Mustafâ Kamal al-dîn al-Bakrî, one of Nâbulusî's students. Shaykh al-Bakrî's writings give evidence, which under the circumstances is not at all surprising, of strong influence on the part of Ibn ʿArabî. This influence is especially marked in all branches of the Khalwatiyya *tarîqa*, to which al-Bakrî belongs: ʿAlî Qarabash, who figures in his "chain of transmission," authored a commentary on the *Fusûs*. It stands to reason that the Mahdî acquired some familiarity with ideas originating in Ibn ʿArabî through this chain. Is that enough to explain the passages in the *Manshûrât*[35] that cite the Shaykh al-Akbar? Nicole Grandin has pointed out that the Mahdists of today mention Ibn ʿArabî's *ʿAnqâ mughrib* as the main source of the Mahdî's doctrine.[36] Chapter 366 of the *Futûhât*, which deals with the "ministers of the Mahdî" (*wuzarâ al-mahdî*), has perhaps also been a contributing factor. But is this a case of direct borrowing from these sources or rather of a judicious use of the anthology *ad usum populi* offered by Shaʿrânî in his *yawâqît* or in one of his other books? In any case, the hypothesis that the Mahdî had access to Ibn ʿArabî's great Qurʾânic commentary is to be excluded: the mentions of this *tafsîr* in the *Manshûrât* come not from one of Ibn ʿArabî's works but rather from a single passage in Qâshânî's commentary (which copyists and editors have long been obstinate in attributing to the Shaykh al-Akbar).[37]

Shaʿrânî is of course not the only one of the first-degree popularizers from whom later authors have drawn their information; we have mentioned Nâbulusî. Although the latter, whose voluminous work has finally begun to be studied,[38] is in fact much more original than he has been credited with being, part of his writings assuredly constitutes a simplified presentation of Ibn ʿArabî's theses. Such is the case for, among others, a small work edited in Damascus in 1969 under the title *Idâh al-maqsûd min wahdat al-wujûd* (Clarification on What Is Understood by the Unicity of Being). It is this treatise and others like it, rather than original texts by the Shaykh al-Akbar, that supply the material for many later formulations. But numerous authors less eminent than Nâbulusî have themselves also been influential mediators. Among representative examples of this literature might be mentioned that of Muhammad b. Fadlallâh al-Burhânpûrî's (d. 1620) *Tuhfa al-mursala ilâ l-nabî*, which attempts to systematically outline Ibn 'Arabî's metaphysics, cosmology, and anthropology in a few pages.[39] This writing by a Gujarati shaykh, which is in some ways to Ibn 'Arabî's doctrine what Sanûsî's *'Aqîda sughra* is to the Ash'arite *kalâm*, was quickly translated into Persian and Turkish, and it gave rise to numerous commentaries (one of which was by Nâbulusî himself) in the Ottoman Empire. It was read by the Emir 'Abd al-Qâdir's entourage, in Damascus, as well as by that of Shaykh 'Abd al-Rahmân 'Illaysh in Cairo.[40] It is still in circulation in India and in Indonesia and also in Turkey and in Arab countries. This "Akbarian breviary" is far from being the only one of its kind.

Closer to home, we should mention Yûsuf al-Nabhânî (d. 1931) among the influential popularizers; his books have been and still are widely read in milieux hostile to the *Salafiyya* and to the Wahhâbîs. The introduction to his famous *Jâmi' karamât al-awliyâ* is nothing more than a summary of chapter 73 of the *Futûhât*, and all his works make abundant references to Ibn 'Arabî, whose defense he offers against the accusations of Ibn Taymiyya and his partisans.[41] Even in present day Damascus a Syrian shaykh, Mahmûd Ghurâb, has begun publication of a series of books, each of which is, on a specific theme (*Al-insân al-kâmil*, *Al-khayâl*, *Al-hubb al-ilâhî*, etc.), a montage of quotations from Ibn 'Arabî—a procedure that reminds one of that used by Sha'rânî—thus quickly allowing the reader to get an idea of the Shaykh al-Akbar's position on the subjects treated.[42] It would not be surprising to have this collection of briefly commentated extracts itself spawn a second-degree popularization.

Even if no mention is made of texts that attempt deliberate and methodical explanations of Ibn 'Arabî's thought, a number of other texts—particularly those coming out of the hagiographical genre—have been and continue to be effective vehicles of this thought. There is hardly a *zâwiya* library in the Arabic speaking world where the famous *Kitâb al-Ibrîz* is not found in either handwritten or printed form.[43] Its author, Ahmad b. al-Mubârak, was the disciple and successor to a great saint from Fez, ʿAbd al-ʿAzîz al-Dabbâgh (d. 1717), whose life and sayings the work recounts. Although al-Dabbâgh may have been *ummî* (unlettered), Ibn Mubârak was himself both educated and a diligent reader of Ibn ʿArabî; implicitly or explicitly, Ibn ʿArabî's ideas are frequently the theme of the two men's discussions. Rather than the *mûrid*, whose knowledge is still all from books, it is the *ummî* master, the inspired visionary, who solves the puzzles of the *Futûhât*. The famous *Kitâb al-Ibrîz*, centered on a charismatic figure whose short life was characterized by marvels, is evidently less intimidating than the works of Ibn ʿArabî or his followers; it is in fact a quite probable source of oral and written diffusion of the Shaykh al-Akbar's doctrine. It is interesting to note in passing that the most recent edition (1984) is preceded by prefaces signed by Syrian religious authorities, providing testimony to the importance of this book and at the same time bolstering its influence.

Besides the hagiographical literature of which, from our point of view, the *Kitâb al-Ibrîz* is a remarkable, though not unique, specimen, mention should also be made of some more austere, yet ubiquitous, writings in *turuq* libraries. A good example is that of the works of Ibn Ajîba (d. 1809), a Shâdhilî-Derqawî author whose audience greatly surpasses that of the members of his *tarîqa*. Like others, he does not propose to systematically explain Ibn ʿArabî's doctrine, but it does underlie his thought, and it clearly influences all that he says about Essence and the Divine Names and their theophanies; and it is reflected in Ibn Ajîba's definitions of the technical terms used in sufism.[44]

Our mention of the *zâwiya* libraries leads us to emphasize the importance, in a study like the present one, of collecting information available on their content. In Algeria, the officers of Internal Affairs had their interpreters compile catalogues early on; thus we have been able to verify the presence there of diverse works by Ibn ʿArabî and many of the works of his glossarists and popularizers. Studies carried out in Damascus and Cairo confirm that this situation is the rule rather than the exception. The presence of these titles in a *zâwiya* certainly does not mean that they are read, less so that they read by all. It does however furnish at least a presumption of interest on the part of successive *shuyûkh* and the

most studious of their disciples, and it does supply information
about the accessibility of materials that might be incorporated into
the oral teaching or literary production of masters.

We will not deal at length with the role—long perceived by
certain researchers—of poems (*qasâ'id*) in the transmission of Ibn
'Arabî's heritage. Easy to memorize even by the unlettered, poems
also have the advantage of giving acceptable expression—since it
can be imputed to poetic license—to ideas that might appear suspect or even blasphemous if presented in discursive form. The verse
of a modern shaykh, cited above, is an example of these audacious
proscriptions on prose. Others are found in the *dîwân* written by
the Moroccan shaykh Al-Harrâq (d. 1845), who was, like Ibn 'Ajîba,
one of the disciples of Shaykh Al-'Arabî al-Darqawî.[45] The poems of
the Egyptian sufis of the seventh century (A.H.), studied by 'Alî Sâfî
Husayn,[46] also offer abundant examples. Annemarie Schimmel, in
several of her works, has well demonstrated the considerable influence of Ibn 'Arabî and his school on mystical poetry in Turkish, Persian, and Urdu.[47] Most, if not all, of these works continue to be
heard in meetings of *turuq*, even those *turuq* in which the use of
theoretical works inspired by Ibn 'Arabî is unlikely, if not completely improbable, due to either lack of the necessary intellectual
qualifications or opposition raised to the Shaykh al-Akbar's think-
ing. A recent anecdote illustrates this point. We are indebted to a
Moroccan researcher, M. Fawzi Skali, for the transcription of
recorded conversations he had during the summer of 1986 with a
number of notable religious figures in the context of an inquiry into
the "spiritual geography" of Fez. Among those interviewed was a
former professor at the Qarawiyyîn. Asked about sufism, he claims
to be quite hostile to "sufi extremists" (*ghulât*), a category that
includes Hallâj, Ibn 'Arabî, Ibn Sab'în, and Muhammad al-Kattânî,
the author of the abovementioned *Salwat al-anfâs*. But at the same
time he affirms his enjoyment of the poems of Ibn al-Farîd,
Shushtarî, or Al-Harrâq, which are recited in sufi meetings: "They
have such subtle, such spiritual meanings!"[48] The coincidence in
the same individual of these two logically contradictory attitudes is
a fact that can often be observed in Muslims who, touched by
reformist currents, present themselves as hostile to sufism, or at
least as partisans of a "moderate" sufism from which Ibn 'Arabî is
obviously excluded.

If the phenomena of transmission via the written word, in prose or in verse, are those which are most easily observable, they are not necessarily the most important. These are perhaps explained by other, less easily detected, phenomena which by virtue of their subtlety have heretofore gone unnoticed. We are referring here to another historical continuity, that of the Shaykh al-Akbar's initiatory chain of transmission (*silsila akbariyya*), uninterrupted up to the present day. Despite certain easily explained confusions, there has never been, properly speaking, a *tariqa akbariyya* in the sense of a formally constituted "brotherhood."[49] But the *khirqa akbariyya* or *hâtimiyya*—in other words, the *baraka*, Ibn ʿArabî's "spiritual flow"—has never ceased to be regularly transmitted and still is today. This ritual investiture of the *khirqa akbariyya* has been received throughout the ages in different manners by individuals belonging to the most diverse *turuq*. Because it was generally quite discreet and always hidden by the much more visible affiliation of the individuals concerned to one or several of the traditional brotherhoods, this initiatory attachment to the Shaykh al-Akbar has often gone unnoticed. A more careful examination shows that it usually has as its effect (besides the eventual appearance of the *nisba* "*al-akbarî*" attached to the name of one shaykh or another) a more particular emphasis on the part of these individuals and their followers on the precepts that define what might be called a "*tarîq akbarî*," a "path," a "method" (and not a *tarîqa* in the sense that this word has today), inspired by the teaching of the Andalusian Master. A meticulous investigation of multiple *silsila* gives evidence of the fact that a number of those who have played major roles in the diffusion of the Shaykh al-Akbar's heritage had received the *khirqa akbariyya*: and we have good reason to believe that on a more modest scale many other lesser-known individuals appearing in these *silsila* also have been effective agents of its maintenance and influence. Numerous though the indirect inheritors of Ibn ʿArabî's legacy may be, it is the direct inheritors who, properly speaking, should be considered as those for whom the heritage was legitimately destined. As for the known figures, we find in these chains of transmission of the *khirqa akbariyya*, for example, names like Suyûtî, Shaʿrânî, Ibn Hajar al-Haytamî, Zakariyya al-Ansârî, Qushshâshî,[50] or, at the end of the Ottoman dynasty, Shaykh Ahmad Gümushkhanevi. The literary relationship with Ibn ʿArabî is thus doubled when there is a case of a spiritual filiation, which should be taken into account in any attempt to interpret the intellectual activities of these authors.

In a work published a few years ago,[51] we were interested in another case that deserves to be mentioned in more than one regard: that of Emir ʿAbd al-Qâdir al-Jazâʾirî, who had the first edition of the *Futûhât Makkiyya* printed at his own expense and under his watchful eye. In his *Kitâb al-mawâqif*, he shows himself to be a profound and subtle commentator on Ibn ʿArabî: this interest in the Shaykh al-Akbar, which appears to have blossomed somewhat late in his life in Damascus, is more easily explained when it is known that in his youth he received the *khirqa akbariyya* from his father, who had received it from his own father, who in turn had had it transmitted by Murtadâ al-Zabîdî (d. 1791). Notice in passing the amazing circuit that sees Ibn ʿArabî's spiritual heritage travel from Murcia, where he was born, to India, where Murtadâ al-Zabîdî was born, to have it carried back to the Maghreb and, finally, to Damascus where the Shaykh al-Akbar and the emir both lived their final days.[52] Such detours do occur: we personally know an *akbarî* born in the Middle East who was joined to Ibn ʿArabî's *silsila* by an Egyptian shaykh; the latter had been initiated by a Syrian who, in turn, had been initiated by a North African. Let us cite one last example of these discreet wanderings, which make intelligible the emergence of Akbarian data in an apparently banal text. In the research done in Fez in 1986 to which we referred above, Shaykh al-Mahdî al-Saqallî (who claims to own nearly sixty of Ibn ʿArabî's works) explained that he had been attached to the "Hâtimiyya," that is, to Ibn ʿArabî's initiatory line, via three different paths and, in particular, by Sîdî ʿAbd al-Hayy al-Kattânî: here we encounter that famous family of *shurfâ* (descendents of the Prophet) to which the author of the *Salwât al-anfâs* also belonged, the latter himself having received the *khirqa akbariyya*, as had many of his relatives. Without being able to expand on it here, we will add only that a number of signs suggest that the end of the nineteenth century saw the beginning of an "Akbarian renaissance" marked by both an increase in attachments to the *silsila akbariyya* and particularly intense intellectual activity regarding Ibn ʿArabî's works.[53] The Wahhâbîs were not mistaken. In the abundant polemic production published in recent years, they have, more hysterically than ever, presented the Shaykh al-Akbar as the *Doctor communis* of sufism whose "bacilli of infidelity" (*jarâthim al-kufr*) have been spread (via disciples, avowed or clandestine) among the *umma*.[54]

At the end of this brief overview, it might be asked why a work as difficult and controversial as that of the Shaykh al-Akbar, more than others that represent the "wisdom tradition" of sufism, has directly or indirectly exercised such considerable influence. Obviously no one can claim to have a historically provable global response to a question of this type. Certainly there are precise factors that help answer the question; for example, the patronage that the Ottoman dynasty accorded the Shaykh al-Akbar. Ibn ʿArabî is said to have predicted (in a sibylline text that he surely did not author, *Al-shajara al-nuʿmaniyya fî l-dawla al-ʿUthmâniyya*[55]) the coming of the Ottomans and, more specifically, their conquest of Syria. The prediction brought him particular veneration by numerous sovereigns and a status that undoubtedly considerably limited the effect of attacks against his doctrine. This Ottoman patronage dates from quite early—it was Sultan Salîm I who, upon his entrance into Damascus, had Ibn ʿArabî's mausoleum constructed—and lasted until the end of the dynasty. However, one must not overestimate the importance of this imperial protection; it is not sufficient to explain Ibn ʿArabî's influence on Indian, Malaysian, or Chinese sufism, for example.

To keep to the order of historical contingencies, a much more satisfying explanation is to be sought in the evolution of sufism and its institutions from the thirteenth century on. The progressive constitution of the *turuq* and their evolution toward the "brotherhood" format in which we have known them since then create a kind of doctrinal "breathing in." The eponymous founders—ʿAbd al-Qâdir al-Jîlânî, Abû l-Hasan al-Shâdhilî, Ahmad al-Rifâʿî, Ahmad al-Badawî, and so on—trace a path, stamp a certain spiritual orientation into their initiatory posterity. They do not propose an organized body of doctrines, and they rarely leave substantial writings. Their oral teachings, which have been recorded by their followers, consist most frequently of disjointed series of insights and precepts. Something would be lacking in this sufism, which is slowly but surely taking shape, were it not precisely for Ibn ʿArabî's work; and, not being able to be claimed exclusively, or even primarily, by any one *tarîqa*, Ibn ʿArabî belongs to the common heritage. His work, unlike all the work that preceded it, presents one characteristic that the method chosen by Shaʿrânî in his *Yawâqît* demonstrates: it has a response to everything. *De omni re scibili*: ontology, cosmology, prophetology, exegesis, ritual, angelology…, it totally embraces the sciences that "those of the Path" could not bypass without putting themselves into peril.

But further horizons must undoubtedly be considered. Ibn ʿArabî does not address only his contemporaries or their immediate successors; nor does he address only the citizens of the *dâr al-islâm* such as it could be traced on the map of his time. In the preface to his famous *Lisân al-ʿarab*, Ibn Manzûr, who was born a few years before Ibn ʿArabî's death, explains that in composing this dictionary he wanted to include all the words of the "language of the Prophet" in the same way that "Noah constructed the Ark, while his people laughed at him." Ibn ʿArabî also built an ark, and it is not fortuitous if, of all his writings, it is this *summa magna* (which the *Futûhât Makkiyya* happen to be) that is the most often read and the most frequently cited. The *Futûhât*, the revision of which Ibn ʿArabî completed two years before his death, represent the majestic synthesis of the secrets of the world above and the world below (*al-asrâr al-mâlikiyya wa l-mulkiyya*) that he transcribed and commented on throughout his life. The role of supreme reference illustrated by the name Shaykh al-Akbar (the greatest of Teachers, the Master par excellence), which was given to Ibn ʿArabî later, was not a posthumous accident. He who claimed the function of "seal of Muhammadan sainthood," according to all the evidence, deliberately assumed the title; he tirelessly enclosed in his work, for the use of those who would live in ages darker than his own, the *amâna*, the sacred repository of which he considered himself the guardian.

1 ❦

"IF ALL THE TREES ON EARTH WERE PENS..."
(QUR'ÂN 31:27)

In the *Futûhât,* Ibn ʿArabî casually recounts an anecdote that might conceivably serve as an exergue to the remarks that follow. The hero of the anecdote is Mâlik, the imam founder of one of the four principle schools of Sunni jurisprudence.

> Mâlik b. Anas was asked: "What is your opinion about the lawfulness of the flesh of the water pig" [*khinzîr al-mâ*: an expression that refers to cetaceans in general, but dolphins in particular]? He replied [*fa-aftâ*: a judicial consultation, not a simple exchange of words] that it was illegal. An objection was made: "Does this animal not belong to the family of marine animals [literally, "fish," whose flesh is lawful]?" "Certainly," he said, "but you called it a pig [*khinzîr*]."[1]

Some might be tempted to class this ambiguous cetacean among the taxonomic fantasies of a maniacal casuistry. But Ibn ʿArabî's mention of it on two different occasions shows it to be something completely different for him. What is in question here is the authority of the name (*hukm al-ism*) and the secret of naming (*tasmiya*), which leads us to the very heart of Ibn ʿArabî's hermeneutics.

Accusations like atheism (*zandaqa*) and libertinism (*ibâha*, in both its philosophical sense and in common usage) are commonplace in heresiology. A close look at the writings hostile to the Shaykh al-Akbar from the thirteenth century up to the present day, however, shows the regular appearance of another accusation: *sacrilege.* The sacrilege in question is *tahrîf maʿâni l-qurʾân,* the "twisting of the meaning of the Qurʾân." The case is seen as early as Ibn Taymiyya, who is practically the founder of "anti-Akbarian polemics" and who supplies the structure for later diatribes.[2] It is also present in Husayn b. al-Ahdâl's (d. 1451) *Kashf al-ghitâ*[3] and in the *Tanbîh al-ghabî*[4] of Burhân al-dîn al-Biqâʿî (d. 1475). The case is again enthusiastically taken up by Sakhâwî (d. 1497), who constructs a catalogue of previous condemnations in his voluminous, unedited *Al-qawl al-munbî*.[5] And, whether they accuse him or praise him, the works of modern university scholars dedicated to Ibn ʿArabî generally echo the opinions of Muslim writers on this point, as is noted in the works of Nicholson,[6] Landau,[7] or ʿAfîfî.[8] Henry Corbin, for his part, often admiringly presented the Shaykh al-Akbar as the man of *bâtin*, the hidden sense—he who shatters the rigidities of the Letter in order to attain, by means of a free esoteric interpretation, a *taʾwîl*, new meanings of Revelation. It does not take much to imagine what use certain Islamic currents are making of this dangerous apology today.

Ibn ʿArabî affirms that "everything of which we speak in our meetings and in our writings comes from the Qurʾân and its treasures." In an unpublished work (*Radd al-matîn*[9]) in which he takes the Shaykh al-Akbar's defense, ʿAbd al-Ghanî al-Nâbulusî underscores, referring to the *auto-da-fe* of Ibn ʿArabî's works barred by certain jurists who sought out heresy with indefatigable zeal, that those who desire to execute such sentences find themselves in a paradoxical situation: if they leave the countless Qurʾânic quotations in Ibn ʿArabî's books that they are tossing into the flames, they end up burning the word of God. On the other hand, if they erase the passages before the burning, then the works to be burned are no longer those of Ibn ʿArabî, for the Qurʾân is such an integral part of them.

In fact, any reader of Ibn ʿArabî notices an abundance of scriptural references page after page. It must further be noted that Ibn ʿArabî's bibliography has an immense lacuna due to the disappearance of the great *tafsîr*, the *Kitâb al-jamʿ wa l-tafsîl fî asrâr maʿânî l-tanzîl* referred to above.[10] But besides the publication of a heretofore unpublished text, the *Ijâz al-bayân*,[11] which is a small *tafsîr*, we are indebted to Shaykh Mahmûd Ghurâb for the recent publication of a collection of four large volumes in which he has regrouped and arranged Ibn ʿArabî's exegetical texts by suras and verses.[12] By virtue of its size alone this impressive anthology suggests that Nâbulusî's observation is not irrelevant.

These quantitative considerations, though deserving of being formulated, are certainly secondary. It is not a question of appealing to the judgment of the *fuqahâ* (or rather, certain of them: in the volu-

minous catalogue of *fatwa* there is no lack of favorable *fuqahâ*[13]).
Instructed by the same methods, a new trial, regardless the out-
come, would be no more than just another judiciary peripeteia. If the
fuqahâ and nothing more are the guarantees of orthodoxy, then the
case is heard. Even though Dhahabî (d. 1348) maintains that the
spread of Ibn ʿArabî's works was relatively late and that his heresies
were noticeable only from the eighth/fourteenth century on,[14] the
author of the *Futuhât*'s difficulties began quite early. The story, told
by comparatively recent biographers, in which his life was in danger
in Cairo in 602/1206 and was spared only by the intervention of one
of Saladin's brothers is probably a fabrication.[15] But other events—
for example the one that led him to write a commentary on his *Tarjumân al-ashwâq*[16]—give evidence that he was under suspicion. It is
true that he did not treat the *fuqahâ* in the kindest of manners:
"They (the *fuqahâ*) have always been to those who have attained
spiritual realization (*al-muhaqqiqûn*) what the pharoahs were to
the prophets."[17] The Mahdî, the "rightly guided one," when he comes
at the end of time, will have no enemies more bitter: "If the sword
were not in his hands, they would give him the death sentence."[18] In
their attempts to please princes and the powerful, they do not hesitate to work out a casuistry that is a mockery of the Sacred Law
whose interpreters they wish they were.[19] If he exposes the too frequently perverse practices of the function of the *faqîh*, Ibn ʿArabî
nevertheless does not call into question either the necessity of *fiqh*—
juridical reflections—or the duty of vigilance incumbent upon the
fuqahâ (even when they speak of saints, when the remarks of the
latter could lead weak souls astray), provided they refrain from con-
demning as infidelity (*kufr*) all that they are incapable of understanding.[20]

But it would take more to appease the anger of a group jealous
and suspicious of these privileges. Two articles appeared in April
1990, one week apart, in the Egyptian daily *Al-Akhbar*. The articles, both quite benevolent, were inspired by recent publications
and respectively entitled "Ibn ʿArabî in France" and "The Ibn ʿArabî
Phenomenon in France." The "Ibn ʿArabî phenomenon," to use the
article's expression, is actually far from being limited to France:
studies on the Shaykh al-Akbar are proliferating throughout the
world including, for example, Japan, the former Soviet Union,[21]
and, as has already been pointed out, Muslim countries.[22] For

whatever reason, basing his arguments on the interest that Western researchers have in Ibn 'Arabî, the author of a brochure recently published in Cairo had been denouncing a "cultural invasion" engendered by these suspect enterprises.

The spread of this criticism was really nothing more than another episode in a very old quarrel: a "Letter to the Minister of Culture," again in the columns of *Al-Akhbar*, signed by Kamâl Ahmad 'Awn (director of the institute of Al-Azhar in Tantâ), reopened the quarrel in November 1975. The author was indignant over the publication of a blasphemous work sponsored by the ministry. The work in question was the critical edition of the *Futûhât* that O. Yahia was preparing. This "letter" was only the first salvo in a furious polemic to which we have already alluded and that has continued for several years.[23] In February 1979, the Egyptian Parlament decided to discontinue the edition in progress, as well as the distribution of those volumes already published. The decision, made under legally questionable conditions, was finally revoked after vehement disputes. What is worth noting is that, when the accounts of this polemic are examined, the majority of those in either camp who publicly took part in the affair had never read Ibn 'Arabî's writings *in extenso*, nor, for the most part, did they know his thought other than through second-hand and generally hostile accounts.

Besides these unfruitful controversies, we should mention a more serious debate on the origin of the patrimony that Ibn 'Arabî left his inheritors. Have the pious servants of God who have taken their inspiration from Ibn 'Arabî's teachings throughout the ages been abused? Is the repository of which Ibn 'Arabî named himself the guardian really the one which is founded upon Revelation? Isn't the affirmation according to which his work "proceeds from the Qur'ân and its treasures" nothing more than a concession dictated by attention to community norms, a concession that would veil quite different sources of inspiration? Is the Qur'ân, for Ibn 'Arabî, a text or a pretext? One might guess that the questions are purely rhetorical for the author of these lines, but they do deserve precise answers.

Plunge into the ocean of the Qur'ân if your breath is sufficiently powerful. And if not, limit yourself to the study of the commentaries on its apparent sense; but in this case do not plunge, for you will perish. The ocean of the Qur'ân is deep, and if he who plunges into it did not limit himself to those places which are closest to the shore, he would never come back toward the creatures. The prophets and the guardian-inheritors [*al-waratha al-hafaza*] take these roles as their goal out of pity for the universe. As for those who remain back [*al-wâqîfûn*], who have reached the goal but have remained there without ever returning, no one profits from them and they profit from no one: they have aimed at the center of the ocean—or rather it has aimed at them—and they have plunged for eternity.[24]

The mention of the "apparent sense" (*zâhir*) also suggests the contrary: *bâtin* (that which is hidden) is the opposite of *zâhir*. Both words belong to the traditional series of Divine Names. But among heresiographers the *bâtiniyya*, and Ibn 'Arabî has often been classified by his adversaries in this outcast category, are those who, in the name of *bâtin* (of the hidden sense that they are attempting to define) revoke the *zâhir* (the obvious) and kill the letter in order to give life to the spirit. However, when taken alone, the interpretation that the just-cited passage best lends itself to hardly stands up if what Ibn 'Arabî says elsewhere about the very process of Revelation to the Prophet is taken into account:

He was told: transmit that which has been revealed to you! And he did not stray from the very form of that which had been revealed to him, but rather transmitted to us exactly what had been told to him: for the meanings that descended upon his heart descended in the form of a certain combination of letters, of a certain arrangement of words, of a certain order of verses, of a certain composition of those suras whose totality comprises the Qur'ân. From that moment on God gave the Qur'ân a form. It is that form that the Prophet has shown, such as he himself had contemplated it...If he had changed something, what he brought to us would have been the form of his own understanding, and not the revelation that he had received. It would not be the Qur'ân, as it came to him, that he transmitted to us.[25]

The preceding allows the reader a glimpse of the importance that the very letter of divine discourse has for Ibn ʿArabî. He says, "Know that God addressed man in his totality, without giving precedence to his exterior (*zâhir*) over his interior (*bâtin*)."[26] If he thus blames those who worry only about legal rules applying to our "exteriors," he is even more severe with the *bâtiniyya* who are preoccupied only with the symbolic meanings of Revelation and who scorn its external meaning: "Perfect happiness belongs to those who join the external meaning with the internal meaning."[27] In his eyes, a little knowledge of the *bâtin* leads away from the *zâhir*, whereas a lot of knowledge of *bâtin* leads back to it.

A number of passages from his work illustrate the absolute sovereignty of the letter to which, we have seen, the Prophet himself is submissive. Having thus alluded to the verse *Wa huwa maʿakum aynamâ kuntum* (And he is with you wherever you are [57:4]) in the *Futûhât* , where he inadvertently used *haythumâ*—which has the same meaning—instead of *aynamâ*, the Shaykh al-Akbar immediately asks God's pardon for having strayed from the literality of the sacred text. "It is not in vain," he says, "that God takes one word away to prefer another to it." Any offense against the letter is thus a form of this *tahrîf*, of the alteration of the Word of God for which the Qurʾân (2:75; 5:13) reproaches the People of the Book.[28] This concern for literal strictness applies also to the hadîth, and Ibn ʿArabî praises those who, calling to mind the words of the Prophet, are careful to not put a *wa* in the place of a *fa*, even though these two particles are often interchangeable;[29] when they are reported "according to their meaning" (*alâ l-maʿnâ*) only, what the Prophet said is not being reported, but only what one has understood of what he said.[30]

This scrupulous attention to the *form* of the Word of God—for the form, being divine, is not only the most adequate expression of the Truth, it *is* the Truth; it is not only the bearer of meaning, it is the meaning—, is that which guides all of Ibn ʿArabî's reading of the Qurʾân. It is not incorrect to consider that the work of the Shaykh al-Akbar, as we presently know it, is in its entirety a Qurʾânic commentary. This commentary is, moreover, a method of interpretation that does not look for what is beyond the letter elsewhere than *within* the letter itself. Thus, just as God is at one and the same time *al-zâhir wa l-bâtin*, "the Apparent and the Hidden," just as universal Reality is similar to the construction known as a Möbius strip (which appears to have two faces, one internal and one external, while in fact it has only one), in this same way it is absurd to distinguish—and *a fortiori* to oppose in the Word of God the letter and the spirit, the signifier and the signified. We are far from an allegoric interpretation in the manner of Philo of Alexandria, for example, as can easily be seen by comparing his commentary on the biblical story of Genesis with that given by the Shaykh al-Akbar in parallel Qur'ânic verses. For Ibn 'Arabî it is the laying bare of each word of divine discourse that renders all of its meaning.

However, there is an obvious paradox: the rigidity of the letter seems to impose a univocal reading. Once it came, Revelation left a message that seemed destined to be nothing more than repeated. Is it then to be concluded that any hermeneutic should be dismissed in advance? To do so would be to forget that "if all the trees on earth were pens, if the seas were ink—and if they were added to by seven other seas—the Word of God would not be exhausted" (Qur'ân 31:27).

The Qur'ân, says Ibn 'Arabî,

is perpetually new for any of those who recite it....But no reciter is conscious of his descent [*nuzûl*], because his mind is occupied with its natural condition. Then the Qur'ân descends upon him hidden behind the veil of nature and produces no rejoicing in him. It is to this case that the Prophet alludes when he speaks of reciters who read the Qur'ân without it going any farther than their throats. That is the Qur'ân that descends upon tongues and not upon hearts. God said the contrary about him who tastes [this descent]: The faithful spirit descended with it [the Qur'ân] upon your heart [Qur. 26:193]. Such a man is he in whom this descent causes an immeasurable sweetness that surpasses all joy. When he experiences it, he is [truly] the person upon whom the ever new Qur'ân has descended. The difference between these two kinds of descent is that if the Qur'ân descends upon the heart, it brings comprehension with it: the being in question understands that which is being recited even if he does not understand the language of Revelation; he knows the significance of that which is being recited even if the meaning that

the words have outside of the Qur'ân are unknown because
they do not exist in his own language; he knows what these
words mean in his recitation, and at the very moment that
they are being recited. The station of the Qur'ân and its state
being what we say, it happens that each one finds in himself
that to which he aspires. It is for this reason that shaykh Abû
Madyan said: the aspirant [al-murîd] is really an aspirant
only when he finds in the Qur'ân all to which he aspires. And
word not endowed with this plenitude is not really Qur'ân.[31]
When the Qur'ân, which is a divine attribute—and the
attribute is inseparable from that which it qualifies—,
descends upon the heart, it is then He Whose Word the
Qur'ân is that descends with it. God said that the heart of his
believing servant contains Him:[32] it is of this descent of the
Qur'ân upon the heart of the believer that the divine descent
in the heart consists.[33]

None of the faithful, no saint will ever hear words other than
those that were heard and transmitted by the Prophet: "The Words
of God do not change" (*lâ tabdîla fî kalimâti Llâh* [Qur'ân 10:64]).
The perpetually revealed Qur'ân is at the same time both rigorously identical to itself—and yet unheard: it continually brings new
meanings to hearts prepared to receive it; none of these meanings
annuls the preceding ones, and all of them were inscribed from the
beginning in the plenitude of the Qur'ân's letter.

It behooves you to distinguish between understanding the
Word and understanding him who is speaking. It is the latter
form of comprehension that must be researched: it is
obtained only when the Qur'ân descends upon the heart,
while the former belongs to the community of the faithful.
Those gnostics who receive their understanding from him
who speaks understand the Word. Those who understand
only the Word do not understand clearly, either wholly or in
part, what he Who spoke meant...The servant whose inner
sight [al-basîra] is enlightened—he who is guided by *a light
from his Lord* [Qur'ân 39:22]—obtains with each recitation of
a verse a new understanding, distinct from that which he had
during the preceding recitation and that that he will obtain

during the succeeding recitation. God has answered the request that has been addressed to him with the words *Oh Lord, increase my knowledge!* [Qurʾân 20:114]. He whose understanding is identical in two successive recitations is losing. He whose understanding is new in each recitation is winning. As for him who recites without understanding anything, may God have mercy on him.[34]

But it is he who speaks, and he alone, who is responsible for the infinite profusion of meanings that wells up during recitation of the Qurʾân. The *ʿabd* (servant) could not reach this goal even with the greatest efforts of his faculties of reflection. Moreover, this effort would not only be in vain; it would deprive him of any chance of being receptive to the meaning that God has destined for him at that exact moment. He must, then, suspend the use of his forces and leave the way open for the Divine Verb, the true Recitant.

It is I, he says, who recite my Book for him with his tongue while he listens to me. And that is my nocturnal conversation with him. That servant savors my Word. But if he binds himself to his own meanings, he leaves me by his reflection and his meditation. What he must do is only lean toward me and leave his ears receptive to my Word until I am present in his recitation. And just as it is I who recite and I who make him hear, it is also I who then explain my Word to him and interpret its meanings. That is my nocturnal conversation with him.[35] He takes knowledge from me, not from his reason and his reflection; he no longer cares to think of paradise, of hell, of accounting for his actions, of the Last Judgement, of this world or of that which is to come, for he no longer considers these things with his intellect, he no longer scrutinizes each verse with his reflection: he is content to lend an ear to that which I tell him. And he is at that moment a witness, present with me; and it is I who take charge of his instruction.[36]

We are shown the modalities of this divine instruction in an exceptional text. The text is that which describes the fundamental event in the course of which Ibn ʿArabî reads the *Futûhât* before writing them. This singular passage, which helps us to understand what Ibn ʿArabî is telling us when he claims to have taken all of his work from the "treasures of the Qurʾân," is that which, after the doxology (khutba) and the introduction (muqaddima),[37] makes up the first chapter of the work.[38] The passage has been studied a number of times, and its contents were commented on in one of our earlier works,[39] but one point must be highlighted because of its direct relation to the purpose of this book. This is where Ibn ʿArabî relates his encounter beside the Kaʿba, near the black stone, with a "young man" (fatâ) described by a number of contradictory attributes. This coincidentia oppositorum clearly means that we are here dealing with a theophany: he is "living and dead," "simple and compound"; he "contains everything" and "everything contains him"; he is "the contemplator and the contemplated," "the knowledge, the knower, and the known." He is "the one who speaks" (al-mutakallim, a term the importance of which will be seen) while at the same time he remains silent (sâmit). From him comes all that Ibn ʿArabî will transcribe in the Futûhât .

Apparently, the "young man" is the manifestation of what the prefatory poem of chapter 2 calls "the august and sublime secret" of the Kaʿba, the "House of God" (bayt Allâh). The Kaʿba is of course the sacred place to which the "illuminations of Mecca" (al-futûhât al-makkiyya) are expressly linked. But several things allow a more precise definition of the young man's identity. Some of these are found in the initial chapter. Others are to be seen some two thousand pages later, in the penultimate chapter (al-bâb al-jâmiʿ, the chapter of synthesis), where Ibn ʿArabî announces that he has encapsulated the quintessence of what the 558 preceding chapters contain. We are not dealing here with a "summary," even though Ibn ʿArabî uses the term mukhtasar (abridgement) in the table located at the beginning of the Futûhât, but rather with a succession of flashes that cast a sometimes blinding light upon jewels encased in the mass of the text. One paragraph, the wording of which is sometimes quite obscure at first glance, corresponds to each chapter of the Futûhât.[40] The one that corresponds to the first chapter[41] informs us that the enigmatic "young man" that Ibn ʿArabî greets at the threshold of the Kaʿba located, according to Ibn ʿAbbâs, in the "umbilicus of the earth"—thus, a visible image of the supreme spiritual center—is the "manifest Prototype," or the "explicit Model" (*al-imâm al-mubîn*): a Qur'ânic expression to refer to the Book in which "all things are numbered" (Qur'ân 36:12), the one in which "nothing is omitted" (Qur'ân 6:38).

In Ibn 'Arabî, the *imâm mubîn*, according to the point of view from which he is seen, is sometimes likened to the divine Pen, or to the guarded Table (*al-lawh al-mahfûz*) upon which the Pen distinctively inscribes the knowledge that it withholds in a synthetic fashion; sometimes he is likened to the Perfect Man (*al-insân al-kâmil*):[42] different names for the same function of mediating between the universe and the impenetrable mystery (*ghayb*) of the divine darkness. But as a passage in chapter 22[43] (to which we shall return) suggests, he is also the Qur'ân itself. One further, clearer, indication comes to us at the moment that the *fatâ* invites the pilgrim to delve with him into the Ka'ba,[44] and where he states: "I am the seventh of what surrounds the universe." This statement, which appears sibylline when taken out of context, is explained by the symbolic correspondance established during a preceding dialogue between the seven prescribed ritual circumambulations of the Ka'ba and the seven names that, in Muslim theology, correspond the the attributes of the Divine Essence. The "seventh," which the young man is identified with, is evidently here the name *al-mutakallim*, "He who speaks." If, in Islamic tradition, the Verb becomes the Book, one sees that, in appearing to Ibn 'Arabî in the guise of the *fatâ*, it appears in the shape of a man.[45]

It is thus *in his very form,* "in the detail of his constitution," that the *fatâ* orders Ibn 'Arabî to decipher the knowledge that he has to pass on to him. The *fatâ* certainly is a book, but a *mutus liber: mutakallim sâmit.* It is his *person* that must be read: "What you see in me, incorporate it in your work and teach it to those whom you love."[46] At that moment the *Futûhât Makkiyya* were born. "A light deep within him," says Ibn 'Arabî, "brought to my eyes the hidden knowledge that he contains and envelops in his being. And the first line that I read, the first secret of this line that I understood is that which I am going to transcribe at present in this second chapter." The second chapter is, quite logically, that which Ibn 'Arabî will devote to the "science of letters" (*'ilm al-hurûf*), that which teaches the fundamental principles of the deciphering of revelation, that which gives the keys to the "treasures of the Qur'ân."[47]

The divinely inspired hermeneutic which, in perpetual renewal, allows the discovery of unprecedented meanings in each recitation holds in the strictest sense to the "body" of words, as we have said. Ibn ʿArabî defines the rules on numerous occasions.

As far as the Word of God is concerned, when it is revealed in the language of a certain people, and when those who speak this language differ as to what God meant by a certain word or group of words due to the variety of possible meanings of the words, each of them—however differing their interpretations may be—effectively comprises what God meant, provided that the interpretation does not deviate from the accepted meanings of the language in question. God knows all these meanings, and there is none that is not the expression of what he meant to say to this specific person. But if the individual in question deviates from accepted meanings in the language, then neither understanding nor knowledge has been received...As for him to whom understanding of all the faces of the divine Word has been given, he has received *wisdom and decisive judgement* [Qurʾân 38:20], that is, the faculty of distinguishing among all these faces,[48]

in other words, that of determining, according to the circumstances, which of the possible meanings is pertinent.

Given the extremely rich polysemy of Arabic vocabulary, rigorous fidelity to the letter of Revelation does not exclude but, on the contrary, it implies a multiplicity of interpretations. Ibn ʿArabî insists on this point on a number of occasions, emphasizing that there is a general rule applicable to all the revealed Books: "Any meaning of whatever verse of the Word of God—be it the Qurʾân, the Torah, the Psalms or the "Pages"[49]—judged acceptable by one who knows the language in which this Word is expressed represents what God wanted to say to those who interpret it so."[50] As a corollary, none of these meanings is to be rejected, regardless how surprising or even how scandalous it might appear, for God, in uttering this verse, had to be aware of the diversity of possible intrepretations for each word or group of words. To deny the validity of this rule is to limit divine knowledge.[51]

However, it must not be forgotten that these instructions are in no way to be understood as an invitation to engage in erudite philological exercises during recitation: "The commentators report that the Qur'ân in its entirety descended as far as the heavens of this world, all at once, and that from there it descended in a shower of stars upon Muhammad's heart. That voyage will never cease as long as the Qur'ân is recited, in secret or aloud. From the servant's point of view, the lasting *laylat al-qadr* [the night of Revelation][52] is his own soul when it is purified."[53] This is the purification by which the being becomes *ummî*.

The word *ummî*, usually translated as "illiterate," appears a number of times in the Qur'ân, in the singular, to refer to the Prophet himself (7:157–58) and, in the plural, to refer to the members of the community toward which it has been sent (62:2). We will not attempt an exegesis of these verses here, for that would lead us too far astray. Let us however keep in mind, by way of clarification, that *ummî* comes from the root *'mm*, from which the word *umm* (mother) is derived, which leads the author of the *Lisân al-'arab* to define *ummî* as "he who is as when his mother gave birth to him."[54]

The eminent theologian Fakhr al-dîn Râzî (d. 1209) one day came upon a saint (*walî*, pl. *awliyâ*) no less illustrious than himself—it was Najm al-dîn Kubrâ—and asked to enter on the Path under his direction. The saint had one of his disciples set Râzî up in a cell and ordered him to devote himself to the invocation. But he did not stop there: we are told that, projecting his spiritual energy (*tawajjuh*) upon Râzî, he stripped him of all the book knowledge he had acquired. Now when Râzî became aware that all the knowledge of which he had been so proud was being suddenly erased from his memory, be began shouting with all his force: "I can not, I can not." The experience stopped there. Râzî left his cell and took his leave of Najm al-dîn Kubrâ.[55]

This anecdotal detour gives a more precise view of the state of *ummiyya*, "spiritual illiteracy." In hagiography, when one speaks of a saint as *ummî*, it is always an uncultured saint or one who is literally illiterate. We have already mentioned one remarkable case, that of 'Abd al-'Azîz al-Dabbâgh. But the examples are numerous. The great Berber saint Abû Ya'zâ, still quite revered today, learned no more of the Qur'ân than the *Fâtiha* and the last three suras, which are among the shortest. He needed an interpreter to converse with his Arabic speaking visitors, and yet that did not keep him from miraculously detecting the errors in recitation of the Qur'ân committed by the imam who led prayer. Abû Ja'far al-Uryabî, the dearly loved first of Ibn 'Arabî's teachers, was an Andalusian farmer who knew neither how to read nor how to count; and we might also remember in this regard the well-known saint Abû Yazid al-Bistâmî, who claims that he had to initiate his initiator, Abû 'Alî al-Sindî, in the elementary rules of ritual practices; or the further case of Abû l-'Abbâs al-Qassâb, one of the great spiritual masters of Transoxiania. In the entourage of Muhammad al-Hanafî, the prestigious figure of Cairan sufism at the end of the fourteenth century, one meets another *ummî* saint, Shams al-dîn Muhammad, also called al-Bâbâ, about whom we are told that he became *qutb al-zamân* (the Pole of his epoch) moments before his death in 1565. Among the teachers of Sha'rânî are two *ummî* saints about whom he spoke at length in two of his works: Ibrâhim al-Matbûlî (whom he did not know personally) and 'Alî al-Khawwâs, always mentioned with affectionate veneration. These individuals—the first was a vendor of chick peas, the second an oil merchant—are seen in the numerous pages that Sha'rânî devotes to them validating or invalidating the prophetic traditions of disputed authenticity, solving subtle problems in unaffected language, and interpreting obscure verses that perplex the exegetes. They know divine decrees and predict the date they will come to pass. A learned and prolific author, Sha'rânî continually appeals to the authority of these to dissect the questions that trouble him.

But for Ibn 'Arabî, who dedicates a chapter of the *Futûhât* to the concept of *ummiyya*, one can be *ummî* without being illiterate from the moment that the intellect is capable of suspending its operations ("For us, *ummiyya* consists in renouncing the use of rational speculation and judgement in order to give rise to meanings and secrets"[56]). As did the Prophet, the virginal receptacle of Revelation, a being should open himself entirely to the lights of grace. This does not imply that all intellectual activity should be forbidden as contradictory to this disposition toward welcoming supernatural illumination: 'Abd al-Karîm al-Jîlî, among many other disciples of the Shaykh al-Akbar, insists, rather, on the importance of books as supports for the *baraka* and as instruments of spiritual perfection,[57] and Nâbulusî, in an unpublished treatise, defends the same point of view.[58]

But there is a time for everything and God does not speak but in the creature's silence. To hear Him, man must thus return to the "state of infancy"—an expression that might after all be the most exact translation of *ummiyya*. This state of infancy is what the Qur'ân describes in the following terms: "God had you come out of the womb of your mothers and you knew nothing" (16:78). Among the possible meanings of a word, of a verse, there is no choice at the end of a mental process: the "true" meaning—that which is true at that very moment for that very being—is that which wells up, in the nakedness of the spirit, from the very letter of divine speech. It is to this letter and to it alone that he whose heart is ready to welcome that "shower of stars," which will cease only on the day that the Qur'ân is no longer recited "in secret or aloud," will listen.

2 ✾

"IN THE BOOK WE HAVE LEFT OUT NOTHING"
(QUR'ÂN 6:38)

In a poem from his *Dîwân*, though taken from the *'Anqâ mughrib*,[1] a work from his youth, Ibn 'Arabî writes: "In awe, I saw an ocean without a shore and a shore without an ocean!"

Although in the context in which they are found these two images lend themselves to another interpretation, it is not incorrect to apply them here to the Qur'ân itself, which the Shaykh al-Akbar, in other passages of his work, expressly describes as an "ocean without shore."[2] If the letter of divine speech can be no more than a "shore without an ocean" for those who do not see perpetual revelation in it, it is unlimited and inexhaustible for "divers with powerful breath." But it is important to understand that the Qur'ân is both the one and the other *at the same time*: the "shore"—the obvious meaning, and the limits that it sets for faith and for works—is never annulled; the Law remains indefeasible in this world, and it is even in it and through it, as we shall see below, that supreme perfection is achieved in man. It is for this reason that Ibn 'Arabî prefers, in conformity with the practice of earlier sufis such as Sahl al-Tustarî and Qushayrî, to speak of *ishârât* (allusions) to refer to his own interpretations of Qur'ânic verses, rather than of *tafsîr*, a word that he reserves for "commentary," properly speaking.[3] The examples of these *ishârât* that we will give, and certain ones that have been the reason for the majority of the attacks referred to above, are thus in no way, let us reiterate, exclusive of the acceptance of meanings founded on prophetic traditions or the consensus of the Companions.

The debate regarding the correct category in which to place the *khinzîr al-mâ*, from the anecdote reported at the beginning of the preceding chapter, directed attention to the importance of "naming" (*tasmiya*). This importance is of course all the greater when it becomes a question of the way in which God refers to himself in the Qur'ân (more specifically, here, the nouns and pronouns

35

that appear in the first sura of the Qur'ân the *Fâtiha*): sometimes one divine name, sometimes another; sometimes the plural *we*, sometimes the singular *I*, and sometimes the *he* that is the pronoun for the "absent person." In a work which remained unpublished for a long time, the *Kitâb al-Abâdila*, Ibn 'Arabî writes notably:

> All reality in the world is a sign that directs us toward a divine reality that is the starting point of its existence and the place of return when it comes to term. When God mentions the world in the Qur'ân, pay attention to the divine name that he employs. In this way will you know to which world he is referring. When God speaks of himself with the singular (I, me) and speaks to you as plural, it means that the verse in question refers to him in his Unicity and to you in your multiplicity...When he speaks of himself as plural, saying for example *Innâ* (certainly, we) or *Nahnu* (we), it means that God is seen in relation to [the plurality of] his names. When he speaks to you in the singular, it means that he is addressing you in relation to one of your constituent elements and not to your totality. Know thus to what part of you the discourse is directed.

Similarly, in the *Futûhât,* he emphasizes the necessity of distinguishing, when one is reciting the Qur'ân, among the different forms of address that God uses in calling upon the faithful. The faithful are sometimes referred to as "those who believe" and sometimes as "those who are endowed with intelligence" or "those who understand," "those who see," and so forth. Now these expressions are not synonymous. The human being is not referred to in the same fashion; the speech is not destined for the same one of the person's constituents. The interior attitude of the reciter must not therefore remain identical, but should rather take into account the choice that God has made of calling upon one of his powers rather than some other.[4]

This concern for considering each of God's words and silences, which characterizes Ibn 'Arabî's interpretations, is certainly not sufficient to convince his adversaries of his orthodoxy, nor is this our purpose here. Nothing better illustrates the impossibility of satisfying the *'ulamâ al-zâhir* by rigorous fidelity to the *zâhir* of Qur'ânic

text than the reading that Ibn 'Arabî does of the famous verse
(42:11) *Laysa ka-mithlihi shay'un*, which might be understood as
meaning: "There is nothing which is his similar." Pages upon pages
would be necessary to analyze in detail the numerous texts where
Ibn 'Arabî evokes this text. In brief, the problem that this verse
poses hinges around the particle *ka*, "as." Is it superfluous, destined
only to reinforce the word *mithl*, "similar"? That is the opinion of,
among others, Qushayrî (d. 1072),[5] to whom we owe the first complete sufi *tafsîr* that has come down to us and for whom this *ka* is
nothing more than a particle devoid of any meaning itself. It is also
the opinion of Fakhr al-dîn Râzî,[6] for whom the *ka* is there *li-l-
mubâlagha* and thus has only an intensive value with no meaning of
its own. Without challenging this way of understanding the verse,
which he considers on numerous occasions in his work, since it is linguistically admissible, Ibn 'Arabî completes it by another one, which
is its exact opposite. God does not speak to say nothing: the particle
ka can thus also preserve all the force of its normal meaning. And
the verse thus means: "There is nothing like His similar"[7]—an interpretation that, for the *fuqahâ*, is supremely blasphemous.

Who is this *mithl*, God's "similar"? It is man—but, of course,
the perfect Man (*al-insân al-kâmil*) inasmuch as he is *khalîfat
Allâh* (God's *locum tenens*) on earth (Qur'ân 2:30, 7:79, 35:39). Ibn
'Arabî, in this commentary, specifically refers to the human being's
theomorphism, citing the hadith *"Inna Llâha khalaqa Adama alâ
sûratihi"* (Certainly, Allah created Adam in his form);[8] and by using
the symbolism of the mirror,[9] itself validated by another hadith:
man is a mirror wherein appears the inverse reflection of truth, of
Divine Reality. That which is *bâtin* (hidden) in God is *zâhir* (apparent) in man. This passage from the *Futûhât* concludes with a triple
exclamation the force of which is lost in translation: *Fa-anta
maqlûbuhu! Fa-anta qalbuhu! wa huwa qalbuka!* (You are His
reflection! You are His heart and He is your heart!).

The hadith just quoted about the creation of Adam, the way
we translated it, recalls immediately the verse in Genesis according
to which "God created man in His own image" (Gen. 1:27). It can
nevertheless be interpreted in another fashion due to the ambiguity of the affixed pronoun coming at the end of the word *surâ*. Nothing really permits a definitive decision as to whether it refers to the

noun *Allâh* or the noun *Adam*. In accord with the aforementioned hermeneutical principle that forbids the exclusion of one linguistically valid meaning in favor of another, Ibn ʿArabî sees both of these possibilities, either in different passages of his work or in the course of a single writing as, for example, in chapter 73 of the *Futûhât*. His response to Hakîm Turmidhî's "questionnaire" contains the following question:[10] What does His word *khalaqa Adama alâ sûratihi* mean? In a work composed in 609/1207, the *Jawâb mustaqîm*, where he included in abbreviated form an answer to Tirmidhî's questions, Ibn ʿArabî took into consideration only the interpretation according to which the pronoun refers to Adam,[11] saying that in so doing he was relying on an "illumination" (*kashf*) while remaining cognizant of the fact that the wording of the hadith included other "aspects" (*wujûh*). In chapter 73 of the *Futûhât* he sees the two grammatically admissible solutions simultaneously. "If an Islamic philosopher [*faylasûf islâmî*: the use of this second word in preference to *muslim* suggests that the philosopher in question's belonging to the Muslim community has a purely statutory character, and that in Ibn ʿArabî's eyes this individual is not integrally really "submissive"] asked me this question, I would reply that the pronoun refers to Adam...for every questioner needs an answer that will satisfy him."

From this point of view, Ibn ʿArabî suggests, the hadith simply means that Adam was instantly created in his definitive form, without passing through the intermediate steps characterized by gestation and growth of human beings. This explanation for the "philosopher" appears at the end of his response to question 143. The beginning of the text gives another: the pronoun in *sûratihi* refers to *Allâh*. Adam was brought into existence "according to the form of the name *Allâh*" (*alâ sûrat al-ism Allâh*). Now the name Allâh synthetically contains all the divine names, and Adam, similarly, contains all of them without exception. Since the universe is but the effect of the unfolding of these names, Adam is consequently "the abridgment of the macrocosm" (*mukhtasar al-ʿâlam al-kabîr*). But Ibn ʿArabî adds that this meaning remains valid even if the pronoun's antecedent is *Adam*. In this case (and it is obvious that the response to the philosopher is an *ad hominem* response that deliberately reduces the field of interpretation), the hadith means that God created Adam in accordance with the form that he had in

Divine Knowledge: which, in fact, is perfectly congruent with the preceding interpretation. It might be added, *à propos* of the use of the word *sûra* (form) by the Prophet, that this passage of the *Futûhât* further entails important remarks about the legitimation by this hadith and by another well-known prophetic tradition ("perfection is adoring God *as* if he were in your sight") of the use of the imaginative faculty (*khayâl*) in the act of adoration.[12]

In the Qur'ân, the divine command to Adam and Eve is not, strictly speaking, that of not eating the forbidden fruit, but rather that of not "approaching the tree" (Qur'ân 2:35). Now the tree (*shajara*) is, for Ibn 'Arabî—a meaning dictated by etymology, and more directly by the meaning of the verb *shajara*, from the same root, in another verse (4:65)—the *tashâjur* (act of dividing).[13] It is this division, this rupture of unity that Adam and Eve should eschew. The metaphysical significance of their disobedience is thus inscribed in the very name of the forbidden object and need not be sought elsewhere.

This interpretation is perfectly coherent with the continuation of the Qur'ânic story as given in sura *Tâ Hâ* (20:121)—in a form that exactly parallels that of Genesis: *Fa-akalâ minhâ fa-badat lahumâ saw'âtuhumâ* (They ate of it and then their nudity became apparent to them). *Nudity* is the usual translation, but the term *saw'âtuhumâ* actually refers to the pudenda, Adam and Eve's sexual organs: in other words, sexual differentiation, the most elementary manifestation, the most evident of the *division*, of the rupture of unity. This is, for Ibn 'Arabî, the unity symbolized by the spherical form that originally was that of the human being.[14] The comparison with what Philo says in the *Legum Allegoriae* about the corresponding biblical episode illustrates quite well the difference between an interpretation that never deviates from the letter and an allegorical transposition.[15]

In sura *Al-kahf*, the sura of the Cavern, the final verse (18:110) can be translated: "He who awaits the meeting with his Lord, let him act piously, and in adoration of his Lord, let him associate no one with Him." We have translated the last word of the verse, *ahad*, by "no one," as is usually the case when it is preceded by a negation (under the circumstances *lâ: wa lâ yushrik bi 'ibâdati rabbihi ahadan*). But *Ahad* is also one of the divine names, referring to God in his being One (*Qul: huwa Llâhu ahad*, "Say: He, Allâh, is one," from sura 112). One can thus also understand this sentence literally—as Ibn ʿArabî does in several passages of his works, most notably in his *Kitâb al-ahadiyya*,[16] the "Book of Unity"—as meaning "He who awaits the meeting with his Lord, let him not associate *Ahad* [let him not associate the One] with adoration of his Lord." For Ibn ʿArabî, the notion of *rabb*, 'Lord,' is correlative with and inseparable from that of *marbûb*, "vassal." It implies a duality that totally excludes the name *Ahad*. According to Ibn ʿArabî's terms, "Unity (*al-ahadiyya*) ignores and refuses you." Now the One, as such, is inaccessible. Man in the act of adoration (*ʿibâda*)—as long as he attaches this act to himself—must address—and cannot address, whatever he might think—only the divine Name that is "his" Lord. That is, he must address only that particular "Face" (*Wajh*) of the Divine which is turned toward him and from which he draws all that he is.

This is the commanding theme of Ibn ʿArabî's doctrine of the knowledge of God, as it is expressed (as in numerous other texts) in a passage from chapter 2 of the *Fusûs al-hikam*,[17] where we again find the image of the mirror: "He to whom he shows himself sees nothing more than his own form in the mirror of Divine Reality (*al-haqq*); he does not see Divine Reality and cannot see It, even if he knows that it is in it that he has perceived his own form...He [God] is thus your mirror wherein you contemplate yourself; and you are his mirror wherein he contemplates his Names and the manifestation of the powers belonging to each of them. And all that is nothing more than him!"

God must be taken at His word. He sent down the Qurʾân *bî lisânin ʿarabiyyin mubîn*, "in clear Arabic" (Qurʾân 26:195). In a verse from the sura of the Light (24:39), the works of the unbelievers are compared to a mirage (*sarâb*) "which the thirsty man believes to be water up to the moment that he arrives at it; then he finds it to be nothing and he finds God by his side" (*fa wajada Llâha indahu*). It is followed by: "and God takes account of him." It is these last words that have drawn all the attention of the commentators, Râzî, for example, and, for them, "he finds God near him" is ultimately nothing more than a figure of style: when the unbeliever discovers that his works were nothing more than an illusion, he will discover at the same time the punishment that a vengeful God has prepared for him.

Ibn ʿArabî reads the verse in a different way. God revealed himself to Moses in the form of fire, in the burning bush, because Moses had gone out in search of fire (Qurʾân 20:10). All need is the need for God, and God shows himself to the creature in the form of his need. The man who, fooled by a mirage, has vainly run in the desert and arrives at the point where he despairs of everything truly finds God, for "it is when you find nothing that you find God. God can be found only in the absence of things [i.e., of second causes] upon which we depend."[18] And God quenches all thirsts, satisfies all hungers. Water is life: God will be life for the thirsty man.

In holding on to the meaning of a key word—refusing to believe, contrary to the implicit assumption of a number of exegetes, that God expresses himself in approximations—Ibn ʿArabî scripturally justifies one essential aspect of his teaching. There is a verse in sura *Al-isrâ* (The Night Journey [17:23]) that says: *Wa qadâ rabbuka allâ taʿbudû illâ iyyâhu* (And your Lord has decreed that you worship only him). Here is what Ibn ʿArabî says about the subject: "*Qadâ* [decree] means "to ordain," "to decide," and that is what explains the worship of false gods. The goal of the worship of any worshipper is in fact nothing other than God. Nothing, if it is not God, is worshipped for itself. The error of the polytheist [*mushrik*] is just that of engaging in a form of adoration that it not prescribed by God."[19] In this regard, he cites the verse where the polytheists, literally, the "associators" (*al-mushrikûn*), state: "We have worshipped them [the false gods, the idols] only that they might bring us closer to God" (39:4). Thus, for the Shaykh al-Akbar, the divine *qadâ* being by definition indefeasible, any creature, whether it wants to or not, whether it knows or not, worships only God (or, more precisely, a divine name, but all the names return to the same Named), whatever the form of the immediate object of the adoration might be. This same idea, on a different scriptural basis, is also strongly developed in chapter 10 of the *Fusûs*,[20] where the point of departure is a verse, to which we shall return, from sura *Hûd* (11:56). The key expression here is that of *sirât mustaqîm*—the "right path." Ibn ʿArabî says: "Men divide themselves into two categories: some walk on a path they know, and whose destination they know; for them, this path is the straight Way. The others walk on a path that they do not know and whose destination they do not know. And this path is rigorously identical to that which, with full knowledge, the first category is travelling." Commenting on this same verse from sura *Hûd* in the *Futûhât*, he exclaims: *Mâ fî l-'âlam illâ mustaqîm!* (There is nothing in this world which is not right and straight!).[21] There is little need to point out that all that raised Ibn Taymiyya's indignation; for him the *qadâ*—in accord with the majority of previous exegeses, that of Fakhr al-dîn Râzî being just one[22]—is a "commandment," a "regulation," and not a decree. This interpretation, according to Ibn 'Arabî's criteria, is evidence of serious confusion between the *amr takwînî*, the existentiating order, which cannot be not executed, and the *amr taklîfî*, the normative order, which can be disobeyed.

In connection with the preceding, we give another example, also related to one of the major perspectives of Ibn 'Arabî's doctrine. This one is a commentary on Qur'ân 7:56, *Wa rahmatî wasi'at kulla shay'in* (And My mercy embraces all things). The commentary is indirect, under the circumstances, since the commentator in this case is none other than Iblîs, the devil. In the *Futûhât* Ibn 'Arabî actually relates a dialogue between Iblîs and a famous ninth-century sufi, Sahl b. 'Abdallâh al-Tustarî (d. 283/896).[23]

> The last thing that Iblîs said to Sahl was this: God said "My Mercy embraces all things," which is an affirmation destined to all. Now, you must have noticed that I am one of those things, without any doubt. The word *all* implies the universality [of this pronouncement] and the word *thing* represents that which is most indeterminate. His Mercy thus embraces me." When Sahl replies: "I did not think that your lack of knowledge would go that far," the response of Iblîs is: "I did not think that you would say that! Do you not know, o Sahl, that limitation [*al-taqyîd*] is your attribute and not his?"

Ibn 'Arabî concludes the story with the following remark: "At that moment I realized that Iblîs possessed incontestable knowledge [literally, a science where no knowledge lacked] *and that, in this problem, it is he who was Sahl's teacher.*"

The theme of the infinity of divine mercy is ubiquitous in Ibn 'Arabî's works. In regard to the idea of *sîrât mustaqîm* used above, and to cite once again chapter 10 of the *Fusûs al-hikam*, we offer the following passage:

"There is no creature that moves [*dâbba*] but that he holds it by the forelock. Certainly, my Lord is on the straight path" [Qur'ân 11:56]. Thus, everything that moves moves on the straight path. From this point of view, then, none is among *those who have incurred his anger*, nor among *those who have gone astray* [Qur'ân 1:7]. Just as straying is accidental, divine anger is also accidental, and all ends up at Mercy, which embraces every thing and which *precedes His Anger*.[24] In effect, everything that is other than God moves [is part of the genus *dâbba*], for everything is endowed with a spirit [possesses life, which is movement].[25] But no being on this earth moves by itself : it moves by following him *who is on the straight path*.[26]

And he pushes criminals [*toward Gehenna*, Qur'ân 19:86]; that is, he pushes those who deserve that toward which they are being pushed, by means of the wind from the west [*rîh al-dabûr*] with which he makes them die unto themselves. He seizes them by their forelocks and the wind—which is only their own passions—pushes them toward Gehenna, toward the separation [*al-buʿd*, "distance"] that they imagined. But when he has thus pushed them toward this place, they in fact arrive at proximity. The [illusory] distance ceases, as does, for them, that which is called "Gehenna" [*musammâ jahannam*, Gehenna retains its name—*ism*—but that which was "named"—*musammâ*—by this name, namely an abyss, a place of exile, has changed its nature].[27]

But Ibn ʿArabî's doctrine on the *Rahma* leads us to examine more closely, among the numerous passages of his works where he makes his position known, a text that, *à propos* of another Qur'ânic verse, presents the interest of placing it in relation to his conception of the *risâla muhammadiyya*, the mission of the Prophet Muhammad. Here we are dealing with his response to the 155th and last of Tirmidhî's questions; its place, at the end of chapter 73—which in itself concludes and crowns the initial section of the *Futûhât*, that which is dedicated to "buds of knowledge" (*fasl al-maʿârif*)—emphasizes its importance.[28] The question itself is about the pardon that is announced to the Prophet in the Qur'ân (48:2). For Ibn ʿArabî, who formulates the same interpretation in a number of other places, Muhammad's impeccability (*'isma*) precludes the belief that he is really the one for whom the announcement is destined: "There is no sin to be forgiven." One must thus conclude that, although the Divine Word is addressed to him (*huwa l-mukhâtab*), it is aimed at his community (*al-maqsûd ummatuhu*). But what is to be understood by "his community"? It is here that the exegesis of a verse (Qur'ân 34:28) according to which Muhammad was sent by God toward men "in their totality" (*kâffatan*) comes into play. The Qur'ânic commentators understand this "totality" as geographically inclusive of the entire human race ("the whites and the blacks"), from the moment of Muhammad's coming. Now, nothing authorizes making relative the breadth of a divine pronouncement that takes the form of an absolute affirmation. Men "in their totality" are not only those who live at the time of the Prophet or after his coming. "It is not necessary for men to see him...Humanity is composed of all men, from the time of Adam to the Resurrection Day...[God] did not say: We have sent you only toward this community [that of the Muslims in the historical sense of the term]. Nor did He say: We have sent you toward men only from today up to the time of the Resurrection." The pardon announced is thus universal, as is Muhammad's mission; that is what confirms the very terms of the Qur'ânic pronouncement: "We have forgiven you of your sin, that which precedes and that which follows." "That which precedes" applies to all human beings who have lived in the period of occultation of the "Muhammadan Reality" (of which previous prophets had been only substitutes [*nuwwâb*] in this world); "that which follows" applies to all those who live and will live from the moment that this Muhammadan Reality becomes manifest in the person of Muhammad.[29] The universality of the *risâla muhammadiyya* thus corresponds to that of the Divine *Rahma*, and it is for this reason that the Prophet is spoken of in the Qur'ân (21:107) as a "mercy for peoples." Let us point out, without elaborating on the point, that the function of Seal of Muhammadan sainthood—that which Ibn 'Arabî claimed for himself—necessarily presents, in virtue of its relation to that of the Seal of Prophecy, a universal character that the Shaykh al-Akbar affirmed in declaring himself "the inheritor of him to whom it was said: We have sent you only as a mercy for the people."[30]

Numerous texts outline more precisely the consequences that

Ibn ʿArabî draws, in rigorous fidelity to sacred text, from the universality of Mercy. Consider, for example, this dialogue with Adam when the Shaykh al-Akbar, during his spiritual ascension, meets him in the first heaven.[31] "Happiness in the life to come," Adam says, "is perpetual, in spite of the difference in stations: for God has placed in each location [Heaven or Hell] that by which its inhabitants will know felicity." Elsewhere, turning toward a Qurʾânic term that has a remarkably ambivalent root (even though this ambivalence cannot be not wanted by God, since it is the Divine Word), he says:[32] "It has been called punishment (ʿadhâb) because it is agreeable (yaʿdhubu) in certain states and for certain beings, since the nature of their composition clamors for it." Let it be understood that these beings are of igneous nature and that a stay in hell is for them a return to the original state of fire. For Ibn ʿArabî, that hell is not necessarily a place of pain is moreover demonstrated by the case of angels who, according to Muslim tradition, live there as guardians, when God would have no apparent reason for punishing them.

It must be emphasized that for these creatures, Mercy is a *maʾâl*, a "finish line," the final point of their evolution. The passages cited above must be in no way interpreted—as a number of polemists have done, in good faith or otherwise—as denying the reality of punishment. Ibn ʿArabî accepts without reservation the explicit meaning of the verses that announce a stay in Gehenna, temporary or eternal, depending on the case, for sinners and unbelievers. But the fact that the stay is eternal does not necessarily mean that the pain is. Pain could not be eternal without the result being an inconceivable limitation in the "Mercy that embraces every thing." "The state of hell," writes Ibn ʿArabî, "will remain what it is, but Mercy will produce [for the damned] a felicity [naʿîm] without the form or the status of the infernal abode being modified: for Mercy is all-powerful, and its authority indefeasible forever."[33] However, that does not imply that there is no difference between the chosen and the damned: *wa baynahumâ ʿinda l-tajallî tabâyûn* (between these and those there is disparity at the time of theophany).[34] The *kâfir* (the infidel, the unbeliever), "will see God without knowing that he sees Him."

The term *kâfir*, which we have just translated in its usual acceptation—that which Ibn ʿArabî kept in the sentence quoted above—, brings us to consideration of a homogenous series of examples of Ibn ʿArabî's paradoxical interpretations, all of which are nevertheless in accord with the hermeneutical rules outlined at the beginning of this book. We have elsewhere stated the tremendous importance, in Ibn ʿArabî's work, of the hagiological doctrine with which these interpretations are linked: the prophetic function (*nubuwwa*) being definitively "sealed" by Muhammad, what is left open to men is the way that leads to sainthood (*walâya*) and, if the metaphysical teaching of the Shaykh al-Akbar intends to describe— to the extent possible by human language—the unique Reality and the secret of its epiphanies, the ultimate goal of his initiatory teaching is that of instructing the aspirant (*murîd*) about the conditions and modalities of the voyage (*sulûk*) that ends in sainthood.

There is no systematic expose of Ibn ʿArabî's hagiology. An overview is possible only via a patient confrontation of the often allusive indications present in the thousands of pages of his work. Nevertheless, in the *Futûhât* there is a text that, when appropriately interpreted, furnishes valuable guideposts, specifically, the long chapter 73 to which we have often referred. The responses to Tirmidhî's questions constitute the second part. The first part, after an introduction that defines the ideas of *risâla* (i.e., the status of the "Messengers" or the "Apostles"), *nubuwwa* (prophethood), *walâya* (sainthood) and *îmân* (faith), takes up two sections itself. We have already extracted considerable data[35] from these pages in a previous book, but some complementary information must be added here.

After the aforementioned introduction, Ibn ʿArabî announces that he is going to write about the *tabaqât al-awliyâ* ("classes" or "categories" of saints). But, as will be seen, the word *tabaqât* covers categories that are not of the same nature, and without distinguishing between them one risks seeing redundancies and contradictions in this enumeration that fog their coherence. The initial section is dedicated to categories that include a fixed number of saints for each period of history. The first of these categories is that of the Poles (*aqtâb*), which at any given moment has one, and only one, titulary. Next come the two imams, the four *awtâd*, the seven *abdâl*, and so on. In total, there are thirty-five *tabaqât*—of which the widest, that of the "Adamics" (*adamiyyûn*), is represented by three hundred *awliyâ*—adding up to a constant number of 589 saints, each of whom is replaced upon his death.

It is at the end of this section[36] that Ibn ʿArabî gives a brief explanation of this unchangeable series of *awliyâ*. For everything involving a precise number in this world there is a corresponding group of saints containing an equal number of individuals. The numbers in question are those that, depending on traditional data, structure the universe: the four directions in space, the five canonical prayers, the seven "climates," the twelve signs of the zodiac, the twenty-four hours of the day, the three hundred divine attributes, and so forth. The thirty-five *tabaqât* thus essentially represent cosmic functions, the totality making up the spiritual hierarchy, which, in permanence, assures the maintenance of the order instituted by divine wisdom. The number thirty-five itself is undoubtedly not fortuitous, being the product of seven and five. Seven, which is the number of heavens and earths (cf., for example, Qurʾân 65:12), symbolizes the sum of the degrees of creation. The number five, on the other hand, has a specific role of protection in Ibn ʿArabî;[37] the role of the number is recognized in Islamic tradition as in other previous traditions, as, for example, in the well-known case of "Fatma's hand," and in the use of the pentacle in theurgic arts, in Bunî.[38]

The second section is dedicated to the description of the 49 new *tabaqât*, which, from one period to another, have a greater or lesser number of *awliyâ*. The knowledge belonging to each age is divided among these *awliyâ*, and if need be it can be be drawn together in one being if, at a given moment, he is the only one present.

After having given, in the first section, a precise and numbered list of the *functions* with a permanent, universal character, what Ibn ʿArabî attempts here is to outline what the *types* and *degrees* of sainthood are (it is definitely not an exhaustive table[39]). He does so, sometimes using one of these criteria and sometimes using the other, without alerting his readers. The type—that is, etymologically speaking, the "imprint"—is that which differentiates one particular modality of spiritual realization from all the others. The characteristic signs are the predominance of certain charismata, the emphasis on certain virtues, the exclusive practice of one special invocation and, especially, the privileged relationship of the *awliyâ* belonging to this particular "family" with one of the

Divine Names. Here a distribution that associates each type to a term borrowed from the Qur'ân or a hadith replaces the "genetic" classification that Ibn 'Arabî uses on other occasions, when he links each form of *walâya* to a determined prophetic model. In this manner a whole series of definitions is linked to the long enumeration of verse 33:35: *al-muslimûn, al-mu'minûn, al-qânitûn* (those who have submitted, those who believe, the devout"), and so on. The interpretation of all these words entails the development of meanings far beyond those usually associated with them. At the top of this list stand the *malâmiyya* (or *malâmatiyya*, but Ibn 'Arabî, who considers this form to be a barbarism, nevertheless uses it on a number of occasions). They are, he says,

> the princes of men of the Path and their imams. The head of the universe, Muhammad, the Messenger of God, is one of their number. They are the sages who put everything in its proper place. They affirm secondary causes where they need to be affirmed, and deny them where they should be denied...What this lower world requires, they grant to this lower world; what the other world requires, they grant to the other world...Their eminence is unknown [down here]. Only their Lord knows them.

Next comes the definition of five other *tabaqât* (*fuqarâ, sûfiyya, 'ubbâd, zuhhâd, rijâl al-mâ*), which are followed by two categories, the *afrâd* and the *umanâ*, which present a number of points in common with the *malâmiyya*, to the extent that one might wonder how to distinguish between them. The *afrâd*, the "solitary," which another chapter of the *Futûhât* purposely refers to as *malâmiyya*,[40] are described here as the "intimates" (*muqarrabûn*, an allusion to Qur'ân 56:11). These are, among men, what the cherubim (*al-karûbiyyûn*)[41] are among celestial spirits: like them, they are forever lost (*muhayyamûn*) in the contemplation of God's majesty and have withdrawn in his presence. They know only him. The Prophet Muhammad, before the revelation of his mission, was one of them. Their station is that of "free prophethood" (*nubuwwa mutlaqa*), which stands between the station of "confirmation of the truth" (*siddiqiyya*) and that of "legislating prophethood" (*nubuwwa shar'iyya*). As for the *umanâ*, the plural of *amîn* (a name used for the Prophet), men who are "dependable," "trustworthy": these are "a group from within the *malâmiyya*," "the greatest of the *malâmatiyya* [*sic*] and their elite. Nothing is known of their spiritual states, for they behave with creatures according to the normal demands of faith...It is at the Day of Resurrection that their eminent degree will appear to creatures, while here below they were unknown among men."

According to Ibn ʿArabî's explanation in chapter 309 of the *Futûhât*, a chapter reserved entirely for them, the *malâmiyya* (sing. *malâmî*), the "men of blame," get their name from the second verse of sura 75, which mentions "the soul that blames itself" (*al-nafs al-lawwâma*).[42] This name applies to them because they do not stop blaming themselves for their imperfections and because they judge none of their actions sufficiently free of impurity to be pleasing to God but especially because they hide their spiritual perfection by mingling with the mass of believers and thus exposing themselves, like the common people, to the blame of the *fuqahâ* and the sufis. But there are degrees within this horizontal type of *walâya*, as there are within all the others. For example, just as Ibn ʿArabî explicitly distinguishes a vertical scale of *tabaqât* at the very heart of the category of *mutassaddiqûn* (those who give alms), there are, among the *malâmiyya*, levels of perfection: the *umanâ* represent a superior degree of the *malâmî* type, and the *afrâd*—themselves divided into two levels—constitute the highest degree. They thus eminently possess all the characteristics of the *malâmiyya* and of the *umanâ*, which explains why they also can be simply called by the latters' names. On the other hand, certain of these *afrâd* can see themselves invested with a function and thus be mentioned under the title corresponding to this function (*qutb, watad, badal*, etc.). Such a title in no way changes their belonging to the "genus" *malâmî*.

The texts we have cited nevertheless suggest that the type *malâmî* is not a type like the others and that it would not be enough to see in the *afrâd* the highest degree of a particular modality of sainthood. There are two quite significant indications in this regard. The *afrâd* are, as has been seen, the *muqarrabûn*, the "intimates"; and their station is that of the *nubuwwa mutlaqa* (which Ibn ʿArabî at times also calls *nubuwwa âmma*, "general prophethood"): nonlegislating prophethood, as distinguished from that

which belongs strictly speaking to the *anbiyâ* and which is "sealed"
by Muhammad but located at a level immediately below the latter.
This *nubuwwa mutlaqa*, a privilege of the *afrâd* and, consequently,
reserved for saints of the type *malâmî*, represents the unsurpass-
able summit of all *walâya*. Those who reach it are to the other
awliyâ "what the Messengers [*rusul*] are to the prophets."[43]

This "station" is the very same one that another term in Ibn
ʿArabî's vocabulary designates, that of *maqâm al-qurba*, "station of
proximity";[44] this is why the *afrâd* are also called *"al-muqarrabûn"*.
The repeated association, under the pen of the Shaykh al-Akbar, of
"solitary" with the idea of "proximity" is itself also extremely revealing, since this idea is that which properly defines—in accord with the
original sense of the root *wly*—the essence of *walâya*. Now, in numerous cases Ibn ʿArabî refers to these *malâmiyya*, who thus represent
the most perfect form of sainthood, as the *kâfirûn*, and he quite systematically ascribes to them the attributes that, in the Qurʾân, are
those of the "unbelievers." Such is particularly the case in chapter 5 of
the *Futûhât*,[45] but also in chapter 73,[46] and in the *Kitâb al-tajalliyât*.[47]
"They are deaf, dumb, blind, and intellectually deprived. They are
deaf, dumb, blind, and irrevocably lost," he writes in this last work.
Reusing terms that, especially in sura *Al-baqara* (2:5–7; 170–71),
describe these "unbelievers" and taking into consideration the original meaning of the root *kfr* ("to hide"), he writes "They are the ones
who hide what has appeared to them in contemplation of the secrets
of union." He then comments on the verses according to which
"whether you warn them or not, they will not believe! God has put a
seal upon their hearts and upon their ears, and there is a veil over
their eyes." "God," he says, has "sealed their hearts" so that there will
no be room in them but for him, he has rendered them "deaf" so that
they will not hear in any word but his word, and it is his light that has
"blinded" their eyes.[48] The *kâfir*, etymologically, is also the "sower,"
thus the interpretation that completes the preceding one: "The
kâfirûn are those who, as the *malâmiyya*, hide their spiritual station.
They are the sowers who hide their seed in the earth."[49]

The stunning transmutation—blasphemous in the eyes of Ibn
ʿArabî's adversaries, it must be said—by which the *kâfir* becomes
the saint par excellence does have its doctrinal foundation, and the
Shaykh al-Akbar explains himself on several occasions. First of all,
he reminds his reader that God describes Himself, in the Qurʾân

and the hadith, using attributes that belong to the imperfect creatures that we are: he "becomes proud," he "forgets," he "is wily," he
"deceives." This well demonstrates that apparently negative qualifications can also have a positive sense and that there is thus nothing surprising about God "hiding his saints under the traits of His
enemies." It is even from this positivity that every name, every
thing, be it noble or ignoble, draws its reality, its *raison d'être*, for
there is no shadow without light: nothing of that which is is without a base *in divinis*, of a *mustanad ilâhî*.[50] Now, "in the Qur'ân or
in any thing, men of intimacy, of beauty, and of Mercy see only perfection and beauty"[51] for it is toward this *mustanad ilâhî* that their
gaze is turned. When they read in the Qur'ân the description of
those who have incurred the wrath of God, they take the words in
the sense that is in accord with their path, and they retain only the
most beautiful meaning. They are thus filled with joy by the same
thing that, for others, is the announcement of punishment (*'adhâb*),
for this is sweetness (*'udhûba*) for them. They are deprived of intelligence (*lâ ya'qilûn*) for the intellect (*'aql*) is, according to etymology, a "bond" from which they are free.[52]

In his response to Tirmidhî's question 154, Ibn 'Arabî, com-
pleting the enumeration of the types of *walâya* appearing at the
beginning of chapter 73 of the *Futûhât*, thus distinguishes several
categories whose names patently refer to the "enemies of God." The
hâsidûn, the "envious," are those who envy divine characteristics
(*al-akhlâq al-ilâhiyya*) and attempt to acquire them. The *sâhirûn*,
the "magicians," are those who have received from God the "science
of letters," which is entirely contained within the initial words of
the first sura of the Qur'ân, the *basmala*, which is for them that
which the *kun!* (the original *fiat!*) is for God.[53] The *zâlimûn*, the
"unjust," are those beings who have chosen to fight against the *nafs*
(the ego) and, in order to conquer it, refuse it the satisfaction of its
legitimate rights by subjecting themselves to the most rigorous of
practices. This is consistent with Qur'ân 35:32, where God mentions, among those whom he calls "our servants," "those who are
unjust toward themselves."

Likewise, "those who are forgetful of their prayers" (Qur'ân
107:5) are the saints whose ritual prayers are no longer their own,
although they perform them on the outside, because God is "their
hearing, their sight, their speech," and in truth it is he who is pray-

ing: their acts no longer belong to them. Those who "refuse [the creatures] their help" (Qur'ân 107:7)—and thus appear to be lacking in that charity that is inseparable from any sanctity—act in such a manner only to distract men's gaze from considering secondary causes and thus turn it toward God, for it is he alone who comes to assist. Those who are "astray" (al-dâllûn) are those who wander (al-ta'ihûn), caught by dizziness (al-ha'irûn) in Divine Majesty: every time they would like to stop to find rest, God bestows upon them a new science about himself that annihilates them. "Those who lead astray" (al-mudillûn) are those who teach their followers the impossibility of exhausting the knowledge of God and lead them toward the perpetual bewilderment of the dâllûn. "Liars" (al-kâdhibûn) attribute to themselves acts prescribed by Sacred Law but know that God is the sole agent: they "lie" to be in accord with the common usage of the believers (whom a truthful language would scandalize and drag into disobedience) and thus hide their spiritual degree.

The Qur'ânic term al-fujjâr, the "debauched," is interpreted by returning to the first meaning of the root fjr, as it appears in verse 76:6. The tafjîr is the act by which spring water is allowed to flow freely. The true fujjâr are, for Ibn 'Arabî, those beings who have accessed the springs of knowledge that God has forbidden to most men because of their natural dispositions. For, if these springs flowed freely, men would be almost all be led (through the effect of an impure look) to profess libertinism (ibâha), incarnationism (hulûl) or other errors that would bring about their loss. The fujjâr, on the other hand, have captured the true meaning of this knowledge. "They have opened a passage to the water of the source, they have drunk of their waters, and they have thus obtained a supplement to guidance and enlightenment."

That this is the setting up of a hermeneutical principle with quite general application rather than a chance series of paradoxes is vigorously expressed at the beginning of the paragraph[54] where Ibn 'Arabî states: "Proceed in a similar manner [to that which precedes] and likewise transpose any characteristic that is worthy of blame in its indeterminate form and that, via an adequate determination, becomes worthy of praise." He promptly demonstrates with an extreme example: "The gravest of blameworthy characteristics is the fact of associating something with God (al-shirk). But there

are 'associators' [or 'polytheists', *mushrikûn*] among the saints."
The exceptional seriousness of *shirk* is evidenced by verses 4:48,
115: of all sins, it is the only one that God cannot pardon. But God
also said (Qur'ân 17:110): "Invoke Allâh or invoke *Al-Rahmân* [the
All-Merciful]. Regardless of the name with which you invoke him,
to him belong the most beautiful Names." The "associator" saints
are those who, taking God's own example, associate with God all
the names with which he has described himself for, although different in a certain sense, they all refer to a single Named One, returning to a single Essence. If you do that, Ibn 'Arabî adds, "it is you
who are the true associator!" (*anta huwa l-mushrik 'alâ l-haqîqa*).
For, in order for there to be true association, those things that one
associates must be associated in everything, and thus they must
have one essence in common. The *mushrik* in the ordinary sense of
the word, the polytheist, attributes different essences to those
things that he associates. He is thus not truly a *mushrik*, and it is
because his *shirk* is a "pretention without foundation" (*da'wâ kâd-
hiba*) that he will be punished.

These examples, which are given because they offer a particularly meaningful illustration of an uncommon kind of exegesis, are
far from exhausting the meanings of the words or verses to which
they refer. The Qur'ân, for Ibn 'Arabî, is a treasure whose abundance is truly infinite; and the *ishârât*, the "allusions" to divine
secrets which can be perceived by those who listen to it in a state of
perfect *ummiyya*, are countless. To some degree, certain ones of
them are communicable, and, among them, there are those that
must imperatively be communicated, since they open the path to
understanding the Qur'ân for those who possess the necessary
qualifications: the *tafjûr*, the piercing that opens a passage for the
waters of a spring, is among the attributes of sainthood, as has
been seen. However, many other secrets transcend the limits of language, and it is up to the individual to experience their flavor
through a personal experience that will never be exactly replicated
by the same person and never be identical for different individuals.
The coming chapters will allow us to sense the extent to which the
Shaykh al-Akbar's teaching is a perpetual discovery of the meanings of what, for him, is perpetual revelation. We say to sense only,
for with the author of the *Fusûs* as with Tirmidhî,[55] what characterizes revelation (*al-wahy*) is its immediacy: no echo exempts one

from hearing the original sound that it reverberates, no gloss, even if inspired, manages to capture in its nakedness the word of divine language upon which it comments.

One more aspect of Ibn ʿArabî's hermeneutics must be mentioned, for it has important practical consequences: the principles that determine, for Ibn ʿArabî, the interpretation of the Qurʾân in its function of establishing the legal rules to which the believer's behavior must be submissive. This problem, which one might think strange for an author often classified in a restrictive manner among the *ahl al-bâtin*, actually occupies a considerable place in his work. The entire translation, exluding notes and comments, of the texts concerning subjects considered answerable to the *fiqh* would undoubtedly fill two large volumes. It is true that most of these texts concern *ʿibâdât*, duties toward God[56] and especially, therefore, prescribed rites. At the end of this book we shall see the main function of these rites on the Path as it leads to sainthood (*walâya*). It will be seen at the same time that the conception of *ʿibâdât* in Ibn ʿArabî ends up embracing all aspects of the Law. But there are also numerous passages that deal with the rules applicable to human relationships (i.e., what the treatises of the *fiqh* classify among the *muʿamalât*). The same is true for the rules applicable to conditions of legitimacy of political power.[57] A few recent works[58] have underscored the interest in this little-explored side of the Shaykh al-Akbar's writings, even though it did previously attract Goldziher's attention.[59] Later in this work we will address the place that *ibâdât* occupy in Ibn ʿArabî's doctrine; at present we will limit ourselves to noting the characteristic traits of his teaching on the matter of *fiqh*.[60]

The most evident is his refusal to admit what is called "closing the door of *ijtihâd*" (the attempt to interpret the *sharîʿa* [the Law]), that is, to consider, as it became customary to do, the end of the third century (A.H.) as a stopping point, as the time when the framework for all juridical reflection was definitely laid out.[61] Consequently, it is also condemnation of the servile attachment of the *fuqahâ* to the interpretations of the founders of their schools of jurisprudence (*madhâhib*), for they go so far as to prefer the opinions of their imams to the Qurʾân itself. "And the first to disavow them on the Judgment Day will be their imam himself!"[62]

A brief parenthetical statement must be made here on the subject of the relations of Ibn ʿArabî with the (today no longer extant) Madhhab Zâhirî school founded by Dâwûd b. Khalaf (d. 270/884). Arab authors, and subsequently Goldziher, have habitually connected the author of the *Futûhât* with this school. The influence of the Zâhirî school on Ibn ʿArabî's thought in matters of law is of course undeniable. It is not by chance that the author of the *Fusûs* and of the *Futûhât* is also the author of an unfinished abridgment of the great Zâhirî Ibn Hazm's *Kitâb al-muhallâ*.[63] And it is of significance that a few years ago the Beirut edition of a treatise by Ibn Hazm, *Ibtâl al-qiyâs*, was based on a manuscript copied by Dhahabî on the edition of this work that Ibn ʿArabî had himself transcribed.[64] But in the eyes of the attentive reader, Ibn ʿArabî is not more Zâhirî than he is Mâlikî or Hanbalî: he is a prefectly autonomous *mujtahid*—or, perhaps, the founder of a *madhhab akbarî*, of an "Akbarian school of jurisprudence," which is, as shall be seen, the most irenic, the most conciliatory of all those that Islam has known. In a number of cases his preferred solution has not been the Zâhirî solution,[65] especially concerning the major issue of reasoning by analogy (*qiyâs*); he has additionally made some quite unambiguous statements. In one of his poems he says:

> I am not one of those who says: "Ibn Hazm said,"
> Or "Ahmad [Ibn Hanbal] said" or "Al-Nuʿmân
> [Abû Hanîfa]."[66]

In another poem he is even more specific:

> They have made me a disciple of Ibn Hazm. But I am not one
> of those who says: "Ibn Hazm said"
> No! And neither am I one of those who invoke the authority
> of someone other than him.[67]

Two rules guide Ibn ʿArabî's reflections on the problems of *fiqh*. The first, he states thus:

> Every thing about which the *sharîʿa* keeps silence has no
> legal status other than original licitness [*al-ibâha al-asliyya*],[68]

which is in accord with the Qurʾânic precept: "Do not ask us about those things that, if they were shown to you, would bring you

wrong" (5:101) and the hadith in which the Prophet states, "Do not
ask me questions as long as I leave you alone!"[69]

In other words, what the Law is silent about is no more fortuitous than what it pronounces. If each word of the *sharî'a* has a
meaning, the absence of a word has one, too; and man, if he is not to
transgress the word of God, is not to fill in God's silence. The "holes"
in the Law are part of its plenitude. The "original licitness of
things" is not less the expression of Divine Will than their eventually illicit character under certain definite conditions.

The second rule further explains the first, and is equally scripturally based. He writes:

> Out of divergence in legal questions God has made both a
> Mercy for his servants and a widening [*ittisâ'*] of what he has
> prescribed for them to do to show their adoration. But the
> *fuqahâ* of our times have restricted and forbidden, for those
> who follow them, what the Sacred Law had widened for them.
> They say to one who belongs to their school, if he is Hanafîte,
> for example: "Do not go looking in Shafi'î for a *rukhsa* [a
> lightening, a dispensation] in this problem that you have."
> And so on for each of them. That is one of the gravest calami-
> ties and one of the heaviest constraints in the matter of reli-
> gion. Now God said that "He has imposed nothing difficult on
> you in matters of religion" [Qur'ân 22:78]. The law has
> affirmed the validity of the status of him who makes a per-
> sonal effort to interpret for himself or for those who follow
> him. But the *fuqahâ* of our time have forbidden this effort,
> maintaining that it leads to making light of religion. Such is
> their role in the fulfillment of ignorance![70]

A tutiorist scruple, a demanding spiritual discipline, can most
often lead the *sâlik* (*viator*) to reserve for himself the the most rigorous of solutions (*al-'azâ'im*). But he must not refuse others the
benefit of more accommodating solutions when, in good faith, a
qualified *mujtahid* finds support for it in the Qur'ân, the sunna of
the Prophet, or the consensus of the Companions. The consequence
of this attitude is that Ibn 'Arabî, when he examines a legal question, mentions all the responses that have been offered by the dif-

ferent schools of jurisprudence, and, if he mentions the one that has his preference, *he validates them all without exception.*

We will offer but one example, although it concerns a fundamental problem in the domain of the source of law. It is the problem of *qiyâs,* reasoning by analogy. Is its use legally permissible? Countless controversies take place over this issue and the Zâhirîs, among others, reject the use of *qiyâs.* Now Ibn ʿArabî, who prefers to not rely on it for himself, refuses to forbid its use by others. But, with the same logic, he opines that "the partisans of *qiyâs*...must not forbid the Zâhirîs from forbidding it."[71]

In summary, then, we have a fundamental principle: the Law is not the cloak or the symbol of *haqîqa,* of a hidden truth that might be reached by transgression. It *is* the *haqîqa:*[72] it thus imposes itself absolutely and up to the last iota on the *ʿârif bi-Llâh* (gnostic)—in the etymological sense of the word—as well as on the *ʿâmma,* the common believers. We also have two rules of application, one of which concerns the "silences" of the Law and the other, its ambiguities. These two rules are dictated neither by considerations of social unity nor by historical convenience. They have their foundation in the Law itself. The God who dictates the Law—and he dictates whether he is speaking or being silent—is also the God who said "My mercy comprehends all things" (*Wa rahmatî wasiʿat kulla shayʾin* [Qurʾân 7:156]). The *fiqh,* human elaboration of the *sharîʿa,* must consequently include and not exclude, open and not close. For the gnostic, this *comprehension,* in the proper meaning of the term, is not opposed to extreme rigor of observance: it is its fruit. Any attempt at reformation of the community, if it is not inspired by this principle and if it is not in accord with these rules, is thus simultaneously disobedience and failure.

3

"It Is To Him That You Will Be Led Back"
(QUR'ÂN 36:83)

In the section of his *Répertoire général* of Ibn 'Arabî's works dedicated to the *Fusûs al-hikam,* Osman Yahia lists more than a hundred commentaries on the *Fusûs,*[1] and this list is far from exhaustive. The heading "commentaries" in the section dedicated to the *Futûhât Makkiyya* is, on the other hand, quite short,[2] and examination of the texts mentioned therein reveals that the attention of their authors is limited to chapters or isolated passages of the work, rather than to the work as a whole. Such is particularly the case with 'Abd al-Karîm al-Jîlî, whose *Sharh mushkilât al-Futûhât* really only deals with the beginning of chapter 559,[3] regardless of what its title implies. The *Sharh-i Futûhât* in Persian, the second volume of which William Chittick recently discovered in the Andra Pradesh Library and which is probably attributable to Muhibbullâh Ilâhâbâdî (d. 1058/1648), is itself no more than a partial and discontinuous commentary. To judge by its title, the *Mulkhis 'ulûm al-Futûhât al-Makkiyya,* by Hasan b. Tu'ma al-Baytimânî (d. 1175/1761–62), mentioned by Murâdî in his *Silk al-durar,* is only a systematic summary, probably somewhat similar to Sha'rânî's *Yawâqît.* Emir 'Abd al-Qâdir al-Jazâ'irî, in his *Kitâb al-Mawâqif,* offers a detailed and meticulous interpretation of a few passages from the *Futûhât,* but if, as is probable, he commented orally on many others for his companions, there is no record of it in his writings. Our bibliography certainly contains lacunae, and within and beyond the frontiers of the Arab world—in Turkey, Iran, India, Malaysia, China, the Balkans—several works, the existence of which is as yet not even suspected, will undoubtedly enlarge it in the future. Let it nevertheless be said that nothing up to the present suggests that one day we will have a complete commentary on the *Futûhât.*

The *Fusûs al-hikam,* a relatively short work that assembles the great themes of the Shaykh al-Akbar's metaphysics in dense formulations, have been a favorite target of polemicists who, from Ibn Taymiyya to the present day, have violently denounced Ibn ʿArabî and his school. For similar reasons, it is on the *Fusûs* that the direct or indirect followers of Ibn ʿArabî have most often produced commentaries. Quite naturally, it is also this work that has most interested Western specialists. But only the *Futûhât* represent the definitive sum of Ibn ʿArabî's teaching seen in its myriad aspects; the countless references to this magnum opus seen in the literature of sufism testify that it has continued to be read and meditated upon: if its dimensions discourage the undertaking of a commentary, it is nevertheless constantly utilized, particularly since its reading is indispensable for a correct understanding of the *Fusûs*. In the introduction to this book we mentioned a few examples illustrative of the *Futûhât*'s influence, as well as the considerable borrowings from the work, among Arab authors. Persian authors, or those of Persian culture, also draw extensively on this superabundant source. Jandî and Haydar Amolî, among others, frequently quote the *Futûhât*.[4] Jâmî does likewise in many of his writings. Moreover, we have a very interesting testimony to the meticulous attention he pays in his attempt to capture the many subtleties of the work. In the *Rashahât ʿayn al-hayât*, a famous hagiographical collection about the early masters of the Naqshbandiyya, the author actually describes an encounter, in 874/1489, between Jâmî and ʿubaydallâh Ahrâr, who was his spiritual master. Jâmî, he recounts, tells Ahrâr that he had encountered problems in certain passages of the *Futûhât* that he could not manage to solve and showed him one of the most difficult. Ahrâr asked him to close the copy of the *Futûhât* that he was holding and then gave him a certain number of explanations. Afterward, Ahrâr said, "Now let us return to the book." The litigious passage, when it was reread, became perfectly clear to Jâmî.[5]

One century later, Ahmad Sirhindî, too often presented as an adversary of Ibn ʿArabî, likewise made, in his *Maktûbât*, frequent references to the *Futûhât*.[6] Such is also the well-known case of his contemporary, Mullâ Sadrâ: even if, in certain of his writings, prudence leads the latter to hide his normally easily identifiable borrowings, the citations that he does use from the *Futûhât* are abundant and sometimes quite long.[7] And, to this quite arbitrary selection, one might add a final example, this one quite recent: we refer to the Ayatollâh Khomeini, whose writings (especially those of his youth) attest to the fact that he was a diligent and perceptive reader of Ibn ʿArabî and, in particular, of the *Futûhât*.[8]

This brief summary could easily be lengthened, and even then it would certainly remain incomplete. Countless glosses, paraphrases, or commentaries produced by readers of the *Futûhât* over the last eight centuries remain for the moment, and perhaps forever, inaccessible. In any case, examination of those works that are known to us brings out a common and rather surprising trait in their authors: on first sight, none of them seems to consider the *Futûhât* as a whole. We often find in them quite perceptive remarks on such and such complex doctrinal theme, on the meaning of passages with delicate interpretations. But the structure of this paramount book—the number and the order of succession of its sections (*fusûl*), and of its chapters (*abwâb*), the subtle and quite rigorous relationships between different parts—never engenders the elucidations one would expect. It thus seems as though the *Futûhât* have always been seen as a cornucopia from which each drew symbols, technical terms, ideas or wordings, according to his inclination and without glimpsing (or allowing us to glimpse) the coherence of the whole and without seeking the secret of its architecture. Similarly, numerous very enigmatic indications given by Ibn ʿArabî—for example, the disconcerting lists of "spiritual sciences" corresponding to each *manzil* (abode), or the precise number of degrees corresponding to each *maqâm* (station)—remain unexplained. This silence of Muslim authors is, it must be said, imitated by Western researchers, among whom, nevertheless, works relating to Ibn ʿArabî are multiplying. Apparently, neither group can see the forest for the trees.

The fact that one finds no answer to these questions among those poets whose work carries a definite "Akbarian" stamp is not surprising: the literary form they have chosen and the nature of their inspiration do not lend themselves to this kind of analysis. Fakhr al-dîn ʿIrâqî, for example, even though he possibly studied the *Fusûs* and the *Futûhât* with Qûnawî, admirably crystallizes the "divine flashes" in his verse. But he is clearly not given to translating what he knows and what he feels into detailed discursive explanations. Such is the case, likewise, with the numerous writers who, after him, will lyrically express the splendor of Ibn ʿArabî's message.

But, to limit ourselves to the first generations of followers, what should be thought of the silence of Qûnawî himself? He was, after all, an exceptionally gifted student of the Shaykh al-Akbar, who left him the autograph manuscript of the final draft of the *Futûhât*. And what of the silence of Jandî, who was a student of Qûnawî's? What about Qâshânî, and Qaysarî? How is is possible to not be surprised at finding only brief and pithy overviews under the pen of ʿAbd al-Karîm al-Jîlî, who presents himself as the explainer of the *Futûhât*'s "obscurities"? Nevertheless, this last author describes the work with admiration, as "the most majestic ever written in the field of this science..., the most brilliant in the immensity of what it embraces."⁹ We do not have the space to review all the authors who might be expected to provide information—or at least to ask questions—suggesting a global approach to Ibn ʿArabî's *summa mystica*. But we do not feel that we err in repeating that they avoid the problems that we are dealing with here. Even if a text presently unknown to us were discovered tomorrow among the writings of Ibn ʿArabî's school, one that deals satisfactorily with these questions, it would remain no less necessary to justify the silence on the issue in the major works composed by the eminent representatives of Ibn ʿArabî's spiritual lineage.

One question must thus be asked: if these individuals, about whose perspicacity and veneration for Ibn ʿArabî there can be no doubt, offer no explanation, could the reason not be that there is nothing to explain? If the structure of the *Futûhât* engenders no remarks from them, is it not because this structure is totally arbitrary and thus resists any attempt at justification? Examination of the table of contents suggests, on first view, an affirmative reply: it is difficult to distinguish any ordered progression, any intelligible articulation of the themes that are there present. The same subject is often treated in a number of different chapters, chapters which are sometimes quite distant from one another and each of which appears to make no reference to the others. Long sections are seen as made up of a total or partial reworking of previous treatises and, thus, of more or less heterogeneous materials.

Moreover, what Ibn ʿArabî himself says appears to authorize this point of view: "Neither this book nor my other works are composed in the manner of ordinary books and I do not write them according to the usual method of authors."¹⁰ Furthermore, he says,

"I have not written a single letter of this book except under the influence of divine dictation."[11] This affirmation (repeated in a number of different instances) of an inspired characteristic of his writings makes one think that it would be vain to try to discern a precise pattern. The Shaykh al-Akbar adds an additional argument to this hypothesis in a reflection regarding the presentation (actually quite disconcerting for the reader) of data relative to the "legal statutes" (*ahkâm*): chapter 88, which outlines the principles (*usûl*) from which these statutes are derived, ought logically, he recognizes, to precede rather than follow chapters 68 to 72, which deal with their consequences; but, he says, "it was not my choice to keep this order."[12] And to illustrate this point, he compares the non sequiturs that are so numerous in the *Futûhât* to those that one sees in the suras of the Qur'ân, where verses follow others whose proximity appears purely accidental. The sentences just cited (and there are many others like them in the *Futûhât*) might consequently encourage one to conclude that a work whose composition obeys unforeseen inspirations is necessarily devoid of internal coherence and that the enigmas that it contains are indecipherable.

We can affirm that this conclusion is radically false. The analogy that Ibn 'Arabî calls to mind (between the abrupt breaks in meaning in the text of the Qur'ân and those of his own book) paradoxically constitutes a first indication in this regard, for, as he explains in another passage, the disorder in the Holy Book is only an appearance: "There is [between consecutive verses seemingly without relationship to one another] a relationship of affinity, but it is extremely secret."[13] "If you join each verse with the one that precedes and the one that follows, the force of the Divine Word will make you see that this verse requires that which accompanies it, and does not attain its perfection but through that which surrounds it. Such is the vision of the perfect among spiritual men."[14] This profound unity in the Qur'ân , which goes unnoticed in the eyes of the common believers, which the *tafsîr* authors themselves are powerless to make us discover, is nevertheless perceived by the gnostic (*'ârif bi-Llâh*). One can thus suspect that, for Ibn 'Arabî, it also exists—and that it is to some extent discoverable—in those *Futûhât* where there is nothing "that does not proceed from an insufflation of the divine Spirit";[15] and one might all the more suspect that it exists for him in that he affirms equally, as mentioned before: "All that of which we speak in our sessions and in our writings procedes from the Qurʾân and from its treasures."[16]

The *Futûhât* in reality are neither a disordered encyclopedia of bookish knowledge, as some have suggested, nor a heteroclite collection of sequences whose juxtaposition might be explained by surprises of inspiration. We would like to demonstrate here how well founded this affirmation is and to show by way of a few examples that it is equally valid for other of the Shaykh al-Akbar's writings.

In his critical edition of the *Futûhât*, Osman Yahia attempts to find an explanation for the number of chapters contained in the six sections (*fusûl*) of the *Futûhât*.[17] His remarks on this subject lead one to think that these different numbers were chosen by Ibn ʿArabî because they had, in Islamic tradition, a symbolic value, but not one that is necessary and intelligible to the nature of corresponding *fusûl*. O. Yahia shows, for example, that the number of chapters of the *fasl al-manâzil* (the section on "spiritual abodes") is identical to that of the 114 suras of the Qurʾân. However, he draws no particular consequence from this observation. The number 114 could have been chosen by Ibn ʿArabî, to some extent, for simple esthetic reasons. However, such is not the case, as shall be seen. Ibn ʿArabî, in this case as in that of other enigmas, offers his reader all the keys that are required: but these keys are deliberately dispersed and, most often, placed in such a way that they are passed over without being noticed.

Let us take a close look at this *fasl al-manâzil*, the fourth of the work and one of the most mysterious. It extends from chapter 270 to chapter 383. From all appearances, it is related at least by its title to one of the first chapters of the *Futûhât* , chapter 22, which is intitled *"fî maʿrifat ʿilm manzil al-manâzil"* (concerning knowledge of the abode of abodes). But this chapter 22, which O. Yahia calls *"bâb gharîb"* (strange chapter), presents a priori more problems than it solves. It contains a list that groups together, under nineteen principal "spiritual abodes" (*ummahât al-manâzil*) a series of secondary *manâzil*, which in turn contain a series of others. The denominations of all these *manâzil* (denominations that are seen to reappear here and there in the *fasl al-manâzil*) are perplexing: *manzil al-istikhbâr, manzil al-halâk, manzil al-duʿâ, manzil al-rumûz*, and so on. None of these designations corresponds to the taxonomy in use in sufi literature to distinguish the stages of the spiritual life.

Like many other terms in his vocabulary, the word *manzil* (literally, "the place where one gets off") is used by Ibn ʿArabî with quite different meanings according to the context. It may refer simply to a "stop," like the one that the Shaykh al-Akbar makes in 597 A.H. between Marrakesh and Salé, at the place called Igîsil, where he is to be given access to the "station of proximity."[18] It applies also to the degrees of paradise, or to the twenty-eight degrees of the universal manifestation, which, in chapter 198 of the *Futûhât* , are described in relation to the twenty-eight letters of the alphabet and to twenty-eight divine names.[19] In the reply to Tirmidhî's first question, the mention of the 248,000 *manâzil al-awliyâ* (abodes of the saints) corresponds to another use of the term: it expresses (248,000 = 124,000 x 2) the double heritage of the Muhammadan saints. It refers to the heritage which they receive from the 124,000 prophets, who, according to tradition, span the course of history, and that which they receive from the Prophet Muhammad himself.[20] At the beginning of the *fasl al-manâzil*, the *manzil* is defined as "the place in which God descends toward you, or in which you descend upon him."[21] This definition is evidently that which should be used here, but it requires a precise technical interpretation which Ibn ʿArabî actually gives and which devolves from the use in the Qurʾân of the root *nzl*, in its nominal or verbal forms, to describe the "descent" of Revelation. This is articulated clearly in chapter 27 of the *Futûhât*, which is not the only indication of its kind: *al-suwar hiya l-manâzil*, "the suras are the abodes," an affirmation that is repeated in the *Tanazzulât mawsiliyya*, among others.[22] There is also an unpublished treatise, written by Ibn ʿArabî in 603 A.H., that is, after he had been working on the *Futûhât* for four years, that is called *Kitâb manzil al-manâzil*[23] and furnishes us with valuable complementary information. The "spiritual abodes" mentioned in chapter 22 are also enumerated with the same, or quite similar, terminology but are to a certain extent topographically situated. For example, one sees, *à propos* of the abodes listed under the heading *manzil al-rumûz*:[24] "Between the *manzil al-istiwâ min al-amâ* [called *manzil al-ityân min al-ʿamâ* in chapter 22] and the *manzil al-tamaththul* there is *Waw manâzil*"—the letter *waw* must obviously be understood here as representing the number 6, its numerical value according to *abjad*. "Between it and the *manzil al-qulûb* there are *Yâ hâ* [15] *manâzil*. Between it and the *manzil al-hijâb* there are *Yâ tâ* [19] *manâzil*. Between it and the *manzil al-istiwâ al-fahwânî* there are *Kaf* [20] *manâzil*."[25]

Cross-checking these different data allows one to identify the "abodes"—that is, the suras—cryptically designated in chpater 22 and in the series of chapters which make up the fourth section of the *Futûhât*. The *manzil al-istikhbâr* (the abode of interrogation) is that which unites the suras beginning with an interrogative formula, like sura 88 (*Hal atâka hadîth al-ghâshiya*). The *manzil al-hamd* (abode of praise), which is subdivided into five *manâzil*, is made up of five suras (1, 6, 18, 34, 35) that begin with *Al-hamdu li-Llâh*. The *manzil al-rumûz* (abode of symbols) includes all the suras that begin with the *hurûf muqatta'a*, the mysterious single letters also referred to as *nûrâniyya* (luminous). The *manzil al-du'â* (abode of calling) is the common name for the suras beginning with the vocative *Yâ ayyuhâ*...The *manzil al-amr* (abode of the commandment) comprises the suras that begin with a verb in imperative mood, like *qul* (Say!). In the *manzil al-aqsam* (abode of oaths) are found the suras beginning with an oath ("By the dawn" "By the sun") and in the *manzil al-wa'îd* (abode of threat), those whose first word is *wayl*, "Woe to." We will not continue this enumeration, the information that follows on the structure of the *fasl al-manâzil* being sufficient for the reader of the *Futûhât* to observe for himself the equivalencies between the names of the "abodes" and the suras. It will be important to remember that the hierarchy of *manâzil* (group of suras corresponding to suras) does not stop there: each *manzil*—each sura—contains in turn other *manâzil*—the verses, each word of which is also an "abode."

If the above observations allow us to foresee an exact correspondance between the 114 chapters of the "section of abodes" and the 114 suras, the order in which this takes place is not yet clarified. Attempting to establish a relationship between the first of these chapters and the first sura, between the second chapter and the second sura, and so on, would be in vain, even if that might appear to be the most probable hypothesis. But the solution to the problem is clearly suggested by Ibn 'Arabî himself at the beginning of chapter 22, where the word *'urûj*, "ascent," and the word *mi'râj*, "ascension," appear in the second and third verses, respectively, of the prefatory poem. It is confirmed by the *Kitâb manzil al-manâzil*, where we find, beginning with the fourth line of our manuscript, *maʿârij* (plural of *miʿrâj* followed shortly thereafter by a sentence about "the ascension from the foot of the mountain up to the summit," while *ʿurûj* and *miʿrâj* appear several times at the end of the text.[26] Let us add that this same treatise, thanks to the precise numbers that he gives about the spacing of "abodes," provides the means of checking the exactness of the solution.

Based on all these indications, is appears that, for Ibn ʿArabî, if Revelation *descends* from God towards humanity, the route for the *viator* is symetrically an *ascending* route that, contrary to the usual order of the Qurʾânic Vulgate, leads the *murîd* from the last sura of the Qurʾân, sura *Al-nâs*, to the first one, *Al-fâtiha*, "the one that opens," the one in which the person is given the ultimate *fath*, definitive illumination. In other terms, it becomes a question of climbing back from the extreme point of Universal Manifestaton (which the last word of the Qurʾân, *al-nâs* [humanity], symbolizes) to its Divine Principle (which is symbolized by the first sura, *Umm al-kitâb* (the Mother of the Book), and, more exactly, the point of the *bâ* in the *basmala*). The inexplicable succession of the chapters then becomes perfectly coherent, and the relationship that we have pointed out becomes demonstrable without exception in each of their texts. In fact, it can be observed in their very titles by anyone who has a familiarity with the Qurʾân. A few examples serve to illustrate: the third *manzil* (chapter 272), *manzil tanzîh al-tawhîd*, the "abode of the transcendence of Unicity," corresponds in an obvious way to the third sura from the last, *Al-ikhlâs*, whose theme is divine unicity; the fourth (chapter 273), *manzil al-halâk*, "abode of perdition," corresponds to sura *Al-masad*, which describes the punishment of Abû Lahab; the sixth sura *suʿûdan*, that is (always counting from the end of the Qurʾân forward) to sura *Al-kâfirûn*, whose theme is the rejection of idolatrous beliefs. The nineteenth *manzil* (chapter 288), "abode of recitation," corresponds via the same rule to sura *Al-ʿalaq*, where the Prophet is ordered to recite the Revelation that the angel is transmitting to him; the forty-seventh (chapter 316), "abode of the Divine Pen," corresponds to sura *Al-qalam*—and so forth up to the one hundred fourteenth and last *manzil*, the *manzil al-ʿazama al-jâmiʿa*, "the abode of Totalizing Immensity," which is the one where the being, having arrived at the end of this initiatory voyage, realizes the secrets of the "Mother of the Book." Given the key, the reader can complete the enumeration.

These brief indications are in any case sufficient to confirm that there is nothing fortuitous in the organization of the *fasl* and that the succession of subjects treated, as singular as it may appear, obeys a precise law. One will not be surprised, for example, to see chapter 366 on the *wuzarâ al-mahdî* (the ministers of the Mahdî) followed without apparent justification by the chapter wherein Ibn ʿArabî describes his ascension from heaven to heaven up to the threshold of the Divine Presence: chapter 366 happens to correspond, according the the schema that we have outlined, to sura *Al-kahf*, whose eschatological character is well known (and emphasized by Ibn ʿArabî, who strongly encourages his readers to recite its beginning in order to protect themselves from the *dajjâl*, the Antichrist), and chapter 367 to sura *Al-isrâ,* which deals with the heavenly ascension of the Prophet. And it will be understood that chapter 336 deals with the *mubâyaʿat al-qutb* (Pact with the Pole), because it is an echo, according to the same logic, to sura *Al-fath,* wherein is mentioned the pact of the Companions with the Prophet at Hudaybiyya (Qurʾân 48:10, 18). Similarly, that the penultimate abode, the *manzil* of the "Seals," deals with the functions of the Seal of Muhammadan Sainthood and with the Seal of Universal Sainthood, would not surprise anyone who remembers that the reference is here in sura *Al-baqara* (sura 2), whose last verses are called in Islam, according to usage that dates from the time of the Prophet, *khawâtim sûrat al-Baqara* (seals of sura *Al-baqara*).

Other enigmas are resolved as soon as the rules that organize the "section of abodes" are understood. We will illustrate this point by referring to two consecutive chapters (273 and 274), chapters that are closely related.[27] The first, that of the *manzil* of "perdition," corresponds, as has been said, to sura *Al-masad* (Qurʾân 111), the second, that of the *manzil* of the "fixed term," to sura *Al-nasr* (Qurʾân 110). Let it be said immediately that the mention of five "rivers" (*anhâr*) at the beginning of chapter 273 is a first allusion to the five verses of the sura. Ibn ʿArabî first mentions, in veiled language, the initial *basmala* (about which he will again speak at the end of the chapter, referring to it symbolically as the "vestibule" [*dihliz*] of this abode). When he himself visits this abode, he sees the Pen—the traditional symbol in Islam of the First Intellect—in the Universal Matrix (that is, in the "Mother of the Qurʾân," the *Fâtiha*) whence he draws his knowledge and the exact place it occu-

pies, that is, a point of color "between red and yellow." It is not difficult to understand that this point is that which, in Arabic writing,
is placed under the letter *bâ*, which is the first letter of the *basmala*[28] and thus the first letter of the first sura of the Qur'ân. The
color attributed to it expresses its medial position between the setting sun and the rising sun, that is, between the "world of secrets"
and the "world of light." It is from the Universal Matrix that the
gnostics, according to Ibn 'Arabî, gain access to the knowledge of
divine transcendence (*tanzîh*). Seventy-two steps—the numerical
value of the letters that make up the *basmala*, according to the
manner of calculating called *"jazm saghîr"*—lead them to the sciences that have been promised to them. The First Intellect, which
is the "master of this *manzil*," takes Ibn 'Arabî by the hand and has
him visit the five "chambers" (a new allusion to the number of
verses). In each of these there are chests (*khazâ'in*). Each of the
chests has locks (*aqfâl*); each lock has keys (*mafâtih*); each key
must be turned a certain number of times (*harakât*).

Next, the the Shaykh al-Akbar describes, one by one, these
chambers and their contents: the first chest of the first chamber has
three locks, the first of these locks has three keys, the first of the
keys must be turned four hundred times, and so forth. These
strange details, which may be disconcerting to the reader, are easily interpreted as soon as one is somewhat familiar with the
method that Ibn 'Arabî uses, a method that is offered in numerous
examples in his works: the chests are the words of each verse, the
number of locks is that of the letters that make up each of the
words, the keys are the graphic signs that make up the letters (diacritical marks and consonant *ductus*), with the number of turns of
the key represented by the numerical value of these same letters
according to *abjad*. The first chest is the word *tabbat*; it is composed
of three letters, which is the number of locks. The first of these
locks is the *tâ'*, which is made up of three graphic signs—thus,
three keys—and whose numeric value is four hundred. Analogous
explanations—where the science of letters (*'ilm al-hurûf*) plays an
important role that chapter 2 of the *Futûhât* expressly announces—
may be given each time that remarks of this kind are encountered,
no matter where, in the work.[29] Those who consider this as nothing
more than a gratuitous intellectual game must at least admit that
it is a game played with rules.

The visit of the *manzil* of "perdition"—it must be remembered
that, for Ibn ʿArabî, it is a question of personal experience with this
abode and not some erudite commentary—is then described in such
a way that one can easily check the exact relationship with the
linking of words and verses in sura 111. In the first "chest," corresponding to the word *tabbat* (may they perish), Ibn ʿArabî discovers
"perilous" (*muhlika*) sciences: these are the speculative sciences,
those of the theologians and the philosophers, but also the secret
sciences (*ʿulûm al-sirr*), which can, if used carelessly, put those who
use them in mortal danger.[30] The second chest contains the "sciences of power" (*ʿulûm al-qudra*), which are obviously related to the
traditional symbolism of the "hands," that is, to the second word of
the sura. The complete translation of the verse is "May Abû Lahab's
hands perish, and may he himself perish!" The third word, the
third chest, is, in Arabic, Abû Lahab's name; despite the fact that
he was one of the enemies of the first Muslims, he was the
Prophet's uncle, and two of Muhammad's daughters married Abû
Lahab's sons. Abû Lahab, which is properly speaking a surname,
means "father of the flame." Opening the third chest, Ibn ʿArabî
sees Gehenna. But, in the center of this infernal fire, he sees a
"green garden" and a man who comes out of the fire and spends an
hour in the garden before returning to the coals. Not knowing that
this "abode" is really sura *Al-masad*, the reader is able to do nothing more than file this vision away without finding any coherent
explanation with what precedes it and what follows it. But, as soon
as the Qurʾânic reference to this passage is perceived, its meaning
becomes apparent: the central garden is nothing more than the
medial letter of *lahab* (flame), which is the *hâ*, the first letter of the
Divine Name *huwa* (he, him). The man who comes out of the flame
to refresh himself in the garden is Abû Lahab himself, who, according to Islamic tradition, will be periodically relieved of his punishment as a reward for the joy he experienced when Muhammad was
born; he had celebrated the birth by freeing a slave.

We will not further extend the description of this *manzil*. The
detailed description of each of the details associated with it would
take considerable space, and would ultimately make complete
sense only to readers who have access to Ibn ʿArabî's own text, to
the Qurʾân, and to its traditional commentaries. What should be
gleaned from this cursory examination is, on the one hand, that the

structure (and not just the content) of Ibn 'Arabî's text is determined by that of the Book—as other examples will prove—and, on
the other hand, that the trip from "abode" to "abode" is really a voyage in the Word of God.

Sura *Al-nasr* (divine assistance), to which the following chapter refers, is one of the last, and most probably even the last complete sura revealed. When he heard it, Abû Bakr—who was to
become the first caliph of the Islamic community—understood that
it announced the approaching death of the Prophet. It is to this that
the names of both the *manzil*, such as it appears at the beginning of
chapter 274 ("abode of fixed term"), and the one by which it is called
when it is mentioned in chapter 22 ("abode of the announcement of
the meeting") allude: it is certainly a question of encounter with the
Supreme Companion (*al-rafîq al-a'lâ*), that is, with God. If the
theme of the *manzil* of sura *Al-masad* is struggle against those passions that lead man to perdition (and this alludes to the beginning
of the "voyage" [*sulûk*], to the beginning of the "spiritual combat"
[*mujâhada*]), then the *manzil* of sura *Al-nasr* refers (as its first
verse says: "When the help of God and victory [*al-fath*] arrive") to
the next stage (that in which divine grace leads to *fath*, to "victory,"
to "opening," to "illumination," which implies initiatory death). It is
for this reason that this chapter mentions the technical modalities
of this second phase, and, in particular, "solitary wandering"
(*siyâha*) and "retreat to a cell" (*khalwa*). The practice of *khalwa*, to
which Ibn 'Arabî devotes a number of treatises,[31] is traditionally
associated with the number forty by virtue of a prophetic tradition
according to which the "sources of wisdom" flow from the heart of
him who has devoted himself exclusively to God for forty days (literally, forty mornings). But it is also notably associated with the
forty nights during which Moses prepared for his conversation with
God (Qur'ân 7:142) and with the forty days that Adam's body
awaited the insufflation of the spirit. It is interesting to note that
this number—which is also the numerical value of *mîm*, the first
letter of *mawt*, death, the subject with which the chapter opens—
represents the total number of words in sura *Al-masad* (17) and
sura *Al-nasr* (23) and corresponds additionally to the forty years
that passed between the birth of the Prophet and Revelation. These
correspondances symbolize the length of the voyage that the *sâlik*
undertakes in pursuit of the Prophet, the voyage that leads to the

"fixed term" (*ajal musammâ*), the event that marks the definitive extinction of the ego.

For reasons to be outlined later, Ibn ʿArabî systematically shuffles the cards, frequently using different names to refer to the same things. Thus, the "chambers" of chapter 273 are sometimes called "rivers" (*anhâr*), "degrees" (*darajât*, a word that itself has different meanings according to its context), "grades" (*martaba*), and so forth. Here we see the appearance of names previously used in chapter 270,[32] like *dînâr* and *qîrât* (carat, a monetary unit representing one twenty-fifth of a *dinar*). The mention of the four dinars (a total of 100 carats), the possession of which corresponds to complete spiritual realization, is once again understandable only if the reader turns toward the chapter's Qurʾânic reference: sura *Al-nasr* contains four verses, including the *basmala* (which, for Ibn ʿArabî, is an integral part of any sura and not just the *Fâtiha*, as is generally thought[33]). These verses are composed of ninety-nine letters, the traditional number of divine names; the hundredth, the supreme Name, is revealed only to the *ʿârif bi-Llâh* (gnostic). Each of the four dinars symbolizes what the Shaykh al-Akbar elsewhere (e.g., at the beginning of chapter 73) calls the *"arkân al-dîn,"* (pillars of the religion): *îmân* (faith), *walâya* (sainthood); *nubuwwa* (prophethood), and *risâla* (the mission of the Apostles). The progressive acquisition of carats and dinars, the stages of which Ibn ʿArabî mentions, corresponds to the esoteric meanings that he perceives in the successive verses of the sura. We will not attempt to gloss this passage of extreme subtlety, but we must nevertheless make two important points. First, the last carat of the fourth dinar corresponds to the Seal of Sainthood. Second, Ibn ʿArabî, as he does on several occasions, emphasizes the fact that *rujûliyya*, "spiritual virility," can be a characteristic of women as well as of men.[34]

Chapter 278 is that of the *manzil al-ulfa*, the "abode of union" or of "assembly," an allusion to the first verse of sura 106 (*Quraysh*) where the union of the Quraysh (the tribe to which the Prophet belonged) is mentioned. But the union dealt with here is that which "joins God with the creature," a union that the first letter of the sura symbolizes, the *Lam-alif*, the figure of the *insân kâmil*.[35] A passage[36] that would otherwise remain somewhat obscure without the benefit of this background information refers to the second verse. Ibn ʿArabî suggests in it that it is in this abode that the "*abdâl* voyage" takes place, referring to those saints who occupy the fourth row of the initiatory hierarchy, counting from the Pole which is its summit. This trip takes place "toward Yemen" and "toward Syria." This second verse therefore unquestionably refers to the "winter caravan" and the "summer caravan" that the Qur'ân speaks of: the caravans that left Mecca each year in the days of the Prophet, in winter toward Yemen and in summer toward Syria. The enigmatic reference to the duration of the *abdâl*'s stay in Yemen and Syria that Ibn 'Arabî gives—twenty-four days and six days respectively—is related to the number of letters in the sura (twenty-four letters up to *shitâ*, "winter," and six for *wa l-sayf*, "and summer").

This manner of reading the Revealed Book may appear somewhat strange and forced. But Yemen—the "country on the right" (in Arabian cartography, the East is above, and thus Yemen, in the South, is on the right)—is also the place whence comes, according to a hadith, the "Breath of the All-Merciful" (*nafas al-Rahmân*).[37] The North, where Syria is located, is *al-shimâl* in Arabic: the left, the side of punishment (Qur'ân 56:9). The voyages of the *abdâl* are thus alternatively oriented toward mercy and toward sternness or, in terms of spiritual states, toward "dilatation" (*bast*) and "contraction" (*qabd*). The regulatory function of the *abdâl*, which is exercised over the seven terrestrial "climates" and leads them to use mercy at times and sternness at others over the creatures that they govern and protect, implies the alternation of these two states. Mecca, because of its central characteristic, is the point of equilibrium "where opposites are united" (*al-jam' bayna l-diddayn*).[38] There are also certain implicit eschatological implications to be considered: the caravan toward Yemen corresponds to the winter solstice, that is, to the birth of Jesus, who is announced by God in Qur'ân 19:45 as "a Mercy on Our Behalf"; Syria, where the Antichrist will receive his punishment, is the place where Jesus is to appear at the end of time[39] as the "seal of universal sainthood."

A further example will illustrate the need to keep in mind that the work of the Shaykh al-Akbar, being drawn from the "treasures of the Qur'ân," and is never perfectly comprehensible unless these treasures are precisely identified. On first sight, one of the problems raised by the *fasl al-manâzil* is that of the sometimes quite long lists at the end of chapters. These are lists of the knowledge, or "sciences," belonging to each "abode." They associate ideas among which one would fruitlessly attempt to establish a link. Reading them leaves one with the impression of being in the presence of an arbitrary catalogue, whose incoherence might be excused only by information of which we have not yet been apprised. Without being able to justify the contents in detail, which would entail the juxtaposition of numerous Qur'ânic citations with entire pages of the *Futûhât*, we will point out only that each of the sciences mentioned relates to the contents of one or more verses corresponding to the *manzil* in question. We thus once again find ourselves faced with statements whose apparent disorder reveals a secret coherence, once the principle that governs their succession is understood. In chapter 329[40] (sura *Al-rahmân*) the "science of understanding the Qur'ân" alludes to verse 4: "He [God] has taught him [man] the explanation." The "science of numbers" corresponds to the word *husbân*, "calculation," in verse 5; the "science of the affirmation of good deeds" refers to verse 13, which comes back as a refrain throughout the sura: "Which of the good deeds of your Lord would you deny?"; the "science of extinction and of permanence," to verses 26–27: "All that is on it [the Earth] will perish and [only] the Face of your Lord will remain." Similarly, in chapter 366[41] (sura 18: *Al-kahf*), the "science of association in Unity" quite explicitly refers to the last verse: "In worship, let him associate no one with his Lord!" The "science of divine descent" relates to verse 1: "Praise to God, who has sent the Book down upon his servant," as is also the case with the "science of the right Word," for the continuation of this verse states that God "has put nothing oblique" in this Book. The "science of the extension of time" echoes verse 25: "And they remained in their cave three hundred years and added nine to that." These few examples—chapter 366 alone could furnish several dozen—are mentioned here as illustrations alone; translation considerably weakens their cogency. Ibn 'Arabî's frequent use of terms identical to those found in the verses corresponding to each science, or of words from the same root, makes the network of Qur'ânic references with these passages from the *Futûhât* even more patent in Arabic.

Before pursuing other aspects of Ibn 'Arabî's work in search of the explanation of its genesis and its architecture, it might be appropriate to return to the question raised at the beginning of this chapter.

Is it truly reasonable to believe that none of the individuals mentioned was able to supply a solution to the diverse problems we outlined? Are we to suppose that they were purely and simply unaware of them? Sunnites or Shi'ites, they all clearly revere the Shaykh al-Akbar, even if they occasionally disagree with one of his positions. They are indifferent to nothing that he writes. The subtle exegeses of his thought, of which their works give so many examples, are fitting evidence that each of his works has been painstakingly examined. Like Jâmî in the example we reported, these writers refuse to resign themselves to not understanding the most obscure, the most ambiguous aspects of the Shaykh al-Akbar's work; with indefatigable zeal they work to resolve these *mushkilât*. It is thus evident that the majority of them, if not all, could neither bypass these problems nor resign themselves to leaving them unsolved. And all the more so, since the solutions, as we believe has been demonstrated, are suggested by numerous indications that could not have escaped them.

Under the circumstances, their silence on the matter could not have been but deliberate. Why then are they silent? At the beginning of his *Nass al-nusûs*, Haydar Amolî expatiates, for ten pages, on the necessity of the secret (*kitmân al-asrâr al-ilâhiyya 'an ghayri ahlihâ*), and he cites Qur'ânic verses, hadith, and a long passage of the *Futûhât* as support for this rule. He also emphasizes the necessity, in order to truly understand the writings of Ibn 'Arabî, of an appropriate spiritual relationship (*munâsaba*) with the author, explaining that such a relationshop is exceptional "even for Poles and those like them." Dhû l-Nûn al-Misrî, a few centuries earlier, gave the same advice with his aphoristic *qulûb al-ahrâr qubûr al-asrâr* (the hearts of free men are the tombs of secrets). The sufi literature of any age abounds in such pithy gems. But is it here truly a question of "divine secrets," to use Haydar Amolî's expression? And what importance should be placed on their being revealed? At the end of the fifth *manzil*, the one that corresponds to sura *Al-nasr*, Ibn 'Arabî, after speaking of the "chambers," of the "chests," of the "locks," and of the "keys," indicates that, if he remains silent on the meaning of these symbolic terms, it is for the purpose of foiling the attempts of the "liar" (*al-kâdhib*).[42] Of course, there is more to understanding the Shaykh al-Akbar's teaching than deciphering the meaning of these words; however, one must solve these quite

simple puzzles, and others like them, to have any chance of pene-
trating the true secrets of his work. And the true secrets are of a
very different nature, not lending themselves to the drawing up of a
banal table of equivalencies. The purpose of these formal obstacles
to the interpretation of the text is both dissuasion—they discourage
a hasty reading coming from impure motives—and awakening: they
stimulate the vigilance of spirits for whom the *Futûhât* are something quite other than a monumental encyclopedia or a collection of
heresies; they lead them to see that this work is inseparable from
the Qur᾽ân from which it draws its substance and its structure.

The discretion of the most eminent interpreters of Ibn ʿArabî
throughout the ages is thus easily explainable, but should not lead
to the conclusion that the solution to problems of this order is
exceptional or unprecedented. A claim today to having discovered
the "keys" of the *Futûhât* would be looked upon as both supremely
comic presumption and abysmal ignorance of Ibn ʿArabî's still
extant tradition: a tradition that has assured the transmission of
these facts and many others. The true heirs of the Shaykh al-Akbar
have never been numerous, but his succession has continued without interruption. As documentary evidence of this statement we
will limit ourselves to the *Kitâb manzil al-manâzil*, the importance
of which has been demonstrated above: the copyist of our manuscript took the trouble of clearly "translating" the emblematic name
of the *manâzil*, adding with his own hand in minuscule but legible
characters between the lines of the text such words as "that is to
say, sura *x*" It is thus evident that he did not need to expect the
arrival of a key to open the locks of the *Futûhât Makkiyya*. But he
certainly could not have forgotten that, these thresholds passed, a
number of walls remained to be passed through.[43]

4 🍂

"ON THE HORIZONS AND IN THEIR SOULS"
(QUR'ÂN 41:53)

We have spent considerable time on the *fasl al-manâzil*, which, among the six sections of the *Futûhât*, is doubly exemplary, by the apparent confusion of its organization and—as soon as its principle is understood—by the linear simplicity of its structure.

Ibn ʿArabî's invitation to consider the series of 114 *manâzil* as the abodes of an "ascent," and thus in ascending order, is clear. If this has been understood, the reader is capable of gradually dispersing the obscurities of the text, since the inverse series of suras supplies the necessary landmarks at each step along the way. The close connections that we begin to see—and that he so strongly emphasizes—between the Qur'ân and the entirety of the Shaykh al-Akbar's work are not always easy to perceive, however. The dimensions of this work keep us from attempting a systematic exploration in these pages. Such an explanation would in any case add no intelligible information, except for those who already have considerable knowledge about the subject. We will nevertheless attempt to extend our investigation to a few other writings, an examination of which will bring us back to the *Futûhât* and to the problem of their structure as a whole.

Certain of these works have thus far not warranted particular comments. They are the ones that, whether or not they take the form of a running commentary, nevertheless have an expressly declared organic relationship with the Qur'ân. Such is the case for the *Ijâz al-bayân fî l-tarjama ʿan al-qur'ân*, recently published by Mahmûd Ghurâb, whom we have already mentioned.[1] Although the greater themes of Ibn ʿArabî's doctrine are obviously not absent, this work is properly speaking a *tafsîr* that concisely, and precisely, explicates the Qur'ânic text verse by verse, as its title suggests.[2] Of a quite different nature, the *Ishârât al-qur'ân*, of which D. Gril is presently preparing an edition, are a collection of quite elliptical "allusions" (*ishârât*). These *ishârât* are based on a verse or piece of a verse taken successively in each of the suras, from the *Fâtiha* to *Al-nâs*. Information gleaned from Ibn ʿArabî about the great commentary, which is no longer extant,[3] tells us that it too follows the traditional order of the suras upon which it comments; according to the author, commentary of each verse is made from the triple point of view of Divine Majesty (*Jalâl*), Divine Beauty (*Jamâl*), and Divine Perfection (*Kamâl*)[4]—this last point of view being the synthesis of the other two.

On the other hand there is in the *Dîwân* a continuous series of 114 poems[5] inspired by "the spirits of the suras" (*arwâh al-suwar*) and whose Qurʾânic source is, here again, quite clear. Ibn ʿArabî states at the end of this collection that these verses were written according to the supernatural inspiration (*wârid*) of the moment, without additions or the intervention of reflection (*fikr*). Let it be noted that the title and the contents of these poems contain hints that may ultimately be seen as valuable; certain similarities of vocabulary direct one's attention to the Qurʾânic references of writings, where they are disguised and risk being passed over unnoticed.

It appears as though the *Kitâb al-isrâ*, the "Book of the Night Journey," which Ibn ʿArabî wrote in Fez in 594 A.H., is the first piece about a spiritual ascension that he composed. In quite different forms, the same theme is later treated in the *Futûhât* (chapters 167 and 367) and in the *Risâlat al-anwâr*, the "Epistle of Lights." In the *Kitâb al-isrâ*, a work composed in assonant prose (*sajʾ*) or in verse, certain elements obviously echo motifs that belong to the literature of the *miʿrâj*, that is, to traditional information that reports the ascension of the Prophet. But the text is constructed in counterpoint to a very precise Qurʾânic sequence. The title suggests that Ibn ʿArabî is referring to sura *Al-isrâ* (sura 17); however, only the first verse of this sura, partially cited by Ibn ʿArabî in the prologue,[6] refers to Muhammad's "night journey." The several characteristic expressions that punctuate the story of this celestial trip are actually borrowed from the seventeen first verses of sura *Al-najm* ("sura of the star," sura 53): the "lotus of the limit" (*sidrat al-muntahâ*), the distance "of two bows, or even closer" (*qâb qawsayn aw adnâ*), or the verb *awhâ* (he has revealed).

This relationship to sura *Al-najm* is confirmed by a passage[7] where the the Shaykh al-Akbar explains that, while suras 2 to 52 represent that part of Revelation that is common to Muhammad and to the previous prophets, the part proper to the prophet of Islam himself extends from sura *Al-najm* to the end of the Qur'ân. This relationship is underscored in another work, the as-yet unpublished *Mashâhid al-asrâr al-qudsiyya,*[8] wherein is found the description of fourteen "contemplations of most holy secrets," the point of departure for which is quite probably the *eighteenth* verse: "and he saw some of the sublime signs of his Lord." The *Mashâhid* generally accompany the *Kitâb al-isrâ* in the manuscript collections, and not by chance: Ibn Sawdakîn, the friend and confidant of Ibn 'Arabî who has left us a commentary on both works (or rather a transcript, as is his custom, of the oral commentary that the author made to him), stresses that the two works are inseparable.[9] It happens that the word *najm*, "star," comes up regularly in the titles of chapters of the *Mashâhid*: "contemplation of the light of existence when the *star* of vision rises," "contemplation of the light of the One when the *star* of confirmation rises," "contemplation of the light of perplexity when the *star* of nothingness rises," and so on. The selection of a word is never fortuitous for Ibn 'Arabî, and less so is its repetition.[10]

Two points deserve to be brought to the forefront concerning the *Kitâb al-isrâ*. The first, several years before the event that constitutes the birth of the *Futûhât Makkiyya*, is an account of a first encounter with the young man (*fatâ*) "whose essence is spiritual and whose attributes are lordly"[11] and before whom Ibn 'Arabî prostrates himself.[12] After a conversation during which he prepares the voyager (*al-sâlik*) for the trials of the path, the *fatâ* disappears: "His essence was hidden to me, but his attributes remained with me."[13] As in the *Futûhât*, he has an initiatory function and the analogy of the roles that he plays in both cases is put into perspective by the mention of the meeting place. In the *Futûhât*, they meet near the Ka'ba, at the "umbilicus of the Earth"; in the *Kitâb al-isrâ* it takes place "at the fountain of Arîn," that is, in a place that, according to Islamic cosmography, also represents the center of the earth, since it is located at equal distances from the four cardinal points.[14] The source of inspiration for the two works is thus identical: it is from the name *Al-mutakallim*, from the Divine Verb, that they both spring; and therefore it is not surprising that at the beginning of the *Futûhât* the reader finds the poem that appears in the prologue of the *Kitâb al-isrâ*, where the *fatâ* makes himself known in these terms: "I am the Qur'ân and the redoubled seven."[15]

see also p. 28 above

On the other hand, there is a significant piece of information—one confirmed by a text to be dealt with later—on the process that leads from contemplation to writing in Ibn 'Arabî. He states in a reply to one of Ibn Sawdakîn's questions that what he recorded in his work is founded on a perception of pure intelligibles (ma'âni mujarrada 'an al-mawâdd): in a second stage, with God's assistance, he clothes these intelligibles with the forms without which they could not possibly be communicated.[16]

Although it is not as explicit as in the works we considered previously, the relation of the Kitâb al-isrâ to the Qur'ân is nevertheless quite clear. Such is not the case for others of the Shaykh al-Akbar's books, and it is to the examination of some of these that we will dedicate the pages remaining. The Kitâb al-'Abâdila, the "Book of the 'Abdallâh," presents itself as a collection of maxims attributed to a series of individuals who are all named 'Abdallâh. Each of their genealogies is detailed by the mention of two degrees of filiation ("son of...son of...") wherein there generally figures one divine name and the name of one prophet (e.g., 'Abdallâh b. Idrîs b. 'Abd al-Khâliq, 'Abdallâh b. Muhammad b. 'Abd al-Wâhid).[17] The specific character of the remarks attributed to them allows us to understand that each "'Abdallâh" here represents a particular modality of spiritual knowledge and sainthood. It is thus useless to attempt a historical identification, for it would be devoid of sense. Throughout the text, it is always Ibn 'Arabî who is speaking, and his introduction leaves no doubt about that fact. He presents himself as the "interpreter" (mutarjim) of the multiple forms of walâya, the one who possesses "all the languages" (jâmi' alsina), a transparent allusion to the function of Seal of Muhammadan sainthood, which he claims. The role of "interpreter" is one that he attributes to himself in several of his works.[18]

A reading of the Kitâb al-'Abâdila uncovers a number of admirably concise formulations of the themes of Ibn 'Arabî's doctrine, and yet it is disconcerting that no logic appears to order the work's successive chapters. But time spent with Ibn 'Arabî's writings shows that it is absolutely essential to be attentive to their beginnings: the titles of books or of chapters, initial doxology or prefatory poems.[19] It is often here that one finds those hints that allow the obscurities of the text to be deciphered. For example, the prologue of the Kitâb al-'Abâdila contains within a span of just a few lines three mentions of the word *jâmi'*, one of which particularly deserves reflection. He writes: "The interpreter in this book is a totalizing son (*ibn jâmi'*) born of a limited father (*âb muqayyad*)." *Jâmi'*, which we have here translated as "totalizing," actually means "he who gathers together, he who unites"; with this meaning, it is one of the divine names on the traditional list.[20] But it also possesses the characteristic of having the numerical value of 114, which is the number of suras in the Qur'ân. Consequently, it can be suspected of being a key to the reading, which a diligent examination of the text confirms, up to a certain point.

The Cairo edition, the only one extant to our knowledge, is unfortunately extremely faulty; on the first page, for example, one finds *banî* for *nabî*. It also contains omissions; comparison with one of the oldest manuscripts has shown that a series of Abdallâh was omitted (it should have appeared between the penultimate and the last chapters[21] of the printed text), and the real number of chapters appears to be 114 instead of 100. As we have not yet examined the autograph manuscript preserved in Istanbul, the only one that would allow definitive conclusions, we will limit ourselves at present to short remarks that are nevertheless consistent with the hypothesis of a Qur'ânic "reading grill." From the very first chapter, a veiled correspondence with the verses of the *Fâtiha* is discovered: considerations on the letter *bâ* refer to the *basmala*; those on the world (*al-'âlam*), to verse 2 ("All praise belongs to God, Lord of the worlds"); "when he speaks to you as plural" (previously cited in chapter 2, above), to verse 4 ("It is you that we worship"); the "request for help" (*talab al-'awn*), to the continuation of that same verse ("To you do we come for help"); the multiplicity of paths and the definition of that which is "right" (*mustaqîm*), to verse 6 ("Guide us on the right path").[22] Similarly, the second chapter corresponds to the second sura: the "absence of uncertainty and of doubt (*rayb*)" immediately calls verse 2 to mind (That is the Book in which there is no doubt"), just as the term *iqâma* (prayer), a little later, resonates with verse 3 ("Those who perform prayer") where the word *muqîmûn* appears (note that *iqâma* and *muqîmûn* share the same root).[23]

Without highlighting all the expressions where a Qur'ânic background can be seen in this chapter, one passage[24] might be noted as an example, a passage where it is easy to recognize an allusion to the dialogue between God and his angels and to the

divine lesson that teaches Adam "all the names," the theme of
verses 30–32 of the sura. A second example is offered in chapter 18,
where it can be seen that the distinction between the status of
prophet (nabî) and saint (walî) refers surreptitiously to the well-
known episode in sura 18 (sura Al-kahf) where Moses and Khadir
meet.[25] In the following chapter, the first paragraph refers to God's
taking charge of the subsistence of his creatures and to the illusion
of "acquisition" (kasb): verse 25 of sura 19 relates the miraculous
bestowal of food to Mary, the mother of Jesus.[26] Chapter 22 lists the
symbolic liquids that were offered to the Prophet at the time of his
night journey (wine, honey, milk, water), beginning with wine;[27]
sura 22 (Al-hajj, v. 2) declares: "You will see men intoxicated, and
[yet] they will not be so." Sura 23 (Al-mu'minûn) deals with the
refusal of the infidels, of all times, to accept that men like them—
men who eat, drink, and attend to their affairs in the market—can
be God's Messengers (v. 23, 33, 47); chapter 23 speaks of the pious
servant who sees only God in this world and who, in the other
world, will also see only God and yet who is placed in a subservient
position here on Earth: "he eats, he drinks, he gets married, he listens to what is said to him, and he replies."[28] Clearly, this is a case
of something other than simple coincidences. A practiced eye could
indentify a number of other items of the same nature in the first
half of the Kitâb al-'Abâdila's printed text. The second half, in its
presently published condition, does not lend itself as easily to the
same kind of parallels. But we have little doubt that, when correctly restored and classified, the text of the entire work will confirm the Qur'ânic character of its structure.

Another of Ibn 'Arabî's writings (of which we do have a correct
text) offers, in both its composition and its content, even more singular aspects than the Kitâb al-'Abâdila; and this one has an even
more important place among the works of the Shaykh al-Akbar. The
Kitâb al-tajalliyât ("Book of Theophanies") was written in Aleppo,
no later than 606/1209,[29] although the exact date of its composition
is uncertain. Theophany (tajallî) is "that which is unveiled to the
heart of the lights of the invisible."[30] With no explanation of their
order of succession, one hundred nine short chapters describe these
tajalliyât, each with a title that describes its precise nature, for
example, "theophany of Mercy," "theophany of Generosity," "theophany of Veracity." In several of them we see Ibn 'Arabî engage in

dialogue with some of the most famous of the *awliyâ* of the past: Shiblî (*Taj.* 56), Junayd (*Taj.* 54, 58, 67), Hallâj (*Taj.* 57), Dhû l-Nûn al-Misrî (*Taj.* 59), Abû Sa'îd al-Kharrâz (*Taj.* 66), Sahl al-Tustarî (*Taj.* 75). The purpose of the work is to instruct the novice on events that might occur along his path. That there is personal experience behind these quite dense statements, formulated in terms as aphoristic as they are categorical, is beyond doubt. But is the movement of the text itself directed by some necessity whose principle and rules can be known to us?

Ibn Sawdakîn's commentary sheds some light on the nature of the experience which the work relates. In 610 A.H., in Aleppo, while Ibn 'Arabî was not present, a man whom Ibn Sawdakîn considered a friend crudely criticized those chapters of the *Tajalliyât* that recounted the author's dialogues with individuals who had been dead for centuries. Upon Ibn 'Arabî's return, his disciple told him of the incident and proffered his own interpretation of these posthumous conversations. Ibn 'Arabî validated the interpretation—but only as far as the *nafs* (the individual soul): as far as heart is concerned, he said, things happen otherwise. "All that has happened between me and these deceased saints," he then explained, "proceeds from a 'holy contemplation' in which my 'secret' [the *Seelengrund*, the *apex animae* of Christian terminology] and that of these individuals met, stripped of all sensible form." He adds: "If I met them in the world of bodies, I would have nothing to add and nothing to take away."[31] The mention of being "stripped" (*tajarrud*) underscores the relationship of this confidence with that which we noted in the commentary on the *Kitâb al-isrâ*, where a similar expression is found. It brings up a trait of spiritual phenomenology that Henry Corbin, obsessed by the "imaginal world," seems to have not noticed: for Ibn 'Arabî, the most perfect illuminating knowledge first takes place in the sphere of intelligibles, of pure spirits free of matter and of form. It is in a second stage, and only then, that it "takes a body" in the *'âlam al-khayâl*, and it is then that it takes on words and images that will allow its transmission to those who do not have access to this universe of pure light.

The oral commentary with which Ibn Sawdakîn continues his recollections, a commentary that is both partial and disconnected, does nevertheless shed light on a number of obscure passages. But despite fleeting allusions whose full sense is captured only when one has understood how the text functions, the commentary does not give us the key that makes deciphering the *Book of Theophanies* possible. It is true that this key is actually hidden only from those who are not completely attentive. Once again, it is suggested as early as the first lines of the work. Signs to orient the attentive reader are present in two expressions: one is *ʿâlam al-barâzikh*, and the other is *maʿqil al-aʿrâs*. *Barâzikh* is the plural of *barzakh*, a Qurʾânic term often translated as "isthmus" and which, more generally, designates any medial place, any intermediary state, any thing that separates and unites two things at the same time. In the vocabulary of sufism, it is applied to the "imaginal world" located between the world of spirits and the world of bodies; it also applies to the status of beings between death and resurrection. The expression *maʿqil al-aʿrâs*, which means the "refuge," or the "sanctuary of fiancées," shows up again in the title of chapter 382 of the *Futûhât*, which is the *manzil* of sura *Al-baqara* (sura 2). This same *manzil*—one of the *manâzil al-rumûz* (abodes of symbols), that is, one of the suras beginning with "luminous letters"—is called *manzil al-barâzikh* in chapter 22. In the *Dîwân*, the poem that corresponds to the sura *Al-baqara* is announced in the title as dealing with "intermediate life" (*al-hayât al-barzakhiyya*).[32] In the *Ishârât al-qurʾân*, sura *Al-baqara* is called *al-baqara al-barzakhiyya*.[33] The first verse of the prefatory poem of chapter 382 ("The science of *barâzikh*; the only ones to attain this are those who join the extremities with the center") points in the same direction. All the above more than suggests that there is privileged relationship between sura *Al-baqara* and the *Kitâb al-tajalliyât*, all the more so since an incidental remark in the prologue suggests that this book actually is part of the *Futûhât*. It can be considered as a complement to chapter 382, the "abode" of *Al-baqara*, and we shall see that the connection in the theophanies that he describes is dictated by that of the verses of the sura.

The connection that Ibn ʿArabî establishes between the idea of *barzakh* and the second sura of the Qurʾân first requires a brief commentary. This connection appears to be based on the repeated presence, throughout *Al-baqara*, of numerous cases of "intermediate status": that of the cow described by Moses (v. 58) being "neither old nor young but between the two" or that of the man (whom commentators often identify as Esdras) who comes back to life at the end of a century (v. 259), or that of four birds that also come back to life (v. 260). It applies even more clearly to the sura itself, due to its intermediate position between the "Mother of the Qur'ân," the *Fâtiha*, and the other suras; and also to the Muhammadan community, which verse 143 calls the "median community" (*umma wasata*).

The prologue of the *Tajalliyât* contains other allusions that act as signposts. One example is that by which this "abode" becomes one of the "abodes of the third talisman" and thus "one of the thirteen." The word *talisman* (*tilasm*) is, according to Ibn ʿArabî, one of the code names of the "luminous" letters (fourteen, of the twenty-eight in the alphabet) that appear at the beginning of twenty-nine suras, either alone, or in a group of two, three, four, or five. The "third talisman" here indicates that sura *Al-baqara* is preceded by a group of *three* letters (*alif, lâm, mîm*), and such is the case for a total of *thirteen* suras.[34] The first theophany ("Theophany of Allusion"), which corresponds to the first two verses ("*Alif—Lâm—Mîm* / That is the Book in which there is, no doubt, a guide for the pious"),[35] comes back to these letters. According to Ibn ʿArabî, the form of the writing (*raqîm*) to which it is an allusion (by the pronoun *that,* [*dhâlika*], which is the demonstrative used for what is far away) is "triangular." One of its "angles" (the letter *alif*, which when written can be joined to no letter that follows it and that is the first letter of the name Allâh) expresses "the supression of any relation of affinity between God and the creatures." The second angle (the letter *lâm*, often likened in traditional exegesis to Jibrâʾîl, the angel of Revelation) "dissipates confusion," while the third (*mîm*, the first letter in Muhammad and a symbolic allusion to the Prophet, who is the model of excellence) makes evident the "way of felicity": the terms used about the second and third "angles" obviously translate the "absence of doubt" (*lâ rayba fîhi*) and the "guidance" (*hudâ*) of the scriptural text.

The title of the second *tajallî*, the "Theophany of the Transcendence in the Freshness of the Eye" (*qurrat al-ayn*), may seem mysterious. But the expression "freshness" or "consolation" of the eye is, for Muslims, an unambiguous allusion to ritual prayer, as it is so called in a very famous hadith upon which Ibn ʿArabî commented at length in the *Fusûs al-hikam*.[36] This chapter thus reveals its relation to the third verse, which mentions "those who perform prayer."

The third *tajallî* is that of the "descent of the mysterious upon those who possess certitude" (*al-mûqinîn*). The "mystery" (*al-ghuyûb*) is that of future life (*al-âkhira*), about which true believers, according to the fourth verse, "possess certitude" (*yûqinûn*).

A line-by-line examination of the text would continue the parallel we have begun here. Omitting a number of details, we have chosen rather to establish some landmarks that make it relatively easy to identify the correspondences between successive theophanies and the verses of *Al-baqara*.

The "Theophany of Confusion" (number 8: *tajallî al-iltibâs*) is the one from which man "learns to know the fine points of ruse and of stratagem...He who contemplates it is sheltered from ruse": a perfectly recognizable echo of verse 9, according to which "[the infidels] attempt to trick God and those who believe. But it is themselves that they deceive and they do not know it." The trickery from which the contemplator is preserved is that of God, the *khayr al-mâkirîn* (Qurʾân 3:54), "the best of those who trick": He tests the faith of the believer who is too quick to believe himself capable of dispelling temptation and who thus wants to "trick God" by claiming an illusory autonomy. The nineteenth *tajallî*, the "Theophany of Burning Glories," alludes by its title to the well-known hadith according to which "God has seventy [or seventy thousand, according to one version] veils of light and of darkness: if he were to remove them, the burning glories of his face would consume whoever was in his sight." "These veils of light and darkness," writes Ibn ʿArabî, "are removed for gnostics: they are the Glories of Generosity [*al-karam*] that shine upon those whom burning does not reach." We thus arrive at verse 20 of the sura: "Lightning might well snatch away their sight."

Verse 26 is usually translated: "They know that it is the Truth (*Al-haqq*) coming from their Lord" or by some similar sentence. But it can also be rendered: "They know that he [alone] is the True One" (or "the Real One"). It is this scriptural text that is the origin of the "Theophany of Veracity" (*sidq*), the twenty-eighth of the work, where one reads: "He whose voyage is through God (*bi l-haqq*), whose arrival is at God and whose return [toward the creatures] is from God and through God, looks at the creatures [here *khalq* must be read rather than *haqq*: the manuscripts show that once again the Hyderabad edition is faulty] as being God [*min kawnihi haqqan*]."

Tajallî number 34 is that of "singularity" (*fardaniyya*). Ibn ʿArabî writes: "God has angels who are engulfed in the light of his majesty and his beauty; they are in perpetual joy and uninterrupted contemplation."[37] He adds that these angelic spirits, the cherubim, have their homologues in the human world: these are the *afrâd* (same root as *fardaniyya*), the "loners" spoken of in the second chapter of this book. This theophany is that which corresponds to verse 34, where the refusal of Iblîs, the devil, to prostrate himself before Adam is reported: in effect, only the cherubim, who do not know that God created the world, who are not even aware of their own existence, were absolved of this prostration. It is for this reason that in another passage from the Qurʾân (38:75) God, asking Iblîs about the motives for his refusal, inquires: "Are you really one of the exalted spirits?" (*Am kunta min al-ʿâlîn?*), those who were not affected by the divine order.

Tajallî number 57 relates a dialogue with Hallâj. "Why," says Ibn ʿArabî, "did you let your house [i.e., your body] be destroyed?" So questioned about his acceptance of torture, Hallâj replies: "I gave it up when the hands of the creatures threatened it...It repulsed me to live in a house over which the hands of creatures had power...It has been said that Hallâj is dead. But Hallâj is not dead. The house has been destroyed but its inhabitant was already gone." The statement is an easily identifiable echo of verse 84, "then you kill one another and chase some of your number from their houses." The end of the dialogue is worth reporting. Ibn ʿArabî then says, "I know something that refutes your argument. He lowered his head, saying: above every individual who is wise, there is one wiser than he (Qurʾân 12:76)." Then Ibn ʿArabî, without further details, concludes the account of this meeting by simply saying, "I then left him and went away." What objection might Ibn ʿArabî have had to Hallâj's argument? According to the *Kashf al-ghayât*, an anonymous commentary of the *Tajalliyât* that should perhaps be attributed to ʿAbd al-Karîm al-Jîlî, this cryptic remark means that "Hallâj had not obtained the *farq al-thânî*." The *farq al-thânî* is the "second separation." The first separation is birth in this world and the forgetting of God produced by it, a forgetting that should be repaired by the return to God, the ascension (*mirʿâj*) that leads the being back to its Principle. The second separation—which is not privative like the first but, rather, represents the fullness of sainthood—is the descent of the saint, once ascension has been completed, toward the creatures in order to guide them. But once returned to multiplicity, it is always the One that the *wâli* is contemplating, his presence in God being in no way affected by his presence among men. That is why the *Kashf al-ghayât* explains Hallâj's imperfection—completely relative—by saying that he failed to perceive *al-irtibât bayna l-haqq wa l-khalq*, "the connection between God and creation."

In the following *tajallî* (number 58), Ibn ʿArabî engages in dialogue with another of the great sufis of past centuries, Dhû l-Nûn. "I am surprised," says the former, "with your words and with those who have repeated them after you, by which God is different from any form that one gives him, from any representation that one makes of him, from any image that imagination gives to him![38]... How could he be absent from that which is, when nothing which is can survive other than through him?" This affirmation of divine immanence is immediately followed, in a move very characteristic of Ibn ʿArabî's thought, by the proclamation of transcendence. The contradiction is logically unsolvable: no image of God, mental or sensual, is "empty" of him; none is him. But here the accent is placed upon the universal presence of God: what is reflected in this amazing passage, as in a mirror, is the famous verse 115 ("To God belong the east and the west, and wherever you might turn, there is the Face of God"), so often quoted by Ibn ʿArabî and one of the scriptural foundations of his metaphysics.[39]

Another reflection, and thus another landmark, is that found in *tajallî* number 81, the "Theophany of Love," connected to verse 165: "Those who believe are stronger in their love for God [than the infidels in their love for what they associate with God]." Theophany after theophany, the *Kitâb al-tajalliyât* is figuratively knotted to sura *Al-baqara*, and the validity of the kind of connections we have been showing here is in most cases confirmed for the reader of Arabic by lexical correlations which a translation can not sufficiently illustrate.

We pointed out the expression "sanctuary of fiancées" above; it appears at the beginning of the work and is also present in the title of the chapter that, in the *fasl al-manâzil*, describes the "abode" of sura *Al-baqara*. This expression is the equivalent of another one, which is found in chapter 30 of the *Futûhât*: speaking of the highest category of *malâmiyya*, that of the *afrâd*, Ibn ʿArabî says that they entered the "tents of mystery" (*surâdiqât al-ghayb*).[40] The "fiancées," whom divine jealousy hides from the sight of creatures, are precisely these "men of blame," hidden in this world because nothing distinguishes them from the common people. God himself hides these individuals in the Qur'ân under the appearance of his enemies, the infidels—those who are "deaf, dumb, blind," those whose hearts are "sealed." In chapter 2 we cited different texts where Ibn ʿArabî applies to the *malâmiyya* terms, all of which have been borrowed from sura *Al-baqara*, that describe the unbelievers. The information above permits us now to add another detail: if *tajallî* number 5 and *tajallî* number 83 deal with the *malâmiyya*, it is because they correspond respectively to verses 6 and 171, where these terms happen to be found.[41]

Given all of this, it can be seen that we are far from any kind of exegesis. What we observe in the *Kitâb al-tajalliyât*, as in most of Ibn ʿArabî's writings, is this "descent of the Qur'ân upon the heart," without which Revelation "goes no farther than the throat." When the words of divine language reach the heart, ever new sciences spring forth like sparks from a flint when it is struck. The theophanies described are born from this encounter with the Word of God *and they cannot be born except from this encounter*: this is why their economy is ruled by the order of suras and verses.

The complementarity between the *Kitâb al-tajalliyât* and the *Futûhât Makkiyya* discretely suggested by Ibn ʿArabî is not an isolated example. We have already witnessed an analogous relationship between the short treatise on the *Manzil al-manâzil* and chapter 22. Michel Valsân, in his translation of the *Kitâb al-fanâ fî l-mushâhada*,[42] had underscored[43] the strict rapport between this work (composed before the part of the *Futûhât* where the *fasl al-manâzil* is found) and chapter 286, on the one hand, and sura 98 (*Al-bayyina*), on the other hand. In both cases it is the "abode" related to this sura that is being dealt with; this *manzil* is the one that, in chapter 22, is called *manzil al-mushâda*, "abode of contemplation." Several other texts take up the same theme,[44] drawn from the first two words of the sura, to such an extent that the reader sees the formation, throughout the entirety of the Shaykh al-Akbar's works, of a veritable network woven from one Qur'ânic reference that constitutes its center. But the discovery is soon made that similar networks are present everywhere in the corpus of Ibn ʿArabî's work and that they are so numerous and complex that an exhaustive map of them could not be made. A few examples will suffice to give a sense of the breadth and density of this weave whose knotting always leads back to the Qur'ân.

The fifth section of the *Futûhât*, the one following the *fasl al-manâzil*, is that of the *munâzalât*, a word whose root is identical to that of *manzil*, but whose sense is one of reciprocity. The definition that Ibn ʿArabî gives of it permits one to interpret it as an encounter between God and man, each having covered half of the distance.[45] The section of the *munâzalât* does not have the same linear character as the preceding section, and there is thus no simple way of identifying the kind of Qur'ânic structure that organizes it. Each of the seventy-eight chapters that make it up is nevertheless in correspondence with a sura.[46] But relying on other works permits a more certain identification of this sura, and at the same time it gradually shows the path taken by one of the "networks" to which we have referred. Furthermore, it permits a deeper understanding of the chapter under consideration.

In the series of Ibn ʿArabî's *Rasâʾil* published in Hyderabad are two short works that, though noteworthy, do not appear to have heretofore attracted the attention of specialists. They are the *Kitâb al-shâhid* (Book of the Witness) and the *Kitâb al-tarâjim* (Book of Interpretations). The "witness" is defined by Ibn ʿArabî in the *Futûhât* ("the permanence of the form of the contemplated in the contemplator") and the *Kitâb al-shâhid* ("that which remains in the heart of the servant after his separation from the station of contemplation").[47] As for "interpretation"—and it is known that this is what Ibn ʿArabî often considers the task that he assigns himself in his writings—it is, broadly speaking, the function of the Perfect Man (*insân kâmil*), the interpreter of the two Books in which God speaks: the Qur'ân and the universe. In the *Kitâb al-tarâjim*, interpretation consists more precisely in translating the secrets that the intellect, purified of all speculative activity, receives from the divine names in the different degrees where they are encountered.[48]

That the *Kitâb al-tarâjim* is in some way closely tied to the *fasl al-munâzalât* is suggested at the beginning of the text:

> Know, my brothers, you who are among men of high aspira-
> tion, among those who raise themselves toward higher
> degrees—for it is to you that I address my words, to you that
> I speak by way of reminding and admonishing, not of
> instructing—that encounters along the way [*munâzalât*]

between the realities of divine names and human realities in
the person of the Perfect Man—whether it is a man or a
woman—are as innumerable as are the orientations [of the
heart toward God] and the divine names themselves.

A little later we read: "The *munâzalât* are not obtained except
through the most perfect conformity to the prescriptions of the
Law"[49] These repetitions of key words are always, for Ibn ʿArabî,
signs worthy of attention.

Each of the sixty-nine chapters that follow this preamble bears
a title that connects it to a divine name: "Interpretation of Magnificence" (*taʿzîm*, or to the name *Al-ʿAzîm*), "Interpretation of Sanctity"
(*taqdîs*, thus attached to the name *Al-Quddus*), and so on. But a
somewhat careful examination of the contents of these chapters
(divided into short paragraphs called "subtlety" [*latîfa*] or "allusion"
[*ishâra*]) shows that, in addition to this rapport with one of the names
of God, each of them has a privileged relationship with a sura of the
Qurʾân, according to a regular progression that, as was the case for
the *manâzil*, is an *inverse* progression from that of the Qurʾânic
suras: chapter 1 corresponds to sura 69 (*Al-haqqa*), chapter 2 to sura
68, and so forth up to the last, which corresponds to the *Fâtiha*. A first
series of rapprochements is thus imposed with the chapters of the *fasl
al-manâzil*, which correspond to these same suras.[50]

Other interconnections—with the 27 chapters of the *Kitâb al-
shâhid* and, as can be seen from indications taken from early in the
text, with different chapters of the *fasl al-munâzalât*—are then
brought to our attention by the recurrence (too frequent to not be
deliberate) of certain words or even certain sentences. Let it be
remembered that this collection of connections, some within the
Futûhât itself and others between the *Futûhât* and other works,[51] is
in each case generated by the sura around which these different
writings are arranged like a star. The arrangement of connections
verifies that the Qurʾân is truly at the very heart of Ibn ʿArabî's
work, as it puts order into an apparently disordered proliferation.
To illustrate the richness and the coherence of this network, let us
look at three further examples of these connections.

Chapter 16 of the *Kitâb al-tarâjim* is entitled *"tarjamat al-
bâtin"*, chapter 23 of the *Kitâb al-shâhid* is the *"bâb al-bâtin"*, and
the resemblance does not stop with the title. The same theme is
dealt with in both cases. But this is not all. In the *fasl al-munâza-*

lât[52] chapter 400 also deals with this theme, and its title contains an expression that is a slight variation (the passing from first person to third person) of a phrase from the *Kitâb al-shâhid*.[53] Chapter 16 of the *Tarâjim* corresponds according to the schema mentioned above, to sura 54 (*Al-qamar*, "The Moon"); it suffices to go back to chapter 330 of the *Futûhât*, which is the *manzil* for this sura[54] to complete the connection. One now sees that the symbolism of the visible face and the hidden face of the moon is used by Ibn ʿArabî to express what these texts outline in other ways: that God hides when the creature is manifest, and becomes manifest when the creature hides. The network is thus summarized in figure 4.1.

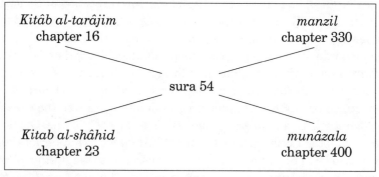

Figure 4.1

According to the same method, figure 4.2 illustrates the similarities between the *bâb al-ʿinâya* (that is, chapter 13 of the *Kitâb al-shâhid*), the *tarjamat al-ʿinâya*, which makes up chapter 49 of the *Kitâb al-tarâjim*, and chapter 412 of the *Futûhât*.[55]

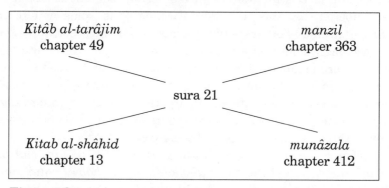

Figure 4.2

In another significant example, chapter 14 of the *Kitâb al-shâhid* and chapter 50 of the *Kitâb al-tarâjim* have their title and subject in common: *qadâ,* "predestination." The two clearly correspond to chapter 413 of the *Futûhât,* which is titled: "Neither He Who Makes a Request of Me nor He Who Does Not Will Escape My Predestination."[56] This sentence is found again word for word at the end of chapter 14 of the *Kitâb al-shâhid.* They are all connected with the *manzil* of sura 20 (*Tâ Hâ*), that is, to chapter 364, which from its very first lines affirms the impossibility of creatures, either in the state of *thubût* (which is theirs in the divine science for all eternity) or when they are enveloped by *wujûd* (when they are "existentiated") to escape the divine order.[57] In the inverse order of the Qur'ânic suras, beginning, then, with sura 69, chapter 50 of the *Kitâb al-tarâjim* corresponds quite well with sura *Tâ Hâ.* A new network can be seen in figure 4.3.

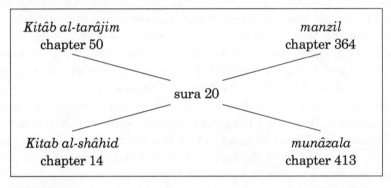

Figure 4.3

Here again, the representation is nothing more than an extremely brief summary; for it to be even close to completed it would require its being enriched by connections with chapters belonging to other sections of the *Futûhât*—chapter six, for example, where each of the "iniatory Poles" is characterized by a verse that is its own particular manner of invocation (*hijjîr*) and where the order of chapters is once again in rapport with a particular order of suras. But Ibn 'Arabî's other works should also be included in such a topographic overview, particularly those that were mentioned previously: the *Kitâb al-'Abâdila, Kitâb al-tajalliyât,* and so on, not to mention, of course the *Fusûs al-hikam,* which alone deserve detailed study. Chapter 12 of the *Fusûs*, for example (on "the wisdom of the heart"), is written into a network where several chapters from the *Futûhât* (chapter 40 in the first *fasl*, chapter 348 in the fourth *fasl*, chapter 405 in the fifth *fasl*) are intertwined with chapter 34 of the *Kitâb al-tarâjim*, the "knot" of this junction being sura *Yâsîn* (sura 36), which is the "heart" of the Qur'ân. Perceiving this common reference is what brings into light the coherence of the ensemble, thus allowing the puzzles to be understood.

The suggestions we have presented here are far from being exhaustive. With them, we simply attempt to illustrate the need for a careful reading of the corpus of Ibn 'Arabî's works, so foreign to those for whom he is nothing but an eclectic philosopher or an incoherent visionary. Identifying in each case the Qur'ânic seed buried in the text from which these luxurious branchings spring is indispensable. Any view should thus be attentive to a staggering but rigorous crisscrossing of pithy allusions, implicit references, and discreet signs. Such detection, which also requires a thorough knowledge of the Qur'ân, is not an easy task. The *Kitâb al-tajalliyât*, whose successive sequences are related to the verses of one sura, is a special case. It is so rich in clues that sooner or later at least some of them are bound to pique the attention of the reader such that, gradually, the majority, if not the totality, of these correspondences can be understood. But even in this case, it must be remembered that the Qur'ânic "seed" can be reduced to a few words: for, in the Qur'ân, each unit—part of a phrase, a verb, a particle—carries its own autonomous meaning, is filled with announcement, and flashes with sparks. In this book's epigraph we gave a passage from the "Theophany of Perfection." This beautiful divine monologue describes the resonance in Ibn 'Arabî's heart of three words: *fa-innî qarîb*, "I am quite near," from verse 185 of *Al-baqara*. Similarly, in chapter 286 of the *Kitâb al-fanâ fî l-mushâhada*, the theme of "extinction of the servant" as a necessary condition of contemplation comes entirely from the initial *Lam yakun* of sura *Al-bayyina*—a statement that out of context expresses the ontological nothingness of the creature—even though other terms taken from this sura are later used on a number of occasions.

If we return to the two examples examined above, where whole texts related to suras 20 and 21, we notice in similar fashion that, among the 135 verses of the first and the 112 of the second, the Qur'ânic seed is reduced to part of verse 129 in sura 20 and three verses (101–103) in sura 21. It will be observed that it is the presence of one verb (*sabaqa*, "to precede") in these two scriptural references that explains the contiguity of the chapters that echo them (49 and 50 in the *Kitâb al-tarâjim*; 363–64 and 412–13 in the *Futûhât*; 14–15 in the *Kitâb al-shâhid*). In each case it is really a question of *qadâ*, the predestination that leads some to felicity (whence the word *'inâya*, "grace"), and others to punishment. Verse 129 of *Tâ Hâ* ("If it had not been for a word already gone forth...") concerns the impious, while verses 101–103 of *Al-anbiyâ* are addressed to the pious servants to whom divine favors have previously been granted (*sabaqat lahum minna l-husnâ*). The pious will consequently be far from Gehenna (regardless of what they do) and will not even hear the hissing; conforming to the eternal decree, they will reside in the place where all their desires will be fulfilled.

It goes without saying that Muslims give the Qur'ân the first place, that the Divine Word rules their faith and their works. And that is even more true for the sufis, whose existence, vowed to God, is centered on his Book: the writings that they have left us and comments that hagiographic tradition has registered for us offer abundant evidence of this fact. But there is much more to it than just that. The Qur'ân's ubiquity in Ibn 'Arabî's work, the permanent role that it plays in his work's development and architecture are of exceptional character. Ibn 'Arabî's doctrine is not simply a meditation on the Qur'ân. It is so organically linked to him that the two are really inseparable. For Ibn 'Arabî, the Word of God is "the Way, the Truth, and the Life." It is in the Qur'ân that the voyage is made that leads man back to his original status, to his divine similitude.

Commenting on the hadith where it is reported that the Prophet demanded of God "Grant me complete Light," he reminds us that light (*al-nûr*) is one of the divine names and adds: "It is for this reason that the sages [*al-hukamâ*] indicated by allusion that the goal that the servant should attempt to reach is to become similar to the divinity [*al-tashabbuh bi l-ilâh*]. As for the sufis, they speak of acquiring divine names. The manners of expression are different, but the meaning is the same."[58]

But *al-nûr* (light) is also one of the names of the Qur'ân: the *theôsis* consists in identifying oneself totally with the Word of God, to "become the Qur'ân." He also writes: "The Perfect Man [*al-insân*

al-kâmil] is the brother of the Qur'ân";[59] or, even more explicitly:
"The Universal Man [al-insân al-kullî] *is* the Qur'ân."[60] After the
death of the Prophet, who was the paradigm of all perfection (*uswa
hasana*), his wife ʿAʾisha said: "His nature was the Qur'ân." Ibn
ʿArabî cites this remark repeatedly; for him, it sums up all that
creatures should aspire to.

In a verse from sura *Fussilat*, it is said: "We will make them
see Our signs on the horizons and in their souls" (41:53). The meaning of the statement for the Shaykh al-Akbar is explained in a
chapter where he deals with *sakîna* ("peace," "serenity," but also,
like the Hebrew *Shekina*, the Divine "Presence"): the *sakîna* that
God sent down for the children of Israel in the Ark of the Covenant
(Qur'ân 2: 248) "was made to come down in the hearts of believers
of Muhammad's community [Qur'ân 48:4], and it is for that reason
and for other similar reasons that it is the best community that has
sprung up among men [Qur'ân 3:110]...What was manifest in other
communities has come down invisibly into this community and
men of spiritual experience have found it in their hearts."

He then explains what distinguishes, among the saints, the
person who is properly a "Muhammadan heir" (*wârith muham-
madî*) from all the others: for the Muhammadan heir, the signs
(*âyât*) are interior.[61]

The word *âyât* is also the word that, in Arabic and in particular in the Qur'ân itself, refers specifically to this eminent category
of signs that constitute the verses of Revelation. It is in us that the
words should be inscribed, it is our very beings that should be the
book in which we decipher them. It thus becomes a question of
becoming like the *fatâ* in Mecca who invited Ibn ʿArabî to examine
the "details of his constitution" and the "order of his form" before
commanding: "Now raise my veils and read what my inscriptions
enclose!" But there is there no appropriation of Revelation on the
part of the man. It is not the man who inhabits the Qur'ân; it is the
Qur'ân that dwells within the man: Divine Word takes possession
of the *ʿârif bi-Llâh* in such a way that the Qur'ân becomes his
"nature." The initiatory voyage (*sulûk*), its abodes, its trials, its
length can be described in a number of ways: certainly, for Ibn
ʿArabî they are nothing more than this possession by the Verb.

This encounter with the *fatâ* we just referred to once again determines, as we have said, the content (the "inscriptions") and the structure (the "order") of the *Futûhât Makkiyya*. We must return to this event in order to clarify, no longer particular aspects of the work, as has already been done, but the disposition of the whole. When Ibn ʿArabî first arrives in Mecca, it is to make a pilgrimage. This pilgrimage requires the performance of a specific rite, that of circumambulation (*tawâf*) of the Kaʿba, the House of God. To forget that the *Futûhât*—the "openings," the "illuminations"—are *Makkiyya*, that they can and do occur only in this sacred place, that the event where they have their genesis is inseparable from the ritual turns that Ibn ʿArabî makes with the *fatâ*, leads only to the worst mistake. When the Shaykh al-Akbar tells the young man "Let me perceive some of your secrets," the answer is "Do the circumambulations in my footsteps."[62] Seven successive theophanies will correspond to these seven circumambulations: "He took before me the form of Life...Then he took before me the form of Sight...Then he took before me the form of Knowledge...Then he took before me the from of Listening...Then he took before me the form of Discourse...Then he took before me the form of Will...Then he took before me the form of Power." The explanation of these transformations follows immediately: "My House that you see here represents my Essence and the circumambulations represent the seven attributes of perfection."[63] These seven attributes are the ones called by the "Names of the Essence": The Living (*Al-Hayy*), The Knowing (*Al-ʿAlîm*), The Wanting (*Al-Mûrid*), The Powerful (*Al-Qadîr*), The Speaking (*Al-Mutakallim* or *Al-Qâʾil*), The Hearing (*Al-Samîʿ*), The Seeing (*Al-Basîr*). Of these names, the six last, according to the Shaykh al-Akbar in another passage,[64] are those to which contingent beings are attached. The first, The Living, is the one by which the others survive and that, present in each of them, remains hidden to created beings.

The arrangement of the *Futûhât* in six sections may be sufficiently explained by the importance with which, in a general way, the number six is seen in the Shaykh al-Akbar's work. This importance is not simply the result of the fact that it is the number of the days of creation (as O. Yahia has shown—as he has also shown that it is the number of dimensions in space). For Ibn ʿArabî, six, which is the first perfect number[65] is above all the symbolic number of the *insân kâmil* (Perfect Man).[66] Effectively, this number expresses the value accord-

ing to the *abjad* of the letter *waw*, which, although not written,
appears, in the existentiating syllable *kun!* (Be!), between the *kâf*
and the *nûn*. And because of that, it is likened by Ibn ʿArabî to
Muhammadan Reality: the "isthmus" (*barzakh*) between *haqq* and
khalq, between the Divine Principle and its manifestation.[67] This
comparison is also based on the grammatical function of *waw*; in Arabic, it plays a copulative role, thus uniting that which is separate.

But in a more specific manner, the explanation of the number
and order of succession of the *fusûl* resides in the number and
nature of the divine attributes (*sifât*) or relational modes (*nisab*)
that creation depends upon; that is, on the six names just listed.
The first section, that of "knowledge" (*maʿârif*), is clearly related to
the name *Al-ʿAlîm* (The Knowing). The second, that of "behaviors"
(*muʿâmalât*), which should be those of the *murîd* (the postulant;
literally, "he who wants") progressing along the Path, appears in
clear relation to the name *Al-Murîd*: when the *murîd* "wants" God,
it is actually that God wants him. The third name in the series, *Al-
Qadîr* (The Powerful), corresponds to the section of "spiritual
states" (*ahwâl*), which divine omnipotence produces in man without his being able to obtain them through his own efforts. The
fourth name is *Al-Mutakallim* (The Speaking): its relationship to
the fourth *fasl*, where each step of spiritual realization is identified
with one of the suras of the Qurʾân, that is, with the Divine Word,
is equally clear, and it suggests the existence of a privileged relationship between the *fatâ* and this section. The following section,
that of "encounters along the way" and of face-to-face discussions
between God and man, corresponds to the fifth name, The Hearing. The sixth *fasl*, finally, that of the "stations" (*maqamât*), is in
explicit rapport with the name *Al-Basîr* (The Seeing). Each of the
"stations" in the sixth *fasl* represents a particular manner of contemplation, but it is God who is both the contemplator and the contemplated at the same time. As for The Living, the seventh name
that sustains and, to a certain extent, contains all the others and
which is thus in reality the first (the theophany "in the form of
Life" comes at the head of the six others when Ibn ʿArabî completes the *tawâf* behind the *fatâ*), it corresponds to the first chapter, the same chapter from which the entire work springs, in the
fatâ's contemplation. Born out of observance of the Law, out of the
performance of a prescribed rite, that of *hajj*, the *Futûhât* repeat

and perpetuate the revolutions of the pilgrim around the House that God, to whom belong "the East and the West," has chosen as a sign of his presence.

5 ❦

"THOSE WHO ARE PERPETUALLY IN PRAYER"
(QUR'ÂN 70:23)

Revelation is not only message: it is also commandment. The message delivers its totality only to the "submissive": to the true *muslimûn*. The Qur'ân opens its "treasures" only to those who apply the Law that it established. There is no illumination without obedience. The *sharî'a* (Law) and the *haqîqa* (the highest and most secret of truths) are inextricably conjoined. They are *bintânî min abin wâhid* (the two daughters of a single father).[1] The *munazalât*, as has been seen, are obtained only by "the most perfect conformity to the prescriptions of the Law."[2] The divine remark, which, as is the case in the fifth section of the *Futûhât*, gives its title to chapter 437 states: "He who knows his part of my Law"—that part which it is his duty to observe at any given moment of his existence— "knows the part of me which comes back to him."[3] In the *Tanazzulât mawsiliyya*, Ibn 'Arabî explains that "the institution of the Law has two causes, in which are two secrets: the first is preserving the order of the world...and its secret is that assisting the believers is a duty for him; and the second is establishing the proofs of servitude by manifesting the magnificence of the Lordship; its secret is the power that his two names exercise."[4] "What he has declared licit, we declare licit; what he has declared a matter of free choice, we also declare likewise; what he blames, we blame; what he recommends, we recommend; what he declares obligatory, we declare obligatory."[5]

The strict relationship between the graces accorded by God and the accomplishment of legal prescriptions is the major theme of a work that the Shaykh al-Akbar composed in eleven days, in Almeria, during the month of Ramadân 595,[6] and completed in Bougie in 597.[7] The work was written for his companion Badr al-Habashî. Ibn 'Arabî said that the book "can make a spiritual master unnecessary," and that "the spiritual master himself needs it," which underscores the importance that he places on the work.[8] Its

101

title, *Mawâqi' al-nujûm*, "The Setting of the Stars," was borrowed from a verse (Qur'ân 56:75) in which the Qur'ân is said to be found "in a hidden Book that only those who have purified themselves touch." The current interpretation, according to which only the Muslim in a state of legal purity can touch a copy of the Qur'ân, is not restrictive, of course. Without deviating from the letter, it is obvious that true access to the "hidden Book" requires more than just formal observance of the rules of ritual ablution. It will be seen that in this matter, as in all others, Ibn 'Arabî does not separate—and *a fortiori* does not oppose—the *zâhir* and the *bâtin*.[9]

The plan of this treatise, as explained by Ibn 'Arabî in his introduction, distinguishes three degrees (*martabât*) to each of which correspond three spheres (*aflâk*): an *islâmiyya* sphere, an *imâniyya* sphere, and an *ihsâniyya* sphere. The association of these names (based on Qur'ânic terms) is supported by a prophetic tradition[10] that defines three hierarchically superimposed stages: *al-islâm* (external submission to the Law), *al-îmân* (internal conviction), and *al-ihsân* (the perfection consisting of "worshipping God as if one saw Him"). Three of these nine spheres (nine being the traditional number of the celestial spheres) are thus quite logically related to the body (*jism*), three with the individual soul (*nafs*), and three with the spirit (*rûh*).

The largest part of the work[11] is dedicated to the seventh sphere (*islâmiyya*) of the third degree, that of sainthood (*walâya*). It deals in great detail with the connection between the fulfillment of the legal prescriptions appropriate to each member and the divine gifts that are their fruits: the charismatic gifts (*karamât*)—ambiguous favors, for they can be a dangerous test for the beneficiary through divine trickery (*makr ilâhî*)—and the *manâzil*, the "abodes" that are the consequence and the gage of authentic spiritual realization. This realization, he explains, is not necessarily accompanied by charisma—which is to his mind quite secondary and eventually dangerous—but he nevertheless judges it necessary to describe them for the use of those to whom these gifts might be given so that they will know how to correctly interpret their nature and origin.

The scriptural foundation of the relationship thus established between the acts of members and supernatural graces is found in a *hadîth qudsî* wherein God says that he is "the hearing, the sight, the hand" of the servant that he loves:[12] for God to be the hearing of the *ʿabd* (servant), it is first necessary that the latter respect the obligations incumbent on this faculty, as is the case for the others. Ibn ʿArabî thus successively examines the case of the seven members submissive to the *taklîf* (prescriptions of the Law). Let it be clarified that he envisions prescriptions of a general character, without specifically taking into consideration the participation of the body in ritual acts, which will be addressed later.[13]

To be obedient to the Law, the eye must turn away from things forbidden and, in a more general sense, from whatever might distract it. For the person who observes these commandments, the charismatic gifts with which he will eventually be gratified are, for example, the vision of hidden things, like the Kaʿba while prayer is performed, or the angels, or the *jinn*; he will be capable of recognizing the *abdâl* or of identifying Khadîr, regardless of the form in which they appear. But that is not the essential: "internal vision" (*basîra*) will be opened. The seer will perceive his own interior "kingdom" (*malakût*) and that of the creatures, whose states and spiritual degrees he knows. He gradually becomes capable of obtaining the *nec plus ultra*, the vision of God.

The ear should refuse to hear calumny, lies, or impious or illicit remarks. Furthermore, it has the duty of dedicating itself to listening to the Qurʾân, or listening to the words of the preacher or the remarks of the spiritual master. It should be attentive to all forms of invocation. If it adheres to these rules, it will be capable of obtaining diverse *karamât*: perceiving the celebration of divine glory (*tasbîh*) by all creatures, including vegetables and minerals; or hearing the instructions of angelic messengers. The corresponding "abodes" are accompanied by even greater privileges, since the servant will finally be able to hear and understand "the Eternal Word" (*al-kalâm al-qadîm*).

The section where Ibn ʿArabî deals with the works of the tongue entails an explanation of the distinction between *karamât* (the miracles of saints) and *muʿjizât* (the miracles of the prophets), of the power of spiritual energy (*himma*), of the different ways of reciting the Book (by the whole being, or by only one part). The tongue is required to abstain from vile words, from lying, from swearing, and from calumny; it is required to devote itself to pious acts in its domain: recitation of the Qurʾân, invocation, the commandment to do good (*al-amr bi-ma'rûf*). The *karamât* engendered by these practices include the ability to predict the future, the ability to speak with an invisible audience, to be understood at extraordinary distances, to bring things into existence by sole virtue of the spoken word—like Jesus, like the chosen ones in the life to come. But especially, and here the divine promise inherent in the hadith quoted above will be recognized, it is God who from this point on is speaking through the mouth of the individual who scrupulously observes the duties of the tongue. Ibn 'Arabî describes two abodes there. In the one, the servant recites the Qur'ân in God's presence. In the other, it is God Who recites the Qur'ân for the servant.

The hand—more precisely, the right hand—must of course abstain from killing and from theft, but also from any useless gesture. It is to be submissive to positive obligations—giving alms, for example, for it symbolizes both power and generosity. Among the numerous corresponding charismatic gifts is included the power to make gold and silver "come out of the air." The true reward, however, does not entail this kind of superior prodigies; it consists rather in seeing the Divine Right inscribe the creatures on the guarded Tablet and thus obtain, in a synthetic form and in a distinctive form, the knowledge of their essential realities. The "Pact with the Pole," described by chapter 336 of the *Futûhât*,[14] takes place in an "abode" dependent upon the works of the hand.

In the long passage about the stomach, the Shaykh al-Akbar cites Qur'ân verse 9:123 ("Oh you who believe, fight against those infidels close to you"). "The lot of the sufi," he writes, "is to consider that this verse refers to his own soul...for of all the "infidels," it is the closest to him. When he has done battle with it and killed or imprisoned it, only then does he occupy himself with other infidels, according to the demands of the station (*maqâm*) that he has attained." This infidel soul possesses two powerful swords—the stomach and sex—which make all creatures subservient. But of these two swords, the one more to be feared is the stomach. When the stomach is tamed, sex is also. In fact, he adds, the body, properly speaking, demands only what is strictly necessary. *Innamâ murâduhu l-wiqâya*: it desires only that which is essential to its preservation, be this food, drink, clothing, or shelter. It is the individual soul, the *nafs*, that demands, in both quality and quantity, all that exceeds this minimum, thus demonstrating its stupidity, since the body that it governs will become carrion, the food excrement, the clothing rags, and the house a ruin. No need of divine instruction to know that; this is a certitude founded on evidence. It is thus important, as God has ordered, to confine oneself to sobriety and to scrupulously consume only legally permitted foods.

Diverse spiritual gifts will sometimes be accorded to those who put these precepts into practice. Signs will advise them of the licit or illicit character of what is to be eaten. Food will multiply in their hands, change its nature according to the desires of those who partake of food with them, or food will come to them in a supernatural manner. Brackish water will become sweet. In certain cases, they will be sated without having eaten, thanks to foods that someone else may have eaten. Works of the stomach will in any case make them penetrate *manâzil*, where they will obtain more valuable spiritual sciences than these phenomena. In the "abode of Abraham" (*manzil ibrâhimî*), these individuals will know the secrets of physical and spiritual germination. In the "abode of Mikâ'îl," the angel in charge of the sustenance of the creatures, they will first contemplate Mikâ'îl as he exercises his distributive function, then God himself, with regard to the names that govern the conferring of the fair share of what each individual deserves. At the end of the voyage, they will end up knowing the Divine Essence, in that it is "the food of foods," that through which every thing is and remains.

Sexual desire in itself is weak. It is the satisfaction of the stomach that fortifies it, and thus there is the need for fasting. "If hunger were for sale in the market place, spiritual aspirants (*al-murîdûn*) should purchase nothing else!" It is mastery of sexual desire (it is not a question of continence, but once again, of conformity with conditions assigned by the Law to the satisfaction of desire) that makes one ready for spiritual paternity. He who controls his sexual desires vivifies beings by his teaching. His words are engraved in those who listen to him—the analogy between the male sexual organ and the pen that writes on the tablet, which itself is a symbol of the female sexual organs, is strongly emphasized.

The foot's duty is to walk toward that which is obligatory (making the pilgrimage, performing collective prayer in the mosque, visiting the sick, and so on) and abstaining from what is forbidden or reproachable. In the lives of the saints, marvels are associated with such obedience: they "walk" in the air, or on water; the earth "folds up" underneath them such that they cover formidable distances with just a few steps. These spectacular gifts are nevertheless nothing more than the expression on the plane of sensation of graces, which are much higher. The true walk in air is domination of the passions (there is here an untranslatable play on words based on the similarity in terms used for air and passion), leading to the *malakût*, the spiritual kingdom. Walking on water is mastering the secret of life (for "it is from water that we [God] have made all living things," Qur'ân 21:30).

We have presented here only a brief outline of the teachings that make up a treatise of more than a hundred pages. It does, nevertheless, give a sense of the exact correlation that Ibn 'Arabî establishes between spirtual realization (*tahaqquq*) and humble, painstaking submission to the *sharî'a*. Another of Ibn 'Arabî's works adds complementary details, which, in this case, concern more the importance of the ritual acts of worship (*ibâdât*) instituted by the Law. The work in question is the *Tanazzulât mawsiliyya*, the angelic "descents of Mosul" written, as the name suggests, in the Iraqi city where Ibn 'Arabî, arriving from Baghdad, stayed in 601 A.H. before going on to Anatolia.[15]

I have placed in this book the subtleties of secrets and the splendors of the sciences of lights. It is constructed on enigma and symbol so that he who attempts an intimate talk [*munâja*] with his Lord, when he observes [in this book] what the fruits of such an encounter truly are, will be conscious of his limits and his powerlessness. But if I have attempted to disguise these divine meanings in an enigmatic speech, it is also out of a jealous concern for keeping away detainers of exoteric science, and to punish them for their refusal—just as God has put a seal on their hearts and their ears and a veil on their eyes [allusion to Qur'ân 2:7] such that they are unable to perceive the smell of the breath of essential truths or to distinguish at all the difference between angelic visits or satanic visits in their hearts.

In this I am in accord with the example of him [Abû Hurayra] who received the science from the infallible Prophet

and stated: "If I divulged it, my throat would be slit," or to
'Alî's [Abî Tâlib] example when he learned what was being
said about him, and said while pointing to his breast: "There
are abundant sciences here. If only I could find someone capable of enduring them."[16]

The use in this introduction of the word *munâja* (intimate talk),
when one is familiar with Ibn 'Arabî's vocabulary, permits the reader
to understand immediately that, among the *'ibâdât*, it is about ritual
prayer (*salât*) that he has chosen to speak. Actually, this word refers
to a hadith: "Each one of you, when you pray, has an intimate talk
with the Lord."[17] Ibn 'Arabî deducts certain important aspects of his
interpretation of *salât* from this hadith, and he uses the hadith frequently when speaking about prayer. This choice of prayer is easily
explained. Among the five pillars (*arkân*) of Islam, the first refers to
faith—the *shahâda*, the testimony to divine unicity and the mission
of the Messenger—and the four others to fundamental works:
prayer, alms, fasting, and pilgrimage. But "the first of his works that
man will be asked to account for on the day of judgment is prayer."[18]
Almsgiving (*zakât*) is a conditional obligation—it is not incumbent
on the poor, who are rather the beneficiaries—and it needs be done
only once per year. The pilgrimage (*hajj*), also dependent on conditions (having the necessary resources, the security of the roads,
physical aptitudes), needs be performed only once in a lifetime. Fasting (*sawm*), for which cases of inability are also foreseen, lasts one
month out of twelve. Prayer is daily and, even though it may be
reduced to a hasty sketch of the prescribed gestures in the case of
those who are ill or elderly, each believer, from the age of reason,
must perform it five times a day.[19] Its daily repetition thus confers on
it a particular importance. In a certain sense, then, prayer contains
the three other works: it is "purification" (the etymological meaning
of *zakât*) and "alms of being," as *zakât* is alms of having; it imposes
the same constraints as fasting since, like fasting, it cuts the person
who prays off from the profane world ("it closes all the doors and the
station that corresponds to it is divine jealousy"[20]); facing in the
direction of the House of God, it is an immobile pilgrimage, just as
the *hajj* is, inversely, a prayer in movement. Ibn 'Arabî, who dedicates countless passages of his work to prayer (and most notably an
immense chapter of the *Futûhât*[21]) especially emphasizes, in the

beginning of the *Tanazzulât*, its *munâja* characteristic; elsewhere he recalls that the successive gestures of a person in prayer recap the "kingdoms of nature": the vertical position is that of the human being, the horizontal position then taken is that of the animal world, and the prostration that turns man toward the earth is indentified with the plant kingdom.[22] Although the text does not mention it, the fourth posture, that of being seated (*julûs*), corresponds quite clearly, from this point of view, to the massive stability of the mineral world. Through this series of positions the believer is to actualize his virtual nature of "abbreviation of the universe," of microcosm, and thus assume the function of "lieutenant," "place holder" (*khilâfa*) that God has assigned him.

The Shaykh al-Akbar deals first with ritual ablution, which, for him, it might be said again, is an autonomous act of worship (*'ibâda mustaqulla*) and not only a preface to prayer.[23] He distinguishes between the perfectly pure "celestial water," which purifies the intellect (*al-'aql*), and "terrestrial water," which purifies the senses.[24] If water is the principle of life, the earth is the matter from which our bodies were created (*mâ khuliqta minhu*): that is why, when water is scarce, the Qur'ân authorizes ablution with dust (*tayammum*).[25] In either case, as can be seen, purification consequently consists in a return to the origin that restores the primordial status of the human being. As for the *ghusl*—complete ablution of the body and not just certain parts of it—which is required to erase the major state of impurity that results from the sexual act, it involves all of man because, in sexual union (*jimâ'*, a word whose root expresses the idea of totalization) the being is as if drowned in a *ghayba kulliyya*, a total absence; it is in exile from itself.[26]

Each element of ritual purification is then commentated: washing of the hands, of the face, of the feet, and so forth. But the intellect must also be cleansed of the representations that it fashions, it must be returned to its primal simplicity: "O intellect, face your place of prayer, that he might recite his Word upon you. Leave your belief (*i'tiqâdaka*) there. Do not reflect while he is speaking to you. Do not think about your response."[27] *I'tiqâd*—the word here translated as "belief"—is not naked faith. Like *'aql* (intellect), this word is formed from a root that means "attach," or "knot." *I'tiqâd* is a ligature, a conception or mental image in which we enclose divine infinity. Returning to *ummiyya*, to illiteracy, to the state of infancy, is a *sine qua non* of hearing divine discourse. The intellect that has welcomed this discourse has no need of responding: it will hear the response that God creates in it.

All of the chapters of the *Tanazzulât* begin with the sentence "The faithful Spirit [*al-rûh al-amîn*, Qur'ân 26:193] descended upon the heart and said," which explains the title given to the work, "[Angelic] Descents." After interpreting the words of the call to prayer (*iqâma*), the faithful Spirit explains the deep meaning of *takbîr* (the recitation of the words *Allâhu akbar!* "Allâh [which represents here the supreme Name] is greatest") with which *salât* itself begins:

> When you are in any state whatever, celestial or terrestrial, you are necessarily under the rule of one of the divine names, whether you know it or not, whether you contemplate it or not. It is this name that rules your movement and your rest; it is through it that you have the status of possible, or that of existent. And this name says: I am God. And it speaks the truth. But it is mandatory that you reply: *Allâhu akbar!*...Know, with absolute certainty, that the Divine Essence never shows itself to you as itself, but only under the form of one of its eminent attributes; and know that you will never know the meaning of the name *Allâh*.[28]

Only this absolute, unconditioned, inaccessible Essence is worthy of worship, and, even though all the attributes may belong to it, even though "all names are those of the same Named," the *takbîr* is a radical refusal to idolize that which is not the Essence itself: it is greater than all that is great, it transcends all transcendence.

The following is a passage on the elevation of the hands, palms facing foreward, a ritual gesture that accompanies the *takbîr* and that, for Ibn 'Arabî, must be repeated in the subsequent phases of prayer:

> The Most High has called you for intimate talk with you, the Munificent has called you to pour out his gifts upon you. Be then humble and poor. Raise your hands in recitation of the *takbîr* each time that you lower yourself or that you stand up again and throw behind yourself what has been given to you in

each theophany...Place in your purse what you have received and claim another gift and a greater light still, for it does not cease to shine. Divine effusion perpetually emanates from the spring of his generosity. Welcome it in that indefeasible indigence of being that remains attached to you when you contemplate him. He does not cease to give, nor you to amass. He does not stop elevating himself, nor you lowering yourself.[29]

Then the faithful Spirit teaches the secret of orientation toward the *qibla*: "Tell your heaven [your spirit] not to veil you by its subtlety, and your earth [your body] not to veil you by its density." The *qibla* within must not hide the exterior *qibla* defined by the Law, and vice versa. In echo to the verse according to which "wherever you turn, there is the Face of God," the angel prescribes: "Be a circular face [*wajh mustadîr*]...so that the orientation [of your body] toward the Kaʿba will not be a screen to orientation in the direction of the divine presence in the heart."[30]

Next come the "secrets of the standing posture and of recitation," that is, of what constitutes the first sequence of *salât*. Muhammad received "the Sum of the Words" (*jawâmiʿ al-kalim*) and the Qurʾân contains all previous revelations. According to the interior state of the reciter, it can thus be perceived in a different way, each modality being the expression of one of its multiple aspects. Thus the injunction:

Know how to distinguish between the Qurʾân [*qurʾân*: the Qurʾân in the sense that it gathers together and sums up] and your *Furqân* [another name of the Qurʾân considered this time in its separating function], between your Torah and your Light [still the Qurʾân seen in the sense that it illuminates], between your Book and your Psalms...The Qurʾân is reserved for the Muhammadan [*mukhtass bi l-muhammadî*], the *Furqân* belongs to it by virtue of its participation in the Mosaic heritage.[31]

The definition of the perfect recitant (he who receives the entire Qurʾân, who embraces all its modalities, all its "readings") is given to us by Ibn ʿArabî in a previous chapter of the *Tanazzulât*:

I contain its Torah, its Gospels and its Qur'ân
[and] I contain its Psalms.[32]

Qur'ânic recitation in prayer obligatorily includes the *Fâtiha*, followed by another sura or another free choice of verses. The *Fâtiha* comes first, with the majority of its sentences making explicit one of the names by which it is traditionally called: "Know that it has two sides and a middle, or two parts and a link between them"—an allusion to the first four verses, which are "God's part," and to the last three, which are "man's part," with the intermediate part, verse 5, being of intermediary nature since it joins God's part ("It is you whom we worship") and man's part ("It is you whom we implore for help"). This double nature of the first sura is put into perspective by the *hadîth qudsi*,[33] in which God says: "I have divided the prayer [here identified with the *Fâtiha*, which is an essential element of prayer] into two parts, between my servant and myself." The text of the *Tanazzulât* affirms this again in different forms a few lines later:

> It is "The One That Opens" [the true meaning of the word
> *fâtiha*] the brilliant theophanies. It is the Doubled One [*al-
> muthannâ*], for it contains the meanings of Lordship and
> servitude at the same time. It is The One That Suffices [*al-
> kâfiyya*], for it includes both trial and security. It is the Seven
> Doubled Ones [*al-sab' al-mathânî*], for it includes the [seven]
> attributes [of the Essence]. It is the Immense Sum [*al-qur'ân
> al-'azîm*], for it envelops the contingent and the eternal. It is
> the Mother of the Book [*Umm al-kitâb*], for in it are found
> felicity and punishment. One of its sides is suspended in
> Divine Realities and the other is attached to human realities,
> while its middle proceeds from the ones and the others.[34]

Of the other suras among which the person who prays might choose after the *Fâtiha*, we are told that they contain "from three to two hundred eighty abodes...that were mentioned in the *Futûhât Makkiyya*." The *fasl al-manâzil* was undoubtedly not yet written at the time that the *Tanazzulât* were composed, but chapter 22 of the *Futûhât*, which is a kind of preface to them, had certainly been written, and it is quite probably this that is being referred to. The identification of the *manâzil* with suras is in any case perfectly clear here, the numbers indicated being those of the verses of the longest sura (*Al-baqara*) and of the shortest (*Al-kawthar*).

As he had already done in the *Mawâqi' al-nujûm* dealing with the works of the tongue, Ibn 'Arabî distinguishes between two recitations: *al-tilâwa al-ilâhiyya* (divine recitation), and *al-tilâwa al-insâniyya* (recitation by the human being), and he shows the difference between them by commentating successively from these two points of view on the first seventeen verses of sura *Al-najm*, the same ones that structured the *Kitâb al-isrâ*.[35] The choice of these verses is not explained, but there is nothing accidental about it. As is known, they describe the ascension (*mi'raj*) of the Prophet. It is in the course of this *mi'raj* that ritual prayer was instituted by God; furthermore, according to a hadith, prayer is the *"ascension of the believer"* [*mi'raj al-mu'min*]. A paradoxical *mi'raj*: it is in lowering himself that the one who prays is raised. "It is in your fall that your elevation comes, and it is in your earth that your heaven is found."[36]

Bowing (*rukû'*) and prostration (*sujûd*) follow recitation in the vertical position.

The first phase of this descent, bowing, where only the upper part of the body is bent, is a *barzakh*, an intermediate spot between heaven and earth, between *rubûbiyya*, the Lordship symbolized by the standing position, and the *'ubûdiyya*, the servile condition soon to be shown via prostration. It thus shows the double nature of man, where the superior realities (*haqqiyya*) and the inferior realities (*khalqiyya*) are joined. That is why, returning to the vertical position after the *rukû'*, he speaks in the name of God, as if he were God, addressing the creatures—and himself in that he is a creature—when he pronounces the ritual words: "God listens to him [servant] who praises him [God]." A hadith[37] teaches us that it is God who, at this moment, pronounces the words through the mouth of the *'abd*.

Once more referring to prophetic traditions,[38] Ibn 'Arabî establishes an analogy between the lowering of the body toward the earth and the descent of God toward the heavens of this lower world during the last third of each night. Lowering himself toward the place of his prosternation, the person who prays is in search of divine proximity. It is said: "Prostrate yourself and come closer" (Qur'ân 96:19) and, according to a *hadîth qudsî*, "he who comes closer to me by a hands length, I come closer to him by a forearm's length." Nevertheless, "just as this fall toward the earth is brief, so also is the theophany corresponding to it prompt to disappear...It has no stability and it is useless to want it to last. It slips away like oil" (*ka l-dihhân*, Qur'ân 55:37).[39]

This chapter on prostration (*sujûd*) once again refers to verse 96:19:

> It is His name, *Al-Qarîb*, "He Who Is Close," which has called you to proximity. You are the lover and not the beloved, which is why he says: [prostrate yourself] and come closer. If you were the beloved, he would say: [prostrate yourself], you are close...Know that in your prostration you are preserved (*ma'sûm*) from Satan, for your prostration subjugates him and he has no power over you. When he observes you in this state, he thinks only of himself [and of his own refusal to prostrate himself before Adam as God had commanded; consumed by the fire in the citadel of his punishment, seeing you obedient and comtemplating the fate that awaits him the day when the Hour of Judgment comes...May God grant that we be, you and I, among those who have prostrated themselves and who have found [*mimman sajada wa wajada*].[40]

In the section of chapter 69 of the *Futûhât* where he deals with prostration,[41] Ibn 'Arabî cites, recommending that the believer imitate the example of the Prophet, the request (*du'â*) that Muhammad made of God while in *sujûd* after pronouncing three times the ritual phrase "Glory to my Most High Lord": "Put a light in my heart, a light in my ear, a light in my eye, a light on my right, a light on my left, a light before me, a light behind me, a light above me, a light under me, give me a light and make me light."

Remember that light (*al-nûr*) is one of the divine names. *Totus ipse lumen.* "The second thing that the person says in prostrate prayer is 'Make me light,' that is, make me you," as Ibn 'Arabî writes. The "proximity" that *sujûd* is to lead to is just another name for *theôsis.* The same passage from the *Futûhât* comes back emphatically to this same theme: "Take me away from myself, and be my being, then will my eye see everything through you."

After standing, bowing, and prostration, the seated posture

(julûs) is the fourth in legal prayer. God "created the heavens and the earth in six days, then he sat upon the Throne" (Qur'ân 57:4) and this divine "seating" (istiwâ) is, to be precise, that of *Al-Rahmân*, the "All Merciful" (Qur'ân 20:5). The consequences that Ibn 'Arabî draws from this analogy in the two chapters where he deals with *julûs*, properly speaking, and then of *tashahhud*, the formula that the *musallî* (the person in prayer) recites in this position, are as follows:[42] "No veil exists that could keep you from attaining the essential realities or from catching subtleties, but for one: viz., the composite nature of the world of sensation. When separation comes and the attachment [of your being] with it ceases..., then the essential realities will shine forth and you will obtain those secrets which are still hidden from you."

But for those who are already separated from the world, who, according to an expression of the Prophet, are "dead before dying," there is no waiting: "You have reached the degree of *istiwâ*—the state of perfect equilibrium—and you have freed yourself from the power of heaven and earth." The sentences that follow are linked together in counterpoint to the elements of the traditional formula of *tashahhud*: "Greet him whose likeness you have become. Then greet him who led you [the Prophet] and through whom he whom you find before you [God] has made you happy by solidly affirming his presence through the vocative particle." Actually, the greeting of the Prophet in the *tashahhud*, is expressed in the second person—gramatically the "person present"—and carries the vocative *yâ ayyuhâ*.

> Then greet, with a salutation which comes from God, yourself and all the beings of your species, for *salâm* [the greeting, but also Peace, one of the divine names] is your Lord and the degree of the name *Al-Salâm* is the place of your theophany [at this specific moment]. Finally, affirm the unicity of the One and deny that there are equals to him [an allusion to the words of the *shahâda* at the end of *tashahhud*]. And then you will need to disappear, for it is in this disappearance that you will obtain what you desired.

To finally leave the state of prayer that he began by the initial *takbîr*, the worshipper must pronounce, while turning his head toward the right: *al-salâm alaykum*. This *salâm* can have different meanings or, in the case where it is said mechanically by a distracted believer, it can have no meaning:

> In prayer there are two categories of Muslims and thus two ways of performing prayer. Those who unite the one with the other are joining together the spiritual realities that correspond to each.
>
> The higher of these categories is that of the worshipper who says *salâm* because he has passed [at the moment he comes out of prayer] from the authority of one name to the authority of another. He is thus greeting the one he is leaving and the one to which he is arriving...
>
> The lesser category is that of the worshipper who greets the All-Merciful because he is leaving him, and the creatures because he is returning toward them...
>
> As for those who belong to neither of these two categories, their *salâm* is worthless: they were not near God, and their greeting is thus not the greeting of one who is departing. They never left the creatures, and thus their greeting is not the greeting of one newly arrived.[43]

The daily ritual act (and the most banal, it might be said), the act that marks the existence of all pious Muslims, is also the one that leads to the highest intimacy with God, to this "proximity" that is another name for the *tashabbuh bi l-ilâh* through which man is reestablished in his original theomorphism. To become "the throne of the Qur'ân"[44] it is necessary to be submissive to the law of the Qur'ân: the *ibâdât* that it prescribes are the place where *walâya*, sainthood, attains its plenitude, and, whatever their merit may be, the spiritual practices added out of free choice to these common obligations cannot in themselves bear comparable fruits. "*Farâ'id* [obligatory acts], are higher and more loved by God than *nawâfil* [supererogatory acts],"[45] says Ibn ʿArabî in one of the numerous texts in which he meditates on the *hadîth qudsî*[46] where God says, "My servant does not approach me by something I love more than by those acts which I have prescribed." Certainly this hadith then mentions the *nawâfil*: "He does not cease approaching me by extra works until I love him. And when I love him, I am his ear with which he hears, his eye with which he sees, his hand with which he grasps." But if *nawâfil* are to a certain extent necessary—in a propaedeutic sense, since they orient the being toward performance of obligatory works, and in a compensatory sense, since they will overwhelm the imperfections of the corresponding *farâ'id* on Judgment Day[47]—they are nevertheless vitiated by their basis in illusion: the *'abd* has nothing and is nothing, and the affirmation of his own will, of a choice, confirms the imposture of the ego. After citing the above hadith, Ibn 'Arabî adds: "If that [that God becomes the hearing, the sight of the servant] is the fruit of supererogatory acts, just think about the fruit of obligatory acts! By these the servant will be God's hearing, and His sight."[48]

Charisma, sciences, epiphanies, all the signs and all the accomplishments are attached to the *farâ'id*, and thus to the Law. Nothing demonstrates this more than the second part of chapter 73 of the *Futûhât*, where the functions, types, and degrees of sainthood are enumerated. Ibn 'Arabî responds to Tirmidhî's famous questions, and in general his responses, often as enigmatic as the questions, constitute, in perfect coherence with the first part, a synthetic explication of his doctrine of *walâya*. It must be understood that the implicit reference in many obscure passages—which allows them to be interpreted—is, once again, a reference to legal prayer and its diverse elements. Thus appears another case of the coincidence of *zâhir* and *bâtin*. The spiritual quest is completed through that by which it was started: observance of the *sharî'a*.

Question number 5[49] says, "Where is the station of men of sessions and discussion located?" [*ahl al-majâlis wa l-hadîth*]. The reply mentions six "presences" (*hadarât*) and indicates a certain number of "sessions" [*majâlis*] for each: eight for the first, the second, and the fourth; two for the sixth; six for the third; four for the fifth. Among these sessions, there are "sessions for meeting" and "sessions for separation." There is, however, a distinction: the "men of discussion," those to whom God speaks (*al-muhaddathûn*), are also "men of contemplation" (*ahl al-shuhûd*); the term *majâlis* is not properly applied to them unless they are considered from the first of these two points of view.

Sessions, discussion, contemplation: although this vocabulary seems less than precise, it is actually still a question of *salât*. The six *hadarât* are the five daily prayers together with the nocturnal *witr* that the Prophet instituted and that is a traditional obligation. The "sessions" (*majâlis*; root *jls*), get their name from the seated position (*julûs*, from the same root), a posture that the person in prayer should take at various times, depending on the prayers. The first "presence" is the prayer at midday, where the seated posture (*jalsa*) comes eight times;[50] the third, that at sunset, where it is repeated six times; the fifth, the one in the morning, where it is repeated four times. Each "session of meeting" corresponds to the intermediate *jalsa* between the two *rak'as*, which is accompanied by recitation of the *tashahhud*. As for the "session of separation," this expression refers to the final *jalsa* (in his reply to question number 8, Ibn 'Arabî specifies that there is only one in any *hadra*), the one that immediately precedes the moment when the worshipper "comes out" of prayer.

Hadîth (discussion), supposes presence (*hudûr*). It is not compatible with contemplation (*shuhûd, mushâhada*), for the latter requires the extinction of the contemplator. If discussion with God is linked to *julûs* (which, by its gestic symbolism, expresses stability, permanence [*baqâ*]), comtemplation is, on the other hand, associated with prostration, where the being lowers himself into his nothingness. Then, and only then, those who pray "see God through Him, and not through themselves" [*bihi lâ bi anfusihim*].[51]

cf
Eckhart

All of this—the identity between *julûs* and *majâlis*, *hadra* and *salât*, *shuhûd* and *sujûd*—remains unexpressed. But there is no lack of evidence: choice of words, the numbers associated with them.[52] It remains for the reader to know how to interpret them. It is in similarly veiled terms that clarification takes place, in questions 9 and 10, of the secrets of prayer in which and by which the *walî* enters into the divine mysteries. "What does intimate talk (*munâja*) open with?" The three less than explicit words used by Ibn 'Arabî in his response represent respectively the call to prayer, the *takbîr*, which begins the state of prayer, and the *basmala*, the initial verse of the *Fâtiha*: that is, the beginning of *salât*, properly speaking. Then transposing the verse (Qur'ân 58:12–13) that commands that any discussion with God's messenger be preceded by almsgiving (*sadaqa*), he adds, "and the best of alms is, for man, to offer himself...so that it is God who speaks to himself by himself and no one listens to him other than him."[53] This total oblation, which will be accomplished in prostration, is required of each *musallî*, and it is only if this condition is satisfied that prayer is truly *munâja*, a dialogue between God and God, where the person praying is only the *locus* of this divine dialogue.

"With what is the dialogue sealed?" A word, which is left unsaid in the response to this question, gives the key to this passage: it is *al-salâm*, the salutation that ends the state of prayer and accompanies the return toward the creatures. The text of the *Tanazzulât* cited above clarifies what the "names"—the one being left, the one being arrived at—that are mentioned here mean. But in a more specific manner, Ibn ʿArabî has in mind the ritual formulas themselves: the name from which one separates is the name *Allâh*, the last to be pronounced in the *tashahhud*; the one that follows it is the one that appears in the final salutation: *Al-salâm*. The one that, according to what Ibn ʿArabî affirms, but without explanation, is "hidden between them" and by which, properly speaking, the prayer closes (since the "greeting" establishes a new state), is the affixed pronoun *hu* of *rasûluhu*, a word that, at the end of the *tashahhud*, attests that Muhammad is his messenger, the messenger of *huwa*, of the divine Self.[54]

Question number 12 appeals to another symbolic designation of *salât*, that which compares it to a voyage—a *vertical* voyage, since it is here an ascension, as suggested by the constant Qurʾânic use of a verb (root *qwm*) that expresses the idea of raising, or erecting, when the duty of *accomplishing* prayer is spoken of. This voyage toward "session and dialogue" must be undertaken "with spiritual aspirations devoid (*mujarrada*) of all that is other than him." This stripping, this purification are not to be taken only in a general sense: technically, it is ablution that is being alluded to. At the end of his answer, Ibn ʿArabî, in clear language this time, distinguishes four voyages, or four abodes of the voyage ("departing from him, toward him, in him, through him") which he identifies with the standing position, bowing, prostration, and the seated position—to the four postures of *salât*, explicitly called by their names. There is little doubt that in the preceding pages it was prayer that he was implicitly referring to, since mention is further made here of the hadith according to which the Prophet found "freshness" or "consolation" in his eye during *salât*.[55]

It can also be noticed that a whole series of replies (the questions numbered 97 to 115) are perfectly intelligible only if one knows how to read the gestures and words of the prayer in filigree, and in apparently abstract wording. The common term in questions 97 and 98 is that of "face" (*wajh*). It is not difficult to guess that Ibn 'Arabî's text there speaks of orientation (*tawajjuh*), which is of course not only orientation of the body toward the *qibla*, although this is certainly included.[56]

Question number 99 is "What is the beginning of praise?" Praise (*Al-hamd*) is one of the names of the *Fâtiha* and the Shaykh al-Akbar, for once, is quite clear. It is all the more evident that is it about this sura that Tirmidhî was inquiring, since the following question is about the *âmîn* (amen) with which the recitation of this sura is completed. The response appeals to the science of letters (the beginning of the "praise" is the *bâ* of the *basmala*, if one takes into consideration the relationship between God and the creature, but it is the first letter, the initial *alif* of the following verse if one considers God in his transcendence) in terms analogous to what is found in chapters 2 and 5 of the *Futûhât*.[57] It is there verified, by the way, that Ibn 'Arabî, when interpreting in terms of ritual acts questions which might be understood in other ways, was not reading a meaning of his own in Hakîm Tirmidhî's questionnaire: Tirmidhî's questions were most often enigmatic, their abstruseness put to the test the spiritual knowledge of those who might take up his challenge. But Ibn 'Arabî's answers are clearly the ones he expected.

Questions 101 and 102 ("What is prostration? What is its beginning?") are likewise quite explicit. "The body," replies Ibn 'Arabî, "prostrates itself toward the earth from which it is made, the spirit before the universal Spirit from which it procedes, the secret (*sirr*) before its Lord." And he adds: "The face [of the one who prays] does not persist in its prostration, but rather raises itself up again, for neither does the *qibla* before which it prostrates itself persist...but the heart never raises itself in this manner, for its *qibla* is its Lord and its Lord remains forever."[58]

In the reply to question 9, Ibn 'Arabî mentions incidentally "those who begin the *munâja* [prayer] by putting on the mantle of Grandeur, and then taking it partially off." Here we recognize the words of the *hadîth qudsî*: "Grandeur is my mantle and magnificence is my loincloth,"[59] but this remark is left without elaboration. The answers to questions 103 to 107,[60] which deal successively with each of the key words of the hadith (grandeur, mantle, etc.), offer a commentary on it that, if its subtleties are deciphered correctly, confirms that Ibn ʿArabî's discourse on sainthood is centered on *ʿibâdât*, and particularly on prayer. "Grandeur" (*kibriyâ*) is an allusion to *takbîr*, which the worshipper recites aloud, proclaiming, "Allâh is the greatest." In this vertical position (*qiyâm*), the *musallî* symbolically assumes—as *khalîfa* (place holder)—the function of sovereignty that properly can belong only to God. But the "mantle of grandeur," which is thus borrowed, must ultimately be given back so that the memory of his ontological indigence is not lost. This is the reason for the bow (*rukûʿ*), in which his stature is diminished by half. The upper part of the body, which is cloaked in the mantle (*ridâ*), is effaced as it becomes horizontal. The only verticality that remains is the lower part of the body, the part covered by the loincloth (*izâr*). The bow is, however, only an intermediate state (a *barzakh*, according to the *Tanazzulât*) toward renunciation of all sovereignty, of all claim of autonomy. The final stage is prostration, falling *fî asfal al-sâfilîn* (Qurʾân 95:5), "to the lowest of the low," an ineluctable vow of absolute servitude.

This explains why, to the question "What is the mantle?" Ibn ʿArabî replies: "The mantle is the perfect servant (*al-ʿabd al-kâmil*) created in the form [of God], who unites in his person contingent realities and divine realities."[61] The Perfect Man (*al-insân al-kâmil*) is this perfect servant, he whose function of place holding (*khilâfa*) is legitimate and who effectively assumes the grandeur of God in his *qiyâm* when, with most men, this position is a mere appearance. He is the "mantle of God" for God is *bâtin fîhi* (hidden in him), covered by him as by a mantle, but he never loses sight of his *ʿubûda* (servitude): if God is as "annihilated in him" (*qad yustahlak al-haqq fîhi*), he is himself obliterated in God.

This meditation on *salât* continues in his dealing with question 109:[62] "What is seriousness (*al-waqâr*)?" Ibn ʿArabî cites, *in fine*, the hadith recommending "serenity and seriousness" to believers when they go to prayer. By choosing the word *waqâr*, Tirmidhî—who also was a *muhaddith*, a specialist in the sayings of the Prophet—invited the understanding that his interrogation was continuing in the narrow line in the previous questions, and it is in this way that the Shaykh al-Akbar took him. But *waqâr* (in Arabic, like *gravitas* in Latin, having the meaning of heaviness) is for him not just an exterior attitude. As he says, just as physical death is preceded by what the Qurʾân calls "inebriation" (*sakarât al-mawt*, "the dizziness of the agonizer"), so also the theophany, which is obtained only by previously passing through another "death," is announced by a kind of oppression, an overbearing weight, a *gravitas* that disposes the being toward acceptance of manifestations of the divine names in prayer.

The notion of "clarity" (*diyâ*) that appears in question 112[63] must also be interpreted in light of another hadith that relates it to prayer or, more precisely, to the ritual act that prepares its performance: *Al-wudû diyâ,* "ablution is clarity."[64] The response—and the two following responses,[65] which, significantly, concern *al-quds* (transcendental purity), and where Ibn 'Arabî distinguishes between an essential purity and an accidental (*aradî*) purity, the latter of which must be continually reestablished—confirms that here we are indeed dealing with the secrets of perfect ablution, that which washes the body and the spirit.

Another series of responses (questions 147 to 151)[66] leads us back, in a completely explicit manner, to the theme of prayer: after the *basmala* (which is for the *'abd* "what the *kun!* the existentiating *fiat!* is for God") they again, one by one, make commentary on the phrases of the *tashahhud*.[67] One example is where the worshipper is to say *al-salâm alaynâ,* "may the greeting [or peace] be upon us." Using as support Qur'ân verse 24:61, which shows that this greeting that believers address to themselves is in fact *tahiyyatan min Allâh,* a greeting that comes from God,[68] he draws the conclusion that the phrase means that man, in prayer, should be "a stranger to himself, present to his Lord." Then *anta tarjumânuhu ilayka,* "you are, for yourself, his interpreter" for, if this condition is fulfilled, it is God who speaks through the mouth of the *musallî.* As for the response to question 154, the next to last, it is entirely dedicated to the "Mother of the Qur'ân," *umm al-kitâb,* to the *Fâtiha,* and thus once again to *salât.*

It would have been possible to present a number of other passages that, in an overt or covert manner, would continually have led us back to prayer, the expression common to all believers—but for the *'ârif bi-Llâh,* to realization—of *'ubûda,* the radical servitude of man. *'Ubûda* is of course the word upon which all this doctrine rests, a doctrine that affirms the superiority of the *farâ'id* over the *nawâfil* and for which supreme liberty is founded on obligation, sainthood on the Law. Ibn 'Arabî defines its meaning as follows:[69] " *'Ubûda* is perfect and immediate conformity to divine order without a hint of disobedience." He makes a distinction—at least in principle, since he often uses one of these terms for the other—between ʿubûda and ʿubûdiyya. ʿUbûda, it will soon be seen why, is an inalterable state. ʿUbûdiyya (bondage) is the condition that this state imposes upon the ʿabd according to the modalities adequate for each moment. To Tirmidhî's question: "What is the number of parts of ʿubûdiyya?"[70] he replies, "Ninety-nine, the number of divine names...for for each of them there is a corresponding, appropriate ʿubûdiyya." Before each of the divine names that successively govern its existence—the universe is no more than their perpetual epiphany—the ʿabd should have the attitude that the nature of this particular name requires, the kind of obedience that is its due. When God manifests himself under his name Al-Razzâq (He Who Provides), the ʿubûdiyya required is not the same as that required by the name Al-Mumît (He Who Causes Death) or the name Al-Muntaqim (the Avenger).

More systematic than Ibn ʿArabî, ʿAbd al-Karîm al-Jîlî, in his commentary on the Risâlat al-anwâr,[71] sets up a strict hierarchy: ʿubûda is the ontological indigence of the ʿabd; ʿubûdiyya consists in remaining conscious at each moment of this ʿubûda. ʿIbâda, which is the third word of the same family and, in Qurʾânic vocabulary, denotes those acts that are due to God (at the first level of which is prayer), is the praxis that devolves logically from this conscience. When Ibn ʿArabî states: "What I ask God for is that he grant me ʿubûda mahda, pure servitude with no trace of lordship in either my body or my spirit,"[72] his words should undoubtedly be read (in order to be completely congruent with what he himself teaches) as ʿubûdiyya rather than ʿubûda, for the ʿabd never comes out of his ʿubûda, whether he knows it or not. Let us note also that the Shaykh al-Akbar's request was granted. He affirms in another chapter of the Futûhât: "I am the pure servant; I know not the taste of lordship."[73] This assertion deserves all the more attention since, in the passage on the "parts of ʿubûdiyya," he says: "I have known not one of the muqarrabûn, the Close Ones, who observes perfectly pure servitude" (ʿubûda, here again, the context of the passage suggests reading it as ʿubûdiyya). According to him, this imperfection has two causes: the first is al-ghafla (inattention), the distraction inherent in the human condition (Adam "forgot" the pact made with God according to the Qurʾân [20:115]); and the second is al-istiʿjâl (haste, an allusion to Qur'ân 17:11). He adds: "What kept me from reaching this station was nothing else than *ghafla*. Between this station and me there is no other veil than that, and it will never be taken away. As for the veil of haste, I hope, praise be to God, that it has already been taken away." Returning to this "station" at the end of his response, he nevertheless exclaims: "I do not give up the hope of reaching it, even though I know that it is impossible."

The expressions that we have used to analyze what Ibn 'Arabî, in many of his works, says about this perfect prayer—which on the outside is nevertheless identical in every way to that of any believer—may sound like a "mysticism of abjection," like one of those paroxysmal forms of humility and penitence with which hagiography is replete. Certainly a "proud saint" would be a contradiction in terms. Humility and repentance are necessary conditions of sainthood. All the masters of sufism, Ibn 'Arabî included, are unanimous on this point. But it must be understood that what is said in the texts we have cited, or in the countless texts about which we have not spoken but where analogous themes abound, is quite another matter. It is not a case of some kind of drunkenness, debasement, or the ecstatic rapture of the flagellant.

If the Shaykh al-Akbar does insist on a rule when he addresses a disciple, it is the rule of sobriety (*sahw*), with the *malâmî*, the *sanctus absconditus*, as its paradigm. This is what explains why, for him, *shatahât* ("locutions theopathiques," to use Massignon's translation) are, in a saint, always a sign of imperfection. Next to *'ubûda*, *'ubûdiyya*, and *'ibâda*, the semantic group to which words like *faqr* (poverty), and *ummiyya* (nakedness of spirit) belong refers not to a psychology of *walâya*, but rather to the metaphysic upon which this psychology is founded.

The definition of *'ubûda* we used above is to be linked to another akbarian notion: this absolute conformity to the divine order is that of the *a'yân thâbita*, what might be called, to borrow a term from Suso and the Rhineland mystics, our "eternal exemplars."[74] In Ibn 'Arabî's doctrine, the "possibles" never have existence, they never leave *thubût*.[75] Their existence (*wujûd*) is no more than a reflection of God, nothing more than a borrowed "coat": "There is there only God; his is the Being (*'ayn al-wujûd*) and the Existent (*al-mawjûd*); he shows himself in "possibles" according to their predispositions...When the divine order of being came [for the *a'yân thâbita*], they found in themselves only the be-ing of God who in them showed himself to himself."[76]

"Existentiation" (*ijâd*) of these immutable haecceities really produces only an effect for them. The effect is the self-consciousness suddenly given to them, for, in God's presence they were previously *mahjûba 'an ru'yati anfusihâ*, they did not see themselves, they were absent to themselves.[77] It is not a coincidence that 'Abd al-Karîm al-Jîlî, in his own definition, cites Qur'ân 76:1: "There was a moment in eternity[78] when man was not mentioned" (or "thought of," *madhkûran*). *Madhkûran*, translated here according to the meaning usually given to the word, means in this verse, for Ibn 'Arabî, *ma'lûman*, "known"[79]—by which it should be understood that man did not know himself yet. At that instant in eternity, we were already all that we are, but we did not yet know that we were.

> The rose which your eye sees here
> Has been budding in God from all eternity,

writes Angelus Silesius in a famous couplet from his *Cherubini-scher Wandersmann*. This rose blooms from eternity without knowing that it is a rose. It knows neither its smell nor its name. It does not know for whom it blooms. Similarly, in this instant in eternity, I did not desire God, I did not want either the same thing or something different from what he wanted. I was in him without knowing that I was myself, without knowing that he was himself. God knew me because he knows himself and in the way that he knows himself.

We should not be put off by the weakness of the language here. The inevitable use of verb tenses introduces a chrolonogy (backing the eternal instant into a past that the present revokes), suggests an event, confers a grammatical being upon our nothing-ness. But the rose, "after" as well as "before," has no being of itself. *'Ubûda* is never our status. It is not a question of acquiring it or returning to it: the *'abd* is constitutionally just that. But the con-sciousness of "being" something, of passing (in obedience to the divine order *kun!* "be") into individual existence *ad extra*, which is really only a metahpor (*isti'âra*), established a separation: the *'abd* perceived himself as distinct from the contingent beings around him, and especially as distinct from God. His knowledge of God began at that moment, which is one of the meanings of the hadith[80] *man 'arafa nafsahu 'arafa rabbahu* (he who knows himself knows his lord).[81] It happens that this knowledge, which unveils his *'ubûda*—he knows from that moment that he has a Lord—veils it at the same time, since true *'ubûda* does not know itself. *'Ubûdiyya*, which for Jîlî is perpetual contemplation by the *'abd* of his *'ubûda*, consists in rebecoming "blind, deaf, dumb"—attributes that describe the *malâmî*, according to Ibn 'Arabî. If *faqr* (poverty) is the silence of the will, if *ummiyya* is the silence of the intellect, then *'ubûdiyya* is the silence of the being.

It is reported via one of the Companions of the Prophet (sometimes Abû Bakr, sometimes 'Umar b. al-Khattâb, sometimes Ibn Mas'ûd, depending on the version) that upon hearing the first verse of the "sura of man," cited above ("There was a moment in eternity when man was not mentioned"), he cried out, "Would that I could be like that!"[82] Ibn 'Arabî expresses the same desire in other terms when he says: "There is in man no quality higher than the mineral quality" (*al-sifa al-jamâdiyya*), the inertia of the stone that moves only if it is moved (by someone or something else). He further says: "Man is more noble in his minerality when he dies and becomes like the earth than in his humanity when he is alive."[83] The Ka'ba is only stone, "it neither feels nor sees, it is devoid of intellect and hearing,"[84] and yet it is the "House of God" and the "heart of the universe." *'Ubûdiyya*, contemplation of *'ubûda*, from that moment in eternity that time cannot abolish, is that mineral state where we no longer know anything, where we no longer know either ourselves or God: for the God that "he who knows himself" knows is not God, since the *'abd* knows God then as "other than himself" and knows himself as "other than him (God)," depriving God of the part of being which he attributes to himself. That God is only an idol fashioned by a measure of smallness, shackled by the ties of his *i'tiqâd*. In the radical nakedness of *'ubûdiyya*, the *'abd* would know neither how to desire God nor how to love nor how to know him. *Deum propter Deum relinquere*. It is God who, in the servant, desires himself, loves himself, and knows himself.

The degree of perfection (*ihsân*), according to Ibn 'Arabî, is reached only by him "whose sun rises in the *Lam yakun*,"[85] in the "it is not," the negation of his illusory being that he reads in the first two words of sura 98, *Al-bayyina* (Evidence), and which is the reply to *kun*. Ibn 'Arabî chooses to isolate these two words from the clause to which they syntactically belong: any element of divine speech—word, letter, diacritical mark—is meaningful in itself, independent of whatever meaning it may have in relation to others. The vibration of this terrific *Lam yakun* actualizes the instant of eternity when "man was not mentioned." It reminds him that the *kun* that brought him into existence did not give him being in itself. The whole *Kitâb al-fanâ fî l-mushâhada* has its point of departure in this segment of a verse, and ends with the hadith about *ihsân*, which, it happens, defines perfection.[86] By means of the introduction of a caesura, which gramatically is no less arbitrary than the one that separates *Lam yakun* from its Qur'ânic context, the expression *in lam takun tarâhu* (If you do not see him) reveals the secret of the vision: what the *ʿabd* hears in this conditional clause is "if you are not [*in lam takun*], you see him."[87]

ʿUbûda, servitude, is the ineluctable status of the creature. *ʿUbûdiyya*, bondage, is the condition resulting from this status; it takes effect only if there is perception of *ʿubûda*. *Perception*, not *acquiescence*, is the operative word here, for pretending to obey, if this were even conceivable, would in itself be disobedience; it would suppose the possibility of a decision, the affirmation of free will.

Based on the two previous words, the last term in the series, *ʿibâda*, which in Arabic belongs to the same linguistic family, might best be translated as "service." The plural of the word (*ʿibâdât*), in the *fiqh* treatises, technically refers to rites and thus corresponds to what might be called "duties toward God." *ʿIbâdât* are distinguished—with some gray areas: marriage is sometimes considered in one category, sometimes in the other[88]—from *muʿâmalât*, a rubric that covers the rules governing human behavior in society. This distinction, if it fulfills a valid, practical necessity in its order, is nevertheless, for the *ʿârif bi-Llâh*, null and void. "Service" is always the service of God; it is he also who prescribes ritual obligations and those imposed on the interactions of creatures.

Sub specie aeternitatis, *ʿibâda* is an ending point. *ʿUbûda* is the principle from which it devolves, and *ʿubûdiyya* is the condition that makes its necessity apparent. For man after the fall, forgetful of his servitude, it is, on the other hand, a starting point. It is through *ʿibâda* that man is to climb back toward his origin, to approach the mystery of his status. When the Prophet comes to find him after the first visit of the angel of Revelation, Waraqa b. Nawfal, a Christian, immediately identifies the angel as *al-nâmûs al-akbar*, the supreme *nomos*, the angel of the Law.[89] The Law institutes service, orders the *'ibâdât*, the acts due to God—regardless who the apparent recipient might be—because the *'abd* no longer remembers his status. It is through service that he will be led back to the servile condition where his servitude becomes evident to him. The superiority of *farâ'id*—of what is done under the constraints of the Law—over *nawâfil* has its source there.

The Qur'ân as a message is the anamnesis of lost truths. The Qur'ân as law is the anamnesis of a disavowed status. The *nâmûs al-akbar* is substituted for the *nâmûs al-asghar*, an internal law from which man has slipped away; little by little, it reclaims its authority. During this period of learning, under the sun of the *Lam yakun* no longer veiled by the cloud of *wujûd 'aynî*, the *'abd* is consumed and ultimately extinguished in a last prostration. In words that Ibn 'Arabî attributes to the Andalusian Ibn al-'Arîf and quotes often (although they should be credited to Al-Ansârî),[90] "then what has never been disappears, and what has never ceased to be remains." From that point on, "there are no longer either obligatory acts nor acts of supererogation."[91] In verses often criticized by his adversaries, which he placed at the beginning of the *Futûhât*, the the Shaykh al-Akbar further says:

> Would that I knew who is subject to obligation!
> If you say: it is the servant, the servant is nonexistent;
> And if you say: it is the Lord, whence would obligation
>   come?[92]

As the rose blooms in God without knowing that it is a rose, without knowing for whom it blooms, the servant—or rather his "eternal exemplar—no longer knows "servanthood." He no longer knows that he has a Lord. Taken to its farthest degree, *'ubûdiyya* is cancelled out, is reabsorbed in *'ubûda*, which is pure presence in God, with no trace of duality. Now the Lord is such only in relation to a servant over whom lordship is exercised. There is no *rabb* (sovereign) without a *marbûb* (vassal).[93] That is why Sahl al-Tustarî said, "Lordship has a secret and if this secret were manifested, Lordship would disappear." "This secret is you!" says Ibn 'Arabî. He immediately adds that Sahl used the conjunction *law*, which, grammatically, is the one that precedes the pronouncement of an unrealizable condition.[94] Actually, this secret cannot manifest itself in this world: extinction (*al-fanâ*) does not bring about the dissolution of human matter. The body remains subject to legal obligation (*taklîf*). On the outside, the yoke of Lordship continues to be exercised. But what is *bâtin* (secret) in this life will be *zâhir* (manifest) in the life to come: at that time the authority of the Law will definitively cease.

If all *ʿibâdât* prepare one to hear the *Lam yakun*—in the *Mawâqiʿ al-nujûm*, it was shown that the fruits of spiritual science are attached to the most humble: visiting the sick, listening attentively to the sermon of the *khatîb*, and so on—*salât* is nevertheless the most central, the one that each day, at the appointed hour, offers the believer the shortest way to the highest contemplation, that of his eternal servitude. This takes place in such a manner that, finally, in his absent eyes, it is God who sees God. In prayer, God precedes the believer. The *musallî*, the person who prays, in the first meaning of the word, is the horse that runs after the winner of the race. This is the way it is defined in the *Lisân al-ʿarab*, the "ark of the language of the Prophet."[95] This meaning is the one retained by Ibn ʿArabî to, once again, draw out of the letter the deepest of truths that it bears. "God prays on us" (*ʿalaynâ*)—a reference to Qurʾân 33:43, which teaches that "It is he who prays on you." "Prayer thus comes simultaneously from us and from him,"[96] Ibn ʿArabî continues, alluding to the hadith cited above where God has divided prayer between himself and his servants. But this God who "prays on us"—who pours out his mercy[97] upon us *before* our own prayer to him and who is thus the First—is also, from another point of view, *al-musallî* (he who comes after), the Last: He follows the servant whose existence precedes his. This God who is second, who draws his being from the being of the *ʿabd* (*ʿan wujûd al-ʿabd*): "the God that the servant creates in his heart by his own speculative thought or by imitation (*taqlîd*) is the divinity conditioned by belief (*al-ilâh al-muʿtaqad*)."[98]

In perfect prayer, God is the first, or rather he is alone. "Praise belongs to God who bestowed upon man his own attributes...while denying the similarity,[99] thus revoking the same thing that he affirms and leaving man to wander, confused, among the rational demonstrations and divinely instituted proofs, and who *then prayed on him before any of man's prayers toward Him*, without there even being a Before."[100] Perfect prayer is, in short, that prayer where the servant lets God pray to God. And for Ibn 'Arabî this is exactly the meaning of the medial verse that, in the *Fâtiha*, "divides" *salât* between God and man: "It is you whom we worship [or rather: "Whom we serve," *na'budu*, if we wish to remain congruent with the translations used on other occasions with the same root—*'ubûda, 'ubûdiyya*, etc.] and it is You Whom we implore for help." This divine help, which can be understood and which is most often taken in a general sense, is, in the eyes of the the Shaykh al-Akbar, that without which worship, or service, is impossible.[101]

Commenting on verse 5 of sura 107 ("Those who are forgetful of their prayers"), Ibn 'Arabî emphasizes[102] that God did not say: "Those who are forgetful of prayer"—for the individuals in prayer fulfill the legal prescriptions. What they have forgotten is *their* prayers: they no longer know that they are theirs—which is what another passage explains as: "When the veil is lifted..., you will see that he who performs his duties toward God is the creator of acts: that is, God himself." Perfect prayer is that wherein the person who prays is *absent*, leaving all the place to God.

This absence may appear paradoxical to the individual who forgets that *'ubûda* is the beginning and the end of *'ibâda*. It may even appear contradictory to other affirmations. In the sura of Degrees (*al-ma'ârij*, plural of *mi'râj*, Qur'ân 70:23) there is praise for "those who are perpetually in prayer," and Ibn 'Arabî identifies this perpetual prayer with a perpetual presence (the *'ârif bi-Llâh*, the gnostic, is, he says, *dâ'im al-hudûr*, whether at rest or in movement).[103] But this presence to God is a presence *in* God: the presence that is forever "blind, deaf, and mute," of the "eternal exemplars," which he alone knows.

When it "descends" upon this world, Revelation comes in the form of sounds and letters, which it shares with the language of people without ceasing to be the eternal and transcendent Word. Likewise, the saint, if he is sent by God to the creatures, is similar to all those in his species. "He eats, he drinks, he gets married, he listens to what is said to him, and he replies."[104] But, under the sun of *Lam yakun*, the servant is no longer anything but a name. Led by the Law from verse to verse, from abode to abode, he who was named by this name has irrevocably crossed the last threshold.

NOTES

Introduction

1. Ibn Hajar al-Haytamî, *Al-fatâwâ al-hadîthiyya* (Cairo, 1970), p. 296. In accordance with standard practice, dates from the Gregorian calendar that cannot be confused with dates from the Muslim calendar (i.e., dates after the 15th century A.D.) are not labeled as *Anno Domini*. Where the calendars do overlap, if there is a possibility of confusion, the date in question is labeled (e.g., 602 A.D.), or the date *Anno Hegirae* is given previous to the date *Anno Domini* (e.g., 1058/1648).

2. Abû l-Alâ ʿAfîfî, *The Mystical Philosophy of Muyhid Din Ibnul ʿArabî*, 2d ed. (Lahore, 1964).

3. *Fus.*, introduction, p. 21.

4. Clément Huart, *Littérature arabe* (Paris, 1932), p. 275.

5. A. J. Arberry, *Sufism: An Account of the Mystics of Islam* (London, 1950), p. 99.

6. Rom Landau, *The Philosophy of Ibn Arabi* (London, 1959), p. 24–25.

7. J. Berque, *Al-Yousi* (Paris, La Haye, 1958). See also C. Geertz, *Islam Observed* (Chicago 1968) (index s.v. Liyusi), on the same subject; P. Rabinow, *Symbolic Domination* (Chicago, 1975); E. Gellner, *Muslim Societies* (Cambridge, 1981), chap. 10.

8. See Berque, *Al-Yousi*, pp. 40, 121–26.

9. Berque, *Al-Yousi*, pp. 123, 126.

10. *Al-bahr al-masjûr* (Mostaganem, n.d.), p. 69.

11. Ibn ʿArabî, *Al-Futûhât al-makkiyya* (Cairo, 1329 A.H.), vol. 1, p. 115; O.Y., vol 2., p. 208–209.

12. Al-Qârî al-Baghdâdî, *Al-durr al-thamîn fî manâqib Muhyî l-dîn* (Beirut, 1959), pp. 27–28; Maqqârî, *Nafh al-tibb* (Beirut, 1968), vol. 2, p. 178.

13. Abû l-'Abbâs Muhammad Zarrûq, *Qawâ'id al-tasawwuf* (Cairo, 1328/1968) (on Ibn 'Arabî, see pp. 35, 41, 52, 129). Cf. also Alî F. Khushaim, *Zarrûq the Sûfî* (Tripoli, 1976), pp. 14, 148.

14. 'Abd al-Wahhâb Sha'rânî, *Al-anwâr al-qudsiyya fî ma'rifat qawâ'id al-sûfiyya*, 2d ed. (Beirut, 1985), vol. 2, p. 28.

15. Fakhr al-dîn 'Alî b. Husayn Wâ'iz al-Kâshifî, *Rashahât 'ayn al-hayât*, 2 vols. (Tehran, 2356), vol. 1, pp. 249–50. The references to Ibn 'Arabî in the remarks of the Naqshbandi masters cited by the author are numerous; in this work see the remarks of, among others, Burhân l-dîn Abû Nasr Parsâ and Muhammad Shams al-dîn al-Kûsawî. The biography of a modern Naqshbandi shaykh (Muhammad Amîn al-Kurdî, who died in 1914) reports behavior similar to that of 'Ubaydallâh Ahrâr: "He used to read me chapters from the *Futûhât*. But if someone came, he closed the book and remained silent" (Muhammad Amîn al-Kurdî, *Tanwîr al-qulûb* (Cairo, n.d.), p. 42.

16. Y. Friedmann, *Shaykh Ahmad Sirhindî* (Montreal-London, 1971). It is interesting to note, regarding the opinion that the Naqsh-bandiyya, an "orthodox" *tarîqa*, were generally hostile to Ibn 'Arabî, that what was true of the masters of old is also true of modern *shuyûkh*. Shaykh Khâlid, who died in 1827, is called *"akbarî l-'irfân"* in a work that came out in the last century ('Abd al-Majîd al-Khânî, *Al-sa'âda al-abadiyya* [Damascus, 1313 A.H.], p. 2). Another work of the same period (Sulaymân al-Hanafî al-Baghdâdî, *Al-hadîqa al-nadiyya*, the *Kitâb asfâ al-mawârid* (Cairo, 1313 A.H.), pp. 60–61) reports that at the death of Khâlid one of his disciples had a vision of Ibn 'Arabî coming out of his tomb to embrace him. The handwritten catalogue of Shaykh Khâlid's library, of which we have a photocopy, confirms that he owned works by Ibn 'Arabî and his principal followers. Regarding the attitude of the first Naqshbandi masters toward Ibn 'Arabî, numerous complementary details are found in Hamid Algar's contribution to the Symposium Ibn 'Arabî held in April 1989 in Noto, Sicily: *Reflections of Ibn 'Arabî in Early Naqshbandi Tradition* (Journal of the Ibn 'Arabî Society, X, 1991, 45–66). On Ahmad b. Idrîs, see R. S. O'Fahey, *Enigmatic Saint: Ahmad b. Idrîs and the Idrîsî Tradition* (London, 1990), pp. 90–106.

17. M. Chodkiewicz, *Le Sceau des saints, prophétie et sainteté dans la doctrine d'Ibn 'Arabî* (Paris, 1986). An English translation of this book is to be published by the Islamic Texts Society, Cambridge, U.K. On Ibn 'Arabî's technical vocabulary, see the valuable work by Su'âd Hakîm, *Al-mu'jam al-sûfî* (Beirut, 1981), which under the circumstances constitutes an indispensable tool for the researcher. Numerous examples give evidence

of the fact that Ibn 'Arabî's typology of sainthood is used by a number of authors to retrospectively interpret the case of sufis previous to Ibn 'Arabî. I have mentioned (*Sceau des Saints*, p. 104) the case of Ayn al-Qudât al-Hamadhânî (d. 1131). There is also the case of Ahmad al-Rifâ'î (d. 1182), whose grandson, to characterize the spiritual type of his grandfather and some of his contemporaries, also refers (without saying so) to Ibn 'Arabî's criteria and wordings, as well as to the idea of 'seal of sainthood' (cf. M. Tahrali, *Ahmad al-Rifâ'î, sa vie, son œuvre et sa tarîqa*, 3d cycle thesis, Paris III, 1973, pp. 134–35; the passages considered appear in 'Izz al-dîn Ahmad al-Sayyâd's *Kitâb al-ma'ârif al-muhammadiyya fî l-wazâ'if al-ahmadiyya* (Cairo, 1888), pp. 59–60.

18. *Fut.* vol. 1, p. 9; O.Y., vol. 1, p. 70. On the meaning of this verse, see below, chap. 4.

19. Al-Kattânî, *Salwat al-anfâs fî man ugbira min al-ulamâ' wa l-sulahâ' bi-Fâs*, lith. ed. Fez, 1316 A.H.; see, e.g., 2d pt., pp. 241, 188, 332–33, 340.

20. See *EI¹*, s.v., Mâ' al-'Aynayn; and B. G. Martin, *Muslim Brotherhoods in 19th Century Africa* (Cambridge, 1976), chap. 5.

21. *Na't al-bidâyât wa tawsîf al-nihâyât* (Cairo, n.d.). Examples of references to Ibn 'Arabî are found on pp. 91–92; to Qâshânî, on pp. 67, 120; to Ismâ'îl Haqqî, on pp. 69–70, 74, 77, 80; to Sha'rânî, on pp. 98, 103, 167.

22. *Jawâhir al-ma'ânî* (Cairo, 1384 A.H.) Ibn 'Arabî (sometimes in the form of al-Hâtimî) is expressly cited in numerous pages (see, e.g., vol. 1, pp. 66, 75, 126, 147, 151, 183, 245–47; vol. 2, pp. 7, 70, 84, 116, 117, 150). But many clear borrowings are not identified as such: such is the case for an anecdote (that of Al-Jawhârî) cited in vol. 1, p. 241, which comes directly from *Fut.*, vol. 2, p. 82.

23. For a characteristic passage relative to the doctrine of sainthood (with mention of the *khatm*), cf. *Jawâhir*, vol. 2, pp. 21, 84–85.

24. *Jawâhir*, vol. 2, p. 37.

25. *Jawâhir*, vol. 2, p. 39.

26. *Jawâhir*, vol. 1, p. 147; vol. 2, p. 143.

27. *Jawâhir*, vol. 1, pp. 183–84; vol. 2, p. 30.

28. *Jawâhir*, vol. 2, p. 25.

29. *Bughyat al-mustafîd* (Cairo, 1380/1959). See, e.g., the treatise on the hierarchy of the *awliyâ'*, pp. 187–94. Ibn 'Arabî is cited numerous times in the work.

30. Printed in the margin of the *Jawâhir.*

31. See Al-Hâjj Umar, *Kitâb al-rimah,* vol. 2, pp. 4, 15, 16.

32. Sha'rânî, *Al-yawâqît wa l-jawâhir* (Cairo, 1369 A.H.) There is printed in the margin of this work, by the same author, another compendium of the *Futûhât, Al-kibrît al-ahmar fî bayân 'ulûm al-Shaykh al-Akbar,* which itself is a summary of a third work by Sha'rânî, the *Lawâqih al-anwâr al-qudsiyya.* On Sha'rânî and his bibliography, consult the work by Michael Winter, *Society and Religion in Early Ottoman Egypt* (New Brunswick, 1982).

33. Cf. Winter, *Society and Religion,* p. 2, and p. 9 n.2.

34. Cf. Mervyn Hiskett, "The Community of Grace and Its Opponents," *African Language Studies* (London), vol. 17, 1980: 99–140.

35. *Manshûrât al-Imâm al-Mahdî,* lith. ed., 4 vols. (Khartoum, 1963), vol. 1, pp. 5–6, 13; vol. 2, pp. 49, 62.

36. Letter, 29 November 1988. Grandin adds that the *'Anqâ mughrib* is, for this reason, widespread today in Sudan in literate Mahdist milieux.

37. The passage to which the *Manshûrât* refer is found (Qur'ân 7:182) in vol. 2, p. 460, of Qâshânî's (although published under the name of Ibn 'Arabî) *Ta'wîlât* (Beirut, 1968). As for Ibn 'Arabî's authentic *tafsîr (Al-jam' wa l-tafsîl fî asrâr ma'ânî l-tanzîl,* RG 172), which included 64 volumes and went as far as sura "Maryam," it appears to have mysteriously disappeared after only a very restricted circulation during a long period of time. At the time of the Mahdî, it was already barely accessible, and only a few exceptional students of Ibn 'Arabî seem to have been able to consult it. The use—or rather the abuse—of Ibn 'Arabî's authority is found at the same time in another heterodox movement, that of Ghulâm Ahmad, the founder of the Ahmadiyya sect, which was clearly inspired by Ibn 'Arabî's ideas about the *nubuwwa mutlaqa* and the *walâya isawiyya.* On this point, see the work by Y. Friedmann, *Prophecy Continuous* (Berkeley, 1989), 3d pt.

38. Thanks to the doctoral thesis of Bakri Aladdin, "'Abd al ghanî al-Nâbulusî, œuvre, vie, doctrine" (Université de Paris vol. 1, 1985), we presently have available a serious bio-bibliographical study, the first part of which is a catalogue of Nâbulusî's works. The role that Nâbulusî played as transmitter of Ibn 'Arabî is perhaps not limited to the Muslim world: a *fatwâ* delivered by him in 1712 in response to a question asked by a Melkite patriarch (probably Athanase Dabbas, d. 1724) makes reference to ideas of *wahdat al-wujûd, a'yân thâbita,* etc. This *fatwâ* is soon to be edited by B. Aladdin.

39. M. Chodkiewicz, "'L'offrande au Prophète' de Muhammad al-Burhânpûrî," *Connaissance des religions* 4, nos. 1–2 (1988): 30–40.

40. It reached the west, through the help of a European student of Shaykh Illaysh, where it was translated in 1911 in a questionable French version; it has since been reedited a number of time, most recently in 1977.

41. Nabhânî, *Jâmi' karamât al-awliyâ* (Cairo, 1329/1911; Beirut, n.d.). For the references to Ibn 'Arabî, see especially vol. 1, pp. 18, 21–25, 36–55, as well as the notice that is dedicated to him, vol. 1, pp. 118–25. Cf. also the *Shawâhid al-haqq* (Cairo, 1394/1974), pp. 418–42 (where he offers long quotes from Sha'rânî; but his knowledge of the works of Ibn 'Arabî is unquestionable).

42. Cf. our review of one of his works (the *Sharh Fusûs al-hikam*) in *Studia Islamica*, fasc. 63 (1984): 179–82. Using the same process M. Ghurâb published (1989) a compilation of Ibn 'Arabî's exegetical texts, in the form of a running Qur'ânic commentary; we will address this further in chapter 2.

43. The *Kitâb al-Ibrîz* was edited a number of times in Cairo (1278 A.H., 1292 A.H., 1317 A.H., 1380 A.H.) and most recently—and most scientifically—in a two-volume edition published in Damascus (1404/1984). A selection from 'Abd al-'Azîz al-Dabbâgh's *fath* story appears in Depont and Coppolani's *Les Confréries religieuses musulmanes* (Paris, 1897), pp. 539–41. A complete translation of the *Kitâb al-Ibrîz*, which is a remarkable spiritual document, is much to be desired.

44. Characteristic examples are found in the two treatises that J.-L. Michon analyzed in *Le Soufi marocain Ibn 'Ajîba et son Mi'râj* (Paris, 1973), pp. 91–104, and in the annotated translation of the *Mi'râj, ibid.*, pp. 173f. Ibn 'Arabî's influence is also present, in a more diffuse yet quite identifiable manner, in Ibn 'Ajîba's commentary on Ibn 'Atâ' Allâh's *Hikam* (*Iqâz al-himam* [Cairo, 1972]). On Ibn 'Ajîba, see 'Abd al-Majîd al-Saghîr's *Ishkâliyyat islâh al-fikr al-sûfî* (Rabat, 1988), chap. 2; despite the author's lack of objectivity, consultation of the book is worthwhile.

45. There are several Moroccan editions of this *dîwân*, without dates. On Al-Harraq, see also the work by 'Abd al-Majîd al-Saghîr cited in note 44 above. Contrary to the author's desire to see the expression of *wahdat al-shuhûd* in these poems, it appears obvious to us that it is *wahdat al-wujûd*.

46. 'Alî Sâfî Husayn, *Al-adâb al-sûfî fî Misr fî l-qarn al-sâbi' al-hijrî* (Cairo, 1964).

47. Annemarie Schimmel, *Mystical Dimensions of Islam* (Chapel Hill, N.C., 1975); *And Muhammad is His Messenger* Chapel Hill, N.C., 1985); *Pain and Grace*, Leiden, 1976; *Islam and the Indian Subcontinent* Leiden, 1980) (cf. index s.v. Ibn 'Arabî).

48. We are indebted to the kindness of M. Fawzi Skali for the transcription of this conversation, as well as for that which he had with Sîdî al-Mahdî al-Saqallî, who will be mentioned further on. These documents are reproduced in Skali's thesis for Doctorat d'État, *"Topographie spirituelle et sociale de la ville de Fès"* (Université Paris VII, 1990).

49. Contrary to the thesis proposed by Abû l-Wafâ Taftâzânî in an article appearing in a memorial volume published in Cairo for the eighth centenary of the birth of Ibn 'Arabî (*Al-kitâb al-tadhkarî* [Cairo, 1969], pp. 295–353).

50. This information is taken from, among other sources, Qushshâshî's *Simt al-majîd* (Hyderabad, 1367 A.H.), p. 105; Murtadâ al-Zabîdî's *Ithâf al-asfiyâ'* (ms. belonging to a private collection); Muhammad al-Sanûsî's *Salsabil al-muʿîn* (Cairo, 1353 A.H.), pp. 70–72; and diverse handwritten *silsila* belonging to private libraries (among which is that of M. Riyâd al-Mâlih, in Damascus).

51. 'Abd el-Kader, *Écrits spirituels* (Paris, 1982), introduction.

52. The name of the emir appears in most modern Middle Eastern or Maghreban *silsila* that we have been able to examine, thus highlighting his central importance in the propagation of Ibn 'Arabî's heritage since the end of the nineteenth century.

53. This activity is translated by numerous Arabic publications. First to be mentioned are the (often mediocre) editions, or reeditions, of authentic works by Ibn 'Arabî (e.g., *Tanazzulât mawsiliyya* [Cairo, 1961, 1986], and *Kitâb al-'Abâdila* [Cairo, 1969]), both of which had remained unpublished up to that time), or of titles that are wrongly attributed to him, but marked by his influence (e.g., *Tuhfat al-safara* (Beirut, ca. 1975); or the inevitable *Tafsîr* that Qâshânî wrote, reedited in Beirut in 1968 under Ibn 'Arabî's name); the monumental critical edition of the *Futûhât*, by O. Yahia (13 vols. have appeared to date) deserves a special category. One might add to the above the critical edition of the *Kitâb al-isrâ* by Suʿâd Hakîm (Beirut, 1988); and the appearance of works *about* Ibn 'Arabî, all the way from the most superficial popularizations (e.g., Tâhâ 'Abd al-Bâqî Surûr, *Muhyî l-dîn b. 'Arabî* [Cairo, 1975]; the series of works by Shaykh Mahmûd Ghurâb mentioned above, etc.) to university-level studies (e.g., Sulayman al-ʿAttâr, *Al-khayâl wa l-shiʿr fî*

tasawwuf al-andalus [Cairo, 1981]; Abû Zayd, *Falsafat al-ta'wîl... 'inda Muhyî l-dîn b. 'Arabî,* Hakim's *Mu'jam* [see infra, note 17], etc.). A fairly complete bibliography covering the last three decades would entail several dozen titles and would be considerably lengthened if it included the works *by* or *about* authors coming out of Ibn 'Arabî's school: Qûnawî, Sha'rânî, Nâbulusî, 'Abd al-Qâdir al-Jazâ'irî, etc. Also to be taken into account are the articles (published in journals but also in the general press, most notably at times when polemics are stirred up by a critical edition of the *Futûhât;* on these polemics, see the article by Th. Emil Homerin, "Ibn 'Arabî in the People's Assembly," *Middle East Journal* 40, no. 3 (1986): 462–77) and several unpublished theses defended in universities in the Arab world. We leave aside here the publications in Western languages or by Western authors, even though they also relate to the "Akbarian renaissance." On this subject, James W. Morris has written an article that might be consulted: "Ibn 'Arabî and his Interpreters" *JAOS,* vol. 106, III, IV, and 107, I.

54. Among these recent Wahhâbî writings let us mention, as typical examples, Sâbir Tu'ayma, *Al-sûfiyya, mu'taqadan wa maslakan* (Riyadh, 1985): see in particular pp. 165–83, 205–45; and the series of works dedicated to *turuq* in the the collection *Dirâsât 'an al-tasawwuf* (Riyadh). See also Mûsâ b. Sulaymân al-Darwîsh's introduction to the collection published under the title *Rasâ'il wa fatâwâ fî dhamm Ibn 'Arabî al-Sûfî* (Medina, 1990).

55. Numerous analogous predictions, the inauthenticity of which is well established, have been placed under Ibn 'Arabî's name for centuries. Such is the case of works like *Sâ'at al-khabar* (RG 642b) and *Sayhat al-bûm* (RG 708). Ibn Khaldûn, in his *Muqaddima* (*Discours sur l'histoire universelle,* trans. V. Monteil [Paris, 1967–6], vol. 2, pp. 702–703), points out other examples. More recently, early in 1991, an obviously apocryphal poem connected with the literature of the *malhamât* was circulating in the Middle East and the Maghreb; it attributed to the Shaykh al-Akbar an apocalyptic interpretation of events occurring in the region. As for the *Shajara nu'mâniyya* (RG 665)—on which there is, among others, a commentary wrongly attributed to Qûnawî—it is interesting to highlight a passage of the *Kitâb al-mawâqif* (Damascus, 1967), vol. 2, p. 709, where Emir 'Abd al-Qâdir describes a visionary encounter in the course of which Ibn 'Arabî accuses as liars all those who call him the author of this work or others like it.

Chapter 1

1. *Fut.,* vol. 1, p. 411 (O.Y., vol. 4, p. 207) and vol. 4, p. 465. For the Arabs, as for the Greeks and the Latins, the cetacean (*ketos, cetus*) is a fat

fish. Imam Mâlik's *fatwâ*, restores it to the class of mammalians, which is taxinomically more satisfactory to zoologists.

2. Cf., for example, *Majmû'at al-rasâ'il wa l-masâ'il*, ed. Rashîd Ridâ, vol. 4, pp. 42–45.

3. Husayn b. al-Ahdâl, *Kashf al–ghitâ* (Tunis, 1964), pp. 192f.

4. Burhân al-dîn al-Bigâ'î, *Tanbîh al-ghabî ilâ takfîr Ibn al-'Arabî*, published in Cairo (1953) under the title *Masra' al-tasawwuf*; see pp. 76, 88.

5. Sakhâwî, *Al-qawl al-munbî* (manuscript, Berlin), spr. 790, f. 24b. For Sakhâwî, the accusation of *ibâha* is aimed not only at doctrine, but also at morals; cf. for example f. 97b.

6. Nicholson, Reynold A., *Studies in Islamic Mysticism* (Cambridge, 1921), p. 149.

7. Landau, Ross, *Philosophy of Ibn 'Arabî*, p. 23 (see intro., note 6).

8. Abû l-Alâ 'Afîfî, *The Mystical Philosophy of Muhyid Din Ibnul 'Arabi*, 2d ed. (Lahore, 1964), pp. 191–94. For a recent study of Qur'ânic exegesis in Ibn 'Arabî by an Arab scholar, consult Nasr Hâmid Abû Zayd, *Falsafat al-ta'wîl* (Beirut, 1983).

9. MS. Zâhirîyya 9872, f. 22b. For Ibn 'Arabî's citation quoted in the preceding sentence, see *Fut.* vol. 3, p. 334.

10. See above, intro., note 37.

11. The *Ijâz al-bayân* was published by Shaykh Mahmûd Ghurâb, according to the *unicum* of Istanbul, in the first volume of the aforementioned work; intro., note 42. The Qur'ânic commentary, in the edited version, ends at verse 252 of sura *Al-baqara*.

12. *Al-rahma min al-Rahmân fî tafsîr wa ishârât al-qur'ân*, 4 vols. (Damascus, 1989). See our summary of this work in the *Bulletin critique des Annales islamologiques*, no. 8, 45–49.

13. On these *fatwâ* see the (nonexhaustive) lists given by O. Yahia in *Histoire et classification*, RG 275, vol. 1, pp. 122–35, and in his introduction to Haydar Amolî's *Nass al-nusûs* (Paris, Tehran, 1975), pp. 48–65.

14. Sakhâwî, *Al-qawl al-munbî*, f. 102. Ibn Hajar al-'Asqalânî (d. 1499), also notes with surprise that the first opinions about Ibn 'Arabî were basically favorable. He says, "it is almost certain that they did not know what is basically well known now about the *Fusûs*" (*Lisân al-mîzân* [Hyderabad, 1329 A.H.], vol. 5, pp. 312–15).

15. See the biography, an excerpt from Maqarrî's *Nafh al-tibb* (seventeenth century), at the end of the *Futûhât* (vol. 4, p. 560). The first mention of this history appears to be in Ghubrînî (*'Unwân al-dirâya* [Algiers, 1970], p. 159). The authenticity of this episode is discussed by Claude Addas, *Ibn 'Arabî ou la quête du soufre rouge* (Paris, 1989), pp. 230–32, a work that we recommend to the reader for all that concerns the life of the Shaykh al-Akbar, only brief details of which will be found in the present volume.

16. Ibn 'Arabî, *Tarjumân al-ashwâq* (Beirut, 1961), p. 1.

17. Ibn 'Arabî, *Rûh al-quds* (Damascus, 1964), p. 98.

18. *Fut.* vol. 3, p. 336.

19. *Fut.* vol. 3, pp. 69–70.

20. See, e.g., *Fut.* vol. 2, p. 79; O.Y., vol. 12, p. 341.

21. Among others, let us mention the recent publication in Tokyo (1987) of a work by Masataka Takeshita, *Ibn 'Arabî's Theory of the Perfect Man*, and, in Leningrad, i.e., St. Petersburg, of the works of Alexander Knysh; in Moscow, Andrei Smirnov is preparing the first Russian translation of the *Fusûs al-hikam*.

22. See intro., note 53.

23. *Ibid.*

24. *Fut.* vol. 1, p. 76; O.Y., vol. 1, p. 328.

25. *Fut.* vol. 3, p. 158.

26. *Fut.* vol. 1, p. 334; O.Y., vol. 5, p. 158.

27. *Fut.* vol. 1, p. 334; O.Y., vol. 5, p. 158.

28. *Fut.* vol. 4, p. 67.

29. *Fut.* vol. 1, p. 248; O.Y., vol. 4, p. 90.

30. *Fut.* vol. 1, p. 403; O.Y., vol. 4, p. 147.

31. Remember that the root of the word *qur'ân* expresses the idea of "gathering together" and "totalization."

32. This famous *hadîth qudsî* is often cited by sufi authors with a chain of transmission going back to Wahb b. Munabbih. However, it does not appear in the collections considered "canonical," and Ibn Taymiyya classifies it among the *isrâ'îliyyât*.

33. *Fut.* vol. 3, pp. 93–94. The idea of the perpetual newness of the Qur'ân is expressed on a number of occasions by Ibn 'Arabî. Cf. e.g., *Fut.* vol. 3, p. 108: "It [the Qur'ân] came down upon the heart of Muhammad, and it does not cease to come down upon the hearts of the faithful of his community up to the Day of the Ressurection. Its descent upon hearts is always new, for it is perpetual Revelation." See also *Fut.* vol. 3, p. 127; *Kitâb al-isfâr* (Hyderabad, 1948), p. 16.

34. *Fut.* vol. 3, pp. 128–29.

35. This mention of the "nocturnal discussion" is an allusion to the hadith according to which God descends toward the sky during the third third of the night; the lines preceding the passage in the *Futûhât* are referring to this hadith.

36. *Fut.* vol. 1, p. 239.

37. See the analysis of these two texts in our introduction to the anthology of the *Futûhât* published as *Les Illuminations de la Mecque*, ed. Michel Chodkiewicz (Paris, 1988), pp. 34–35.

38. *Fut.* vol. 1, pp. 47–51; O.Y., vol. 1, pp. 215–30.

39. Cf. Meyer, "The Mystery of the Ka'ba," *Eranos Yearbooks*, XXX, vol. 2, pp. 149–68; H. Corbin, *L'Imagination créatrice dans le soufisme d'Ibn Arabî* (Paris, 1958), pp. 213–15; Addas, *op. cit.*, pp. 241–43; Chodkiewicz, introduction to *Illuminations de la Mecque*, by Ibn 'Arabî, pp. 46–48 (see note 37).

40. Let it be added that in different editions of the *Futûhât* the order of succession of these paragraphs presents numerous anomalies; without the order being corrected certain passages remain completely unintelligible.

41. *Fut.* vol. 4, p. 327.

42. Cf. for example *'Uqlat al-mustawfiz*, in Nyberg, *Kleinere Schriften des Ibn al-Arabî* (Leiden, 1919), p. 52; *Fut.* vol. 4, p. 83, 287. The identification of the *imâm mubîn* as the *insân kâmil* is, although expressed without the latter term being used, perfectly clear in the passage from chapter 559, to which we were referring in the preceding note; the identification is confirmed by the commentary of 'Abd al-Karîm al-Jîlî, *Sharh mushkilât al-Futûhât* (manuscript), p. 10. Ibn 'Arabî explains (in *Fut.* vol. 2, p. 394) the reasons a same reality can be referred to by different names.

43. *Fut.* vol. 1, p. 180; O.Y., vol. 3, p. 149.

44. *Fut.* vol. 1, p. 51. O.Y., vol. 1, p. 229.

45. To understand the coherence of these successive identifications it must be remembered that, for Ibn ʿArabî, the Perfect Man or the Universal Man (*al-insân al-kullî*) and the Qurʾân are "brothers" (*Fut.* vol. 3, p. 94) and are even purely and simply assimilated, the one into the other (*Kitâb al-isfâr*, p. 17). On the seven divine names envisioned here, see among others *Fut.* vol. 1, p. 204; O.Y., 13, p. 238 and *Fut.* vol. 2, p. 493; *Inshâ al-dawâʾir*, ed. Nyberg, p. 28. In Ibn ʿArabî these names are not always classified in the same order, and *al-mutakallim* is sometimes replaced by *al-qâʾil*, "He Who Says." The information given here on the encounter with the *fatâ* will be elaborated upon below, at the end of chapter 4.

46. *Fut.* vol. 1, p. 50; O.Y., vol. 1, p. 230. The last words of the sentence cited ("record it in your work and teach it to all those whom you love") appear in the 1239 A.H. edition of the *Futûhât*, which is based on the text of the first edition of the work, but the words are absent from the edition prepared by Osman Yahia.

47. Selections from this second chapter, accompanied by a long introduction, were translated by Denis Gril in Ibn ʿArabî, *Illuminations de la Mecque*, pp. 439–87.

48. *Fut.* vol. 4, p. 25.

49. The "Pages" (*suhuf*, sing. *sahîfa*) is a Qurʾânic term (20:133; 53:36; 87:18) that globally refers to revelations previous to that of Muhammad, when these are not mentioned by their specific names. It goes without saying that the principle raised by Ibn ʿArabî here applies only to the revealed Book—whichever—if it is known in the same language in which it was revealed, since its translation into another language vitiates its character as Divine Word and gives it an interpretation that, even if correct, is necessarily restrictive.

50. *Fut.* vol. 2, p. 119; O.Y., vol. 13, p. 92.

51. *Fut.* vol. 2, p. 28; O.Y., vol. 11, p. 420.

52. The *laylat al-qadr*, which gives its name to sura 97, is traditionally celebrated on the twenty-seventh of the month of Ramadân. For Ibn ʿArabî, the Book descended as *qurʾân* (by which, according to the etymology of the word, Revelation in its synthetic aspect should be understood) during the month of Ramadân, and as *furqân* (Revelation in its distinctive mode) during the night of the fifteenth of the month of Shaʿbân. It is this night in the month of Shaʿbân—identified with that "in which all wise

things are decided" (Qur'ân 44:4)—which is for him the *laylat al-qadr* (*Fut.* vol 3, p. 94). Elsewhere he specifies (*Fut.* vol. 3, p. 159; vol. 4, p. 486) that the night does not come on a fixed date but circulates throughout the year.

53. *Kitâb al-isfâr*, p. 15.

54. *Lisân al-'arab* (Beirut, n.d.), vol. 12, p. 34.

55. On the sources of this anecdote, see Fritz Meyer, *Die Fawâ'ih al-gamal wa fawâtih al-galâl* (Wiesbaden, 1957), pp. 45–46. According to another version (Tâsh Kabrizadé, *Miftâh al-sa'âda* [Hyderabad, 1329 A.H.], vol. 1, pp. 450–51), it is rather during this retreat that Râzî is supposed to have received the supernatural inspiration that guided him in the composition of his great commentary on the Qur'ân.

56. *Fut.* vol. 2, p. 644.

57. 'Abd al-Karîm Jîlî, *Marâtib al-wujûd* (Cairo, n.d.), pp. 8–12.

58. Nâbulusî, *Kitâb al-rusûkh fî maqâm al-shuyûkh* (manuscript, Berlin), We 1631, f. 189b.

Chapter 2

1. Ibn 'Arabî, *Dîwân* (Bûlâq, 1855), pp. 31–32; Ibn 'Arabî, *'Anqâ mughrib* (Cairo, n.d.), p. 24.

2. *Fut.*, vol. 2, p. 581.

3. See especially chapter 54 of the *Futûhât*, vol. 1, pp. 278f. ; O.Y., vol. 4, pp. 262f. On Tustarî's hermeneutics, see G. Böwering, *The Mystical Vision of Existence in Classical Islam* (Berlin, New York, 1980), pp. 135f.

4. Ibn 'Arabî, *Kitâb al-'Abâdila* (Cairo, 1962), p. 42 (analogous remarks, also relative to the *Fâtiha*, are found in *Ijâz al-bayân*, pp. 29–30); *Fut.*, IV., p. 105.

5. Qushayrî, *Latâ'if al-ishârât* (Cairo, 1971), vol. 5, p. 354. Rûzbehân Baqlî (d. 606/1209) in his *tafsîr* (*'Arâ'is al-bayân* (Indian lith. ed., 1315/1899), vol. 2, pp. 229–30) does not address the *ka* problem, but keeps only the verse's affirmation of divine transcendence.

6. Râzî, *Tafsîr* (Tehran, n.d.), vol. 27, pp. 150–53. Râzî also criticizes the connection between this verse and Qur'ân 16:60 (*wa li-Llâhi l-mathal al-a'lâ*), which lends itself to an interpretation analogous to that which Ibn 'Arabî gives to Qur'ân 42:11. On the interpretations of Muqâtil and Tabarî, see C. Gilliot's article "Muqâtil, grand exégète..." *Journal asiatique* 1–2 (1991): 56–57.

7. Regarding the passages of Ibn ʿArabî's writings relative to this verse, let us mention, among others, *Fut.* vol. 2, p. 563; vol. 3, p. 165; vol. 4, pp. 135–36; *Fus.*, vol. 1, pp. 70–71, 111, 182.

8. On this hadith and its variants, cf. Muslim, *birr*, 115; *janna*, 28; Bukhârî, *istiʾdhân*, 1.

9. The idea of man (*al-insân al-kâmil*) as mirror of God and God as mirror of man is developed in the first and second chapters of the *Fusûs* (see in particular *Fus.* vol. 1, pp. 63, 61f.). It is also presented in the *Futûhât* (vol. 1, p. 163; vol. 4, p. 430). See also (*Fut.* vol. 3, p. 112; O.Y., vol. 2, p. 190) the interpretation of the hadith: *Al-muʾmin mirʾat al-muʾmin* (Tirmidhî, *birr*, 8); the interpretation is based on the fact that *al-muʾmin* is one of the divine names and thus this tradition—which is generally translated "the believer is the mirror of the believer"—can be interpreted as meaning that God is the mirror of the believer, and, conversely, that the believer is the mirror of God. Ibn ʿArabî (*Kitâb al-ʿAbâdila*, p. 160) interprets in an analogous manner the hadith according to which "the believer is the brother of the believer" (*al-muʾmin akhu l-muʾmin*).

10. This question is numbered 143 in the *Futûhât* (*Fut.* vol. 1, pp. 123–24; O.Y., vol. 13, pp. 125–31), and 149 in the critical edition by B. Radtke of Tirmidhî's text. We are indebted to Pr. Radtke for having given us in advance the pages of his book (presently in press in Beirut) containing the questionnaire.

11. Hakîm Tirmidhî, *Kitâb khatm al-awliyâ*, ed. O. Yahia (Beirut, 1965), p. 314.

12. We have already touched on this theme in *Sceau des Saints*, pp. 97–98 (see intro., note 17).

13. *Fut.* vol. 2, p. 218. Cf. Râzî, *Tafsîr*, vol. 3, pp. 5–6, where the connection between *shajara* and *tashâjur* is mentioned without commenting on the consequences. See also Qurtubî, *Al-jâmiʿ li-ahkâm al-Qurʾân* (Cairo, 1933), vol. 1, p. 260; Qushayrî, *Latâ ʾif al-ishârât*, vol. 1, p. 92. Baqlî (*ʿArâʾis al-bayân*, vol. 1, p. 21), however, suggests an interesting connection between Adam and Eve's tree and the Burning Bush (in Arabic, also *shajâra*; cf. Qurʾân 28:30). To the negative meaning of *shajara* based on the etymology which Ibn ʿArabî holds here, there symetrically corresponds a positive meaning tied to visual symbolism, the tree having an obvious axial character: the tree is also the perfect man, according to a definition that Ibn ʿArabî gives in his *Kitâb istilâh al-sûfiyya* (Hyderabad, 1948), p. 12. On the other hand, one does not have to take into consideration the data that can be found in the treatise entitled *Shajarat al-kawn*, a work often attrib-

'Arabî but should be returned to its true author, 'Abd al-Salâm
ı. Ghânim al-Maqdisî (d. 678/1280), as shown by the research of
Alaoui Mdaghri (DEA memoire, Sorbonne nouvelle, 1990). For
ːal interpretation of the tree (in relation to Qur'ân 14:24–25),
. Nwyia's analysis (*Exégèse coranique et Langage mystique*
36), pp. 336–38) of a passage of the ninth-century *tafsîr* of Abû l-
ūrî.

14. Cf. *Tadbîrât ilâhiyya*, ed. Nyberg, p. 225 in the Arabic text.

15. Philo of Alexandria, *Commentaire allégorique des Saintes Lois
après l'œuvre des six jours*, trans. Father Claude Mondésert, bk. 3 (Paris,
1962). Let it be remembered that Philo, if he allegorizes freely when he is
engaged in exegesis of the scriptures, emphasizes the necessity of not
neglecting the letter, of being concerned about "careful search for the invis-
ibles and faithful guarding of the visibles" (*De Migratione Abrahae*, cited in
J. Daniélou, *Philon d'Alexandrie* [Paris, 1958], p. 113). The difference
between Philo and Ibn 'Arabî is that for the latter it is in the letter itself
that one should search for both the "visible" and the "invisible." The direct
or indirect followers of the Shaykh al-Akbar do not always observe the
principle of such rigorous hermeneutics. Qashânî, for example—whose
tafsîr is so often attributed to Ibn 'Arabî—does not hesitate to allegorize.

16. Ibn 'Arabî, *Kitâb al-ahadiyya* (Hyderabad, 1948), p. 3.

17. *Fus.* vol. 1, pp. 61f; *Fut.* vol. 4, p. 2.

18. On Qur'ân 24:39, see *Fut.* vol. 1, p. 193; vol. 2, pp. 269, 338, 455.
On Qur'ân 20:10 regarding Moses, see *Fus.* vol. 1, pp. 212–13. Baqlî (*'Arâ'is
al bayân*, vol. 2, p. 87) briefly suggests, in his commentary on Qur'ân 24:39,
an interpretation analogous to that of Ibn 'Arabî.

19. *Fut.* vol. 1, p. 405; O.Y., vol. 6, p. 163; *Fut.* vol. 4, p. 106; Ibn
'Arabî, *Kitâb al-masâ'il* (Hyderabad, 1948), p. 14.

20. *Fus.* vol. 1, p. 108.

21. *Fut.* vol. 2, p. 563.

22. Taymiyya, *Majmû'at al-rasâ'il*, vol. 1, p. 173; vol. 4, p. 795; Râzî,
Tafsîr, vol. 20, pp. 183–84.

23. *Fut.* vol. 2, p. 662. Cf. the commentary on this dialogue by 'Abd
al-'Azîz al-Dabbâgh (*Kitâb al-Ibrîz* [Cairo, 1961], p. 361).

24. Allusion to a *hadîth qudsî* encountered in several canonical collections, present in this form or with the variant *ghalabat* ("My mercy is

greater than my anger"). Cf., e.g., Bukhârî, *tahwîd*, 55, *tawba*, 14–16; Ibn Mâjah, *Zuhd*, 35.

25. For Ibn ʿArabî there are no "inanimate" beings: according to the Qurʾân, all things give glory to God and thus possess life. Cf. *Fut.* vol. 2, p. 678; vol. 3, pp. 264, 324, 333; vol. 4, p. 289.

26. *Fus.* vol. 1, p. 106.

27. *Fus.* vol. 1, pp. 107–108. For Dâwûd Qaysarî (d. 751/1350), *Sharh Fusûs al-hikam* (Bombay, 1350 A.H.), p. 194, the "western wind"—which comes from where the sun sets—is the breath of the dark material world, and it thus pushes them toward the east, that is, toward the light. It makes them "die unto themselves" and thus leads them into *fanâ* (the extinction of the ego). On this passage from the *Fusûs*, see also Qâshânî's commentary (Cairo, 1321 A.H.), p. 127.

28. *Fut.* vol. 2, p. 138; O.Y., vol. 13, pp. 264–68. This question is numbered 162 in Tirmidhî's text, as edited by B. Radtke. On the same theme, see also chapter 337, dedicated to the *Manzil Muhammad* (*Fut.* vol. 3, pp. 140–46), where the six privileges of the Prophet are commented upon.

29. Concerning "Muhammadan Reality," its occultation and manifestation, see Chodkiewicz, *Sceau des saints*, chap. 4. Concerning the (generally quite brief) commentaries on Qurʾân 34: 28 by other authors, see, e.g., Râzî, *Tafsîr*, vol. 25, p. 258; Qushayrî, *Lataʾif al-ishârât*, vol. 5, p. 183; Qurtubî, *Al-jâmiʿ li-akhâm al-Qurʾân*, vol. 14, p. 300; Ismâʿîl Haqqî, *Rûh al-bayân* (Istanbul. 1330 A.H.), vol. 7, p. 294; Sayyid Qutb, *Fî zilâl al-qurʾân* (Beirut, 1977), vol. 5, p. 2906. Like Ibn ʿArabî, Jîlî (*Nasîm al-Sahar* [Cairo, n.d.], p. 17) emphasizes that Qurʾân 21:107 means that the Mercy in question is not reserved "for Muslims and believers," that is, for the historical Muslim community.

30. *Fut.* vol. 4, p. 163. See also *Fut.* vol. 4, p. 153, where Ibn ʿArabî mentions a vision of the Divine *Rahma* that he had in Fez in 593 A.H., which he maintains he is incapable of transcribing. Concerning this aspect of the function of the Seal, refer to Addas, *Ibn ʿArabî*, pp. 340–43 (see chap. 1, note 15).

31. *Fut.* vol. 3, p. 346.

32. *Fut.* vol. 3, p. 25.

33. *Fut.* vol. 4, p. 248. Ibn ʿArabî clarifies (vol. 4, p. 120) that it is divine mercy that keeps the damned in hell once their punishment is com-

pleted, for, as he says, "if they were placed in paradise they would suffer" because of the incompatibility of their nature with the order of heaven.

34. *Fus.* vol. 1, p. 94. Concerning Gehenna and its inhabitants, see chaps. 61 and 62 of the *Futûhât*.

35. Chodkiewicz, *Sceau des saints*, chap. 6. The first part of chapter 73, to which we are referring here, corresponds to *Fut.* vol. 2, pp. 2–39, and to O.Y., vol. 11, pp. 247–493.

36. *Fut.* vol. 2, p. 16; O.Y., vol. 11, p. 237.

37. *Fut.* vol. 3, p. 321 (the first verse of the poem), and vol. 4, p. 175. More precise information can be obtained in the *Ishârât al-qur'ân fî 'âlam al-insân* (p. 28), of which D. Gril, who is presently preparing the edition, has been kind enough to furnish us with the proofs. Information may also be found in *Tanazzulât mawsiliyya* (Cairo, 1961, under the title *Latâ'if al-asrâr*, p. 55). Although it cannot be reduced to that, Ibn 'Arabî's affirmation according to which 5 "preserves itself and preserves others" evidently alludes to the well-known mathematical property of the number, a property illustrated by the following: $5 \times 5 = 25$; $25 \times 25 = 625$; $625 \times 625 = 390,625$, etc.

38. Cf. E. Doutté, *Magie et Religion de l'Afrique du Nord* (Algiers, 1908; Paris, 1984), pp. 183–84, 325–27; E. Westermarck, *Survivances païennes dans la civilisation mahométane* (Paris, 1935), pp. 39, 50f. It would at any rate be erroneous to see only a popular practice there: independent of the remarks of Ibn 'Arabî, it can be noted that the groups of five *nûraniyya* letters appearing at the beginning of sura 19 and sura 42 play, for analogous reasons, an important role in certain forms of prayer and, e.g., in Abû l-Hasan al-Shâdhilî's *Hizb al-bahr*. Let us note that these two groups are particularly related to certain eschatological data and that they constitute a protection against the *Dajjâl* ("the Imposter"), i.e., against the Antichrist.

39. *Fut.* vol. 2, p. 39; O.Y., vol. 11, p. 491.

40. *Fut.* vol. 1, p. 201; O.Y., vol. 3, p. 257.

41. The oldest attested form of this word in Arabic is *qarûbiyyûn*, with a *qâf*, which underscores the idea of proximity expressed by the word *muqarrabûn*. Pseudo-Dionysius the Areopagite places "Thrones, cherubim, and seraphim...immediately next to God in a proximity *superior* to that of the others" and adds that "the name cherubim shows moreover the ability to know and to comtemplate God, to receive the highest gifts of His light" (*La Hiérarchie céleste*, chaps. 6 and 7, in *Œuvres complètes du Pseudo-*

Denys l'Aréopagite, trans. M. de Gandillac [Paris, 1943]). On the angelic hierarchies in Ibn 'Arabî, see *Fut.* vol. 2, p. 250.

42. *Fut.* vol. 3, pp. 34–37. The apparently disconcerting position of this account in the *Futûhât* will be explained in chapter 3 below. For the present we have deliberately left aside the term *malâmiyya* by previous authors; on this subject see R. Deladrière's article in the forthcoming Acts of the *Mélamis et Bayramis* symposium, Istanbul, 1987. For a more complete analysis of Ibn 'Arabî's material on the *malâmiyya*, see Chodkiewicz, *Sceau des saints*, chap. 7.

43. *Fut.* vol. 2, p. 53; O.Y., vol. 12, p. 150. On the *nubuwwa mutlaqa*, see also *Fut.* vol. 1, p. 150; O.Y., vol. 2, pp. 357–60; *Fut.* vol. 2, p. 3; O.Y., vol. 11, pp. 251–55; *Fut.* vol. 2, p. 85; O.Y., vol. 12, pp. 386–87.

44. In *Fut.* vol. 2, pp. 260–62, Ibn 'Arabî describes his own arrival at this "station." This text has been translated by D. Gril in Ibn 'Arabî, *Illuminations de la Mecque*, pp. 339–47, with an introduction and notes that supply important details on the idea of *qurba*.

45. *Fut.* vol. 1, pp. 115–16; O.Y., pp. 206–10. From this passage comes the inspiration for Shaykh Ahmad b. 'Aliwâ's commentary on sura *Al-baqara* which was mentioned in the introduction to this volume.

46. *Fut.* vol. 2, p. 134; O.Y., vol. 13, pp. 245–49.

47. Ibn 'Arabî, *Kitâb al-tajalliyât*, ed. O. Yahia, in the journal *Al-Mashriq* 1967: p. 372, *tajallî* no. 83. The relationship of this *tajallî*—as is the case with the *tajallî* no. 5 (*Al-Mashiq* 1966: p. 683)—with the *malâmiyya* is not the least bit fortuitous, as shall be explained in chapter 4.

48. *Fut.* vol. 1, p. 215; O.Y., vol. 2, pp. 208–209.

49. *Fut.* vol. 2, p. 136; O.Y., vol. 13, pp. 245–46. Cf. also (II, pp. 591–92) chapter 275—a chapter that, as we shall soon see, corresponds to sura *Al-kâfirûn*—, where the *malâmiyya* are, on the other hand, assimilated into the five "Holy Letters" (*hurûf muqadassa*), that is, into those that, in writing, are never joined to the *alif*.

50. On the "abode" that joins friends (*awliyâ*) and enemies of God, see *Fut.* vol. 3, pp. 475–83. Cf. also here the final remark of note 4, chapter 5. On the idea of *mustanad ilâhî*, see for example *Fut.* vol. 3, pp. 94, 528; vol. 4, p. 174; *Kitâb al-tarâjim*, p. 4: "all reality in this world is linked (*marbûta*) to a divine reality that preserves it." In the section from chap. 10 of his *Talbîs Iblîs*, where he criticizes the sufi exegesis, Ibn al-Jawzî reproaches Junayd (regarding his interpretation of Qur'ân 2: 85) with the same thing that later

censors were to object to in Ibn ʿArabî: namely, interpreting in terms of praise the Qurʾânic phrases that express reprobation.

51. *Fut.* vol. 2, p. 136; O.Y., vol. 13, p. 246.

52. On the *ʿaql*, see *Fut.* vol. 3, p. 198; *Fus.* I, p. 122.

53. *Fut.* vol. 2, p. 135; O.Y., vol. 13, pp. 243–45. Ibn ʿArabî specifies that only the *basmala* of the *Fâtiha*, and not that, however rigorously identical, of the other suras of the Qurʾân can play this role. He illustrates his remark with the case of a saint from Seville, Fâtima bint Ibn al-Muthannâ (on whom, see *Rûh al-quds*, section 54; *Fut.* vol. 2, p. 347), who, with a single recitation of the Fâtiha, gained supernatural powers and was astonished that all Muslims did not have the same powers available to them. On the subject of the "positivity" of the term *al-sâhirûn*, he recalls that the magicians of Firʿawn (the biblical Pharaoh) continue to be called by this name in the Qurʾân after their conversion to the true faith, which would be inconceivable if this word had only a pejorative connotation.

54. *Fut.* vol. 2, p. 138; O.Y., vol. 13, p. 261.

55. *Al-wahy huwa l-surʿa, Fut.* vol. 2, p. 78; O.Y., vol. 12, p. 330. On this meaning of the word *wahy*, cf. *Lisân al-ʿarab* (Beirut, n.d.), vol. 15, p. 382. See P. Nwyia's analysis (*Exégèse coranique*, pp. 154–56), of an unedited text by Tirmidhî on this subject.

56. Such is particularly the case for chaps. 68 to 72 of the *Futûhât*, which deal respectively, and in great detail, with ritual ablution, prayer, alms, fasting, and pilgrimage.

57. We dealt briefly with this theme, to which we intend to return later, by speaking about "the foundations of political legitimacy in Ibn ʿArabî," in a round table discussion, "The Struggle Against the Unjust Sovereign in Islam," held at the Maison des Sciences de l'Homme in May 1986.

58. See the texts translated and presented by Cyrille Chodkiewicz in "La loi et la voie," part 4 of Ibn ʿArabî, *Illuminations de la Mecque.*

59. I. Goldziher, *Die Zâhirîten* (Leipzig, 1884); English trans. *The Zâhirîs*, 2d ed. (Leiden, 2d ed. 1971), pp. 161f, 169f, 174.

60. Ibn ʿArabî claims (*Fut.* vol. 1, p. 334; O.Y., vol. 5, p. 159) to have planned, if God gave him a long life, to dedicate a huge work to all legal questions, but he needed to limit himself, in the *Futûhât*, to dealing only with the essential. Shaykh Mahmûd b. Mahmûd Ghurâb published an anthology of Ibn ʿArabî's texts relating to *fiqh* (*Al-fiqh ʿinda l-Shaykh al-Akbar* [Damascus, 1981]). This anthology, quite summarily annotated and completely without references, is unfortunately of little use to researchers.

61. *Fut.* vol. 3, p. 336.

62. *Fut.* vol. 1, p. 494; O.Y., vol. 7, pp. 289–90.

63. On this short work, see Yahia, *Histoire et Classification*, RG 275. A copy of the work is said to be held by M. Saʿîd al-Afghanî in Tunisia (see p. 17 of his introduction to the work mentioned in note 64). This manuscript, about which Mr. Saʿîd Afghani gives no reference information, does not appear in the catalogue done by R. Deladrière on Ibn ʿArabî's MSS preserved at the Zaytûna (*Arabica*, vol. 13, 1966, pp. 168–72). On the veneration that Ibn ʿArabî had for Ibn Hazm, cf. the vision reported in his *Kitâb al-mubashshirât*, MS. Fâtih 5322, f. 90b.

64. Ibn Hazm, *Ibtâl al-qiyâs* (Beirut, 1969).

65. By way of example, and remaining at the level of the *furûʿ* (later a typical case in the domain of *usûl* will be seen), let us point out that Ibn ʿArabî is at variance with the Zâhirîs on the subject of ablution, which he considers not only as a condition (*shart*) of the validity of prayer, but as an *ʿibâda mustaqilla*, an "autonomous act of adoration." Similarly, he judges as "blamable" only things that, for the Zâhirîs, invalidate prayer (the wearing of forbidden clothing, for example). Let it be noted in passing that the idea of *tasmiya* to which we referred at the beginning of chap. 1 is, for Ibn ʿArabî, very near to what it is for Ibn Hazm. On the other hand, the fundamental distinction in Ibn ʿArabî among *amr/irâda/mashiʾa* (a distinction analogous to that which certain Mâturîdîtes make) separates him clearly from Ibn Hazm, for whom *irâda* and *mashiʾa* are synonyms.

66. Cited in Ibn al-ʿImâd, *Shadharât al-dhahab* (Beirut, n.d.), vol. 5, p. 200.

67. Ibn ʿArabî, *Dîwân*, p. 47 (see chap. 2, n. 1).

68. *Fut.* vol. 2, p. 165; O.Y., vol. 13, p. 466.

69. Bukhârî, *Iʿtisâm*, 2; Muslim, *Hajj*, 411, etc. Ibn ʿArabî explicates the meaning of this hadith in *Fut.* vol. 2, p. 562.

70. *Fut.* vol. 1, p. 392; O.Y., vol. 4, p. 79.

71. Cf. *Fut.* vol. 1, p. 472; O.Y., vol. 7, pp. 137–38; *Fut.* vol. 2, pp. 162–63; O.Y., vol. 13, pp. 445–50; *Fut.* vol. 2, p. 507; vol. 3, p. 335. In this last passage, Ibn ʿArabî explains that *qiyâs* cannot find its justification except in the absence of the Prophet, who is, par excellence, the interpreter of Divine Law. Now, for the "people of unveiling" (*ahl al-kashf*), the Prophet, he says, is always present—which is obviously not a Zâhirî argument.

72. *Fut.* vol. 2, p. 563.

Chapter 3

1. RG 150. The list of commentaries is found in vol. 1, pp. 241–55. The explanations found below—and those that will be encountered later in the text—on subjects dealt with in this chapter are not by any means to be credited to us. We are indebted to Michel Valsân for the first hints that led us to these remarks on the structure of the *Futûhât*. Our learned friend Abdelbaki Meftah has assisted the honing of our interpretations on numerous points. We are additionally indebted to a number of individuals who still today are in charge of transmission of the *khirqa akbariyya*, for without their support our efforts would have been in vain. The solution to one of the problems examined here had already been presented in our introduction to the *Illuminations de La Mecque* (p. 29 and p. 493, n. 38). The themes of this chapter, approached first in our seminar at the École des hautes études in 1985–86, have been discussed in several papers: "Ibn ʿArabî and Western Scholarship" (Institut néerlandais, Feb. 1990); "The Qurʾân in the Work of Ibn ʿArabî" (Congrès international pour le 750ᵉ anniversaire de la mort d'Ibn ʿArabî, Murcia, Nov. 1990); "The *Futûhât Makkiyya* and Their Commentators: Some Unresolved Enigmas" (Conference on the Legacy of Persian Sufism, London, SOAS, Dec. 1990). The text of this chapter is a synthesis of these different presentations.

2. RG 135. The list of commentaries is found in vol. 1, pp. 232–34.

3. Jîlî's commentary has been published in Cairo (1988) by Atif Jûda Nasr, from a manuscript belonging to a private collection and a manuscript belonging to Dâr al-Kutub. The text, identical to that of our personal manuscript of this work, comments on the paragraphs from chapter 559 corresponding to the first ten chapters of the *Futûhât*. Another edition has been published more recently (1991) in Kuwait by Dr. Yûsuf Zaydâr.

4. Cf. Jandî, *Sharh Fusûs al-hikam* (Mashhad, 1982); Haydar Amolî, *Nass al-nusûs*, ed. H. Corbin and O. Yahia (Tehran, Paris, 1975); and *Jâmiʿ al-asrâr* (in H. Corbin and O. Yahia, *Philosophie shiʿite* [Tehran, Paris, 1969]). See for example, in the last work, pp. 440ff., a long quote from chapter 366 of the *Futûhât*.

5. *Rashahât ʿayn al-hayât*, vol. 1, pp. 249–50.

6. *Maktûbât-i Imâm-i Rabbanî* (Lucknow, 1889). Sirhindi's attention is drawn not only by doctrinal ideas expressed in the *Futûhât*, but also by anecdotes reported there; see, e..g., in letter no. 58 (where he critiques *tanâsukh*—metempsychosis), the story of a visionary encounter at the Kaʿba between Ibn ʿArabî and a man belonging to a human race previous

to our own (cf. *Fut.* vol. 3, pp. 348, 549). As Y. Friedmann notes (*Shaykh Ahman Sirhindî* [Montreal, London, 1971], p. 64), the *mujaddid* "recommends the study of Ibn 'Arabî's works and considers them indispensable for the proper appreciation of his own spiritual insights."

7. Such is the case in *Al-hikma al-muta'âliyya fî l-asfâr.* On this problem, see James W. Morris's introduction to his translation of *Al-hikma al-'arshiyya* (*The Wisdom of the Throne* [Princeton, 1981]), a work where explicit mentions of the *Futûhât*, although rarer, are not exceptional: in *Wisdom of the Throne*, see, e.g., pp. 178, 234–35, 239–40.

8. We are referring particularly to the following works of the Ayâtollâh Khomeini: *Sharh du'â al-sahar* (Beirut, 1982); *Misbâh al-hidâya* (Beirut, 1983); *Ta'lîqât alâ sharh Fusûs al-hikam* (Qom, 1986).

9. This remark appears in the third line of our manuscript copy of Jîlî *Sharh mushkilât al-Futûhât.*

10. *Fut.* vol. 1, p. 59; O.Y., vol. 1, pp. 264–65.

11. *Fut.* vol. 2, p. 456.

12. *Fut.* vol. 2, p. 163; O.Y., vol. 13, p. 450. Similarly, chapters 61 (on Gehenna) and 65 (on Paradise) have a "complement" in chapter 371.

13. *Fut.* vol. 3, p. 200.

14. *Fut.* vol. 4, p. 137. See also vol. 2, p. 548.

15. *Fut.* vol. 3, p. 101.

16. *Fut.* vol. 3, p. 334.

17. O.Y., vol. 3, pp. 37–38.

18. *Fut.* vol. 2, p. 270.

19. The description of these twenty-eight degrees, which are also to be placed in relationship to the lunar "abodes," is given in sections 11 to 38 of this chapter. Their list appears at the beginning (*Fut.* vol. 2, pp. 397–99). On the *manâzil* as degrees of paradise (in correspondence with the verses of the Qur'ân), see *Fut.* vol. 3, p. 435.

20. *Fut.* vol. 2, p. 59; O.Y., vol. 12, p. 57.

21. *Fut.* vol. 2, p. 577.

22. *Fut.* vol. 1, p. 192; O.Y., vol. 3, p. 212; Ibn 'Arabî, *Tanazzulât mawsiliyya*, p. 98. See also *Fut.* vol. 2, pp. 40–41; O.Y., vol. 12, pp. 56–65,

where the expression "110 and some *manâzil*" is an allusion to the number of suras.

23. MS. Fâtih 5322, f. 60b–66.

24. MS. Fâtih, f. 61b.

25. The copyist of this manuscript obligingly added in figures, between the lines, the numeric values expressed in letters in the text.

26. These different pieces of information appear respectively in f. 60b, 61a (line 19), f. 65a, and 65b.

27. *Fut.* vol. 2, pp. 582–90.

28. We do not have space here to enter into a detailed explanation of the symbolism of *bâ* and the subscript dot. We refer the reader to chapters 2 and 5 of the *Futûhât* (of which D. Gril has translated excerpts in the last part of Ibn 'Arabî, *Illuminations de la Mecque*, dedicated to the "science of letters") and to the short epistle entitled *Kitâb al-bâ* (RG 71), composed in Jerusalem in 602 A.H. and published in Cairo in 1954.

29. It is likewise by reference to the *'ilm al-hurûf* that interpretations should be made, e.g., in the series of chaps. 74–185 (Tirmidhî, *Futûhât*: *fasl al-mu'âmalât*, 2d ed.) of the number of degrees (*darajât*) corresponds to each of the spiritual categories (*ârifûn, malâmiyya*) and their subdivisions (*ahl al-uns, ahl al-adâb*), or even of the number of stages pertaining to the *ahl al-anwâr* (for whom the numerical values to take into consideration are those of the Eastern *abjâd*) and to the *ahl al-asrâr* (for whom the numerical values are those of the Maghreban *abjâd*). All these numbers, and more generally, all those that appear in the works of Ibn 'Arabî, come out of a perfectly intelligible calculation. To dissipate the idea of strangeness that a Western reader can feel today when faced with the use of these arithmetical procedures, analogous to those found in the Kabbalah, one must return to the idea of *tasmiya*, of "nomination": no name is coincidental, nor does it come out of a simple convention among the speakers of a language; the name has, along with what it designates, an essential relationship. As is the case for the other Semitic alphabets, each of the letters of the Arabic alphabet also represents a number—which the later use of Indian numerals will not erase, any more than "Arabic numerals" will succeed in wiping out the use of "Roman numerals" (which are letters, also) in the West. The perception of phonetic values and that of numeric values (both signifying the nature of that which is "named") does not require the laborious mental operation that they usually impose on a Westerner, but are rather done simultaneously.

30. These "secret sciences" can nevertheless play a positive role, and Ibn 'Arabî mentions the case of one of the Companions of the Prophet, Hudhayfa b. al-Yaman, who had the gift of detecting hypocrites. The Shaykh al-Akbar states on numerous occasions that he has vowed to never use powers associated with these sciences and specifically that of the science of letters (*Fut.* vol. 1, p. 190; O.Y., vol. 3, p. 202; *Fut.* vol. 3, p. 584).

31. Concerning the *khalwa* see, in addition to chaps. 78 and 79 of the *Futûhât* (translated by M. Valsân in *Études traditionnelles* no. 412–13 (1969): p. 77–86), the *Kitâb al-khalwa* (RG 255) and the *Risâlat al-anwâr* (RG 33), upon which we commented in chapter 10 of Chodkiewicz, *Sceau des Saints*. On the idea of *khalwa* in sufism, see H. Landolt's article, *EI²*. The practice of *arbaʿiniyya*, the forty-day retreat, based on a hadith (absent from the canonical collections) cited by Abû Nuʿaym al-Isfahânî, is described in detail in chaps. 26, 27, and 28 of Suhrawardî's *ʿAwârif al-maʿarif*.

32. *Fut.* vol. 2, p. 574.

33. Cf. *Fut.* vol. 4, p. 137.

34. Our concern for mentioning this aspect of Ibn 'Arabî's doctrine has, in the past, caused us criticism on the part of certain Muslim readers. Let it be recalled that affirmations of the same nature are found repeatedly, for example, in chap. 73 where, as we have said, types of sainthood are described. The author, after giving the name of such and such category of *awliyâ*, often adds a remark in this sense (*wa minhum al-rijâl wa l-nisâ*, or a similar phrase). Still more explicit is a sentence (*Fut.* vol. 3, p. 89) where he says that all the degrees (*marâtib*), including that of the Pole (*al-qutbiyya*), are as accessible to women as to men. It is significant that this sentence appears in chapter 324, which corresponds to the *manzil* for sura 60 (*Al-mumtahina*), a sura several of whose verses refer to the status of Muslim women and whose penultimate verse, in particular, concerns the pact that women, the same as men, have with the Prophet. Historically, the pact in question here is the one made in Hudaybiyya in the year 6, but it is at the same time, in sufism, the prototype and the scriptural justification of the initiatory pact. On this subject, see also, e.g., *Fut.* vol. 4, p. 494; *Mawâqiʾ al-nujûm*, pp. 115–16; *Kitâb al-tarâjim*, pp. 1 and 39.

35. *Fut.* vol. 2, p. 641. As Ibn 'Arabî reminds the reader at the beginning of chap. 322 (*Fut.* vol. 3, p. 81), the word *quraysh* itself contains, by virtue of its etymology, the idea of assembly (*ijtimâ*).

36. *Fut.* vol. 2, p. 604.

37. Ibn Hanbal, vol. 2, 541.

38. *Fut.* vol. 3, p. 327.

39. *Fut.* vol. 3, pp. 109–10. On the relationship between Jesus and the Yemenite angle of the Ka'ba, see *Fut.* vol. 1, p. 160; O.Y., vol. 2, p. 401. Christian data on the date of Jesus' birth are taken up by Muslim historiography (see, e.g., Mas'ûdî, *Murûj al-dhahab* [Cairo, 1964], vol. 1, p. 63). Syria's name, for Arabic geographers, includes the totality of the Levant, consequently including Lebanon and Palestine. On the function of Jesus at the end of time, numerous data are presented in the *'Anqâ mughrib* and cryptically confirmed by the several passages (mutilated and disfigured in printed editions) composed in a secret alphabet, of which certain commentaries allow deciphering. Bakri Aladdin is preparing a critical edition of this work. Other information is to be found in chap. 366 of the *Futûhât*. Let us point out that it is Jesus who is referred to in this chapter: by reason of his birth without an earthly father, he escapes the normal human condition. It is to this that the sentence (*Fut.* vol. 3, p. 328) according to which the "ministers of the Mahdî will have a guardian (*hâfiz*) "who is not of their kind" is alluding (in reference to Qur'ân verses 18:18 and 18:22).

40. *Fut.* vol. 3, pp. 107–10.

41. *Fut.* vol. 3, pp. 338–40.

42. *Fut.* vol. 2, p. 590.

43. The copy is dated 937/1531. Copies of other works by Ibn 'Arabî, collected together with that of the *Manzil al-manâzil* in MS. Fâtih 5322, were done by the same copyist. Annotations in other manuscripts, not all of which are found in public libraries, prove that the copyist of the *Manzil al-manâzil* was not an isolated case.

Chapter 4

1. See chap. 1, notes 11 and 12. According to L. Massignon, cited by O. Yahia (cf. RG 268), an autograph manuscript of this work exists in Baghdad; it can be supposed that this manuscript is more complete than the one (Dogmulu, 9, f. 1b–179b) used by Ghurâb, for the latter stops at the end of sura 2, as we have said. Several things said by Ibn 'Arabî in the text and in the *Futûhât* lead one to think that, although it is not an entire *tafsîr*, the *Ijâz al-bayân* was to cover far more than just the first two suras (see, e.g., *Fut.* vol. 3, p. 64).

2. *Gharadunâ al-tanbîh wa l-îjâz wa mâ yadullu 'alayhi l-lafz* (ed. Ghurâb, p. 136).

3. See intro., note 37.

4. Ibn ʿArabî, *Fihris* (in Ibrâhîm al-Qârî al-Baghdâdî, *Manâqib Ibn ʿArabî*, ed. S. Munajjid [Beirut, 1959], p. 47, no. 6). This detail is missing in the text of the *Ijâza* edited by A. Badawî. Another difference: the version of the *Fihris* given in the *Manâqib*, undoubtedly later, states that this *tafsîr* goes up to sura *Maryam* (sura 19), not just up to verse 60 of sura *Al-kahf* (sura 18). The interpretation that Ibn ʿArabî gives of verses 6 and 7 of sura 2, such as we related in chapter 2, offers a characteristic example of what may be the commentary on the Qurʾân "from the point of view of Beauty," the point of view prevalent in saints of the Christic type, as was pointed out in Chodkiewicz, *Sceau des saints*, p. 102. The "point of view of Majesty" is Mosaic, and the "point of view of Perfection" is Muhammadan.

5. Ibn ʿArabî, *Dîwân*, pp. 136–71. These poems, too, are linked together according to the traditional order of the suras. With the exception of a hemistich (p. 157, in the first verse of the poem dedicated to sura *Al-rahmân*) which is found in the *Futûhât* (vol. 3, p. 483), we have up to the present found no trace of these poems in any other of Ibn ʿArabî's works; in the *Dîwân*, however, texts taken from other sources are often found (e.g., *Mawâqiʿ al-nujûm*, *Kitâb al-isrâ*, *Futûhât*). R. Deladière, to whom we are indebted for correspondence about a long, as yet unedited work on the sources of the *Dîwân*, has confirmed this point.

6. Ibn ʿArabî, *Kitâb al-isrâ*, ed. S. Hakîm (Beirut, 1988), p. 52. Besides this edition, preferable by far to that published in Hyderabad in 1948, we have consulted MSS. BN 6104, f. 28b–58b, and Fâtih 5322, f. 97–108 (in the collection compiled by the copyist mentioned in chap. 3, note 43).

7. Ibn ʿArabî, *Kitâb al-isrâ*, p. 177; on the seventeen first verses of sura 53, see also Ibn ʿArabî, *Tanazzulât mawsiliyya*, pp. 98–100. We will return (see below, chapter 5) to the relationship between these verses and the modalities of spiritual ascension in Ibn ʿArabî's doctrine.

8. *Mashâhid al-asrâr al-qudsiyya*, MS. BN 6104, f. 11–28b (not mentioned by O. Yahia); Shehit Ali 1340, f. 88b–108b (we owe the opportunity to examine this last manuscript to the kindness of Mustafa Tahrali, who made a copy of it for us by hand).

9. Ibn Sawdakîn's commentary, entitled *Kitâb al-najât min hujub al-ishtibâh*, forms part of MS. Fâtih 5322 (f. 169b–201 for the *Kitâb al-isrâ*, f. 201–214 for the *Mashâhid*). On the inseparable character of these two works, see f. 169b and 201a. Let us point out that the *Risâla fî l-walâya* edited in Cairo (in the journal *Alif*, 1985, pp. 7–38) by H. Taher is no more

than the beginning of the *Mashâhid* (f. 1–13 of MS. BN 6104). S. Hakîm is preparing an edition of the very beautiful commentary of the *Mashâhîd* done by Sitt al-ʿAjam bint al-Nafîs, which begins with the account of a vision during which Sitt al-ʿAjam converses with Ibn ʿArabî before an assembly of prophets (see MS. Berlin We. 1833, f. 2b–3). It is worth mentioning that Sitt al-ʿAjam states *in fine* that she *voluntarily* refrains from explaining the structure of the *Mashâhid al-asrâr*.

10. The double symbolism of "risings" and "settings" which play an important role in another of the Shaykh al-Akbar's works, the *Mawâqiʿ al-nujûm* (Cairo, 1325 and 1384 A.H.), would require explanations that we are unable to give here. Ibn ʿArabî, according to Ibn Sawdakîn's commentary, interprets the first verse of *Al-najm* ("By the star, when it sets") by comparing it to Qurʾân 6:76–78, verses in which Abraham successively observes the settings of celestial bodies: stars, moon, sun.

11. Ibn ʿArabî, *Kitâb al-isrâ*, p. 57.

12. Ibn ʿArabî, *Kitâb al-isrâ*, p. 67.

13. Ibn ʿArabî, *Kitâb al-isrâ*, p. 68

14. Ibn ʿArabî, *Kitâb al-isrâ*, p. 57

15. Ibn ʿArabî, *Kitâb al-isrâ*, pp. 58–59; *Fut.* vol. 1, p. 9; O.Y., vol. 1, p. 70. The poem, in the version given by the *Kitâb al-isrâ*, includes two additional verses. The first verse cited here is that which we mentioned in the introduction (*Anâ l-qurʾân wa l-sabʿ al-mathânî*) and which we have found an echo of in a poem by a present day Algerian shaykh. Other passages of the *Kitâb al-isrâ*, where the *fatâ* is not named, supply complementary information on the subject. We intend to return to this theme in a future work.

16. *Al-najât min hujub al-ishtibâh*, f. 171b.

17. Ibn ʿArabî, *Kitâb al-ʿAbâdila* (Cairo, 1969), p. 39. This edition, based on three manuscripts about which the editor (p. 38) supplies only quite vague information, leaves much to be desired, as we will explain below. We have used the Shehit Ali Pasha MS. 2826 (f. 7–61b), which is dated 721 A.H.

18. See, e.g.,, *Fus.* vol. 1, p. 47. The title of the famous collection of poems, *Tarjumân al-ashwâq*, "The Interpreter of Desires," is equally significant, as is that of the *Kitâb al-tarâjim*, about which we will speak later.

19. He underscores the importance of the poems that introduce the chapters of the *Futûhât* in *Fut.* vol. 2, p. 665, and vol. 4, p. 21.

20. On this divine name, see D. Gimaret, *Les Noms divins en islam* (Paris, 1988), pp. 300–301.

21. MS. Shehit Ali Pasha 2826, f. 57–60.

22. Ibn ʿArabî, *Kitâb al-ʿAbâdila*, pp. 42–43. However, let it be noted that chap. 72 (pp. 181–83), as our friend Abdelbaki Meftah has pointed out, also presents itself as an allusive commentary on the *Fâtiha*. The structure of the work appears thus quite complex and should be analyzed in a more detailed manner, using a more reliable text.

23. Ibn ʿArabî, *Kitâb al-ʿAbâdila*, pp. 43–44.

24. Ibn ʿArabî, *Kitâb al-ʿAbâdila*, p. 48.

25. Ibn ʿArabî, *Kitâb al-ʿAbâdila*, p. 82.

26. Ibn ʿArabî, *Kitâb al-ʿAbâdila*, p. 83. The idea of miraculous food is also associated with Mary in Qurʾân 3: 37, and it represents, in the Qurʾân, a characteristic of the kind of sainthood that she incarnates.

27. Ibn ʿArabî, *Kitâb al-ʿAbâdila*, p. 87.

28. Ibn ʿArabî, *Kitâb al-ʿAbâdila*, pp. 90–91.

29. Here we again are indebted to Abdelbaki Meftah, who has drawn our attention to several important points raised in the following pages of this chapter. The edition of the *Tajalliyât* to which we are referring is that of O. Yahia, published in the journal Al-Mashriq (1966–67). The Hyderabad edition is, as usual, defective. We have also had the use of the copy of the *Tajalliyât* included in the MS. Beyazit 1686 (f. 38b–52b) and of Ibn Sawdakîn's commentary, Fâtih 5322, 1–37.

30. *Istilâh al-sûfiyya*, definition no. 80. On the idea of *tajallî*, see also chap. 206 of the *Futûhât* (vol. 2, p. 485).

31. Ms. Fâtih 5322, f. 1b–3a. According to Ibn ʿArabî (*Fut.* vol. 2, pp. 117–18; O.Y., vol. 13, p. 74) the look of God upon his saints is turned toward this "secret" (*sirr*).

32. Ibn ʿArabî, *Dîwân*, p. 137.

33. *Ishârât al-qurʾân*, p. 3.

34. Six of them are preceded by the group *alif-lâm-mîm*, five by *alif-lâm-râ*, two by *tâ-sîn-mîm*.

35. Another caesura in the second verse, traditionally admitted for the same reason as the one taken into consideration in our translation, sug-

gests a slightly different meaning. Our choice is here dictated by that of Ibn ʿArabî as it is for the translation of the demonstrative *dhâlika*, which Ibn ʿArabî interprets as referring to the group of three letters that precedes it.

36. *Fus.* vol. 1, pp. 214f.

37. See above, chap. 2, notes 39–40; *Fut.* vol. 4, p. 312.

38. This saying of Dhû l-Nûn is also reported, without commentary, in the work that Ibn ʿArabî dedicated to the great Egyptian sufi, *Al-kawkab al-durrî fî manâqib Dhî l-Nûn al-Misrî.* Translated into French by R. Deladrière as *La Vie merveilleuse de Dhû l-Nûn l'Égyptien* (Paris, 1988), p. 168.

39. Concerning this verse, see, e.g., *Fut.* vol. 3, p. 161. Ibn ʿArabî draws a legal conclusion from it, also (*Fut.* vol. 1, p. 404; O.Y., vol. 4, p. 157): the divine order to turn in the precise direction of the *qibla* for prayer is in effect only when one is able to determine the direction; but, by virtue of Qurʾân verse 2:115, which, for Ibn ʿArabî, is not abrogated by the verses that prescribe orientation towards the Kaʿba, the worshipper who does not know where the *qibla* is can pray facing any direction. Classical exegesis is usually much more restrictive and more often considers this verse as abrogated. Concerning debates on this subject, see Tabarî's *Tafsîr* ed. Mahmûd Shâkir and Ahmad Shâkir, (Cairo), vol. 2, pp. 526–36.

40. *Fut.* vol. 1, p. 201; O.Y., vol. 3, p. 257. The word ʿarâʾis is also used by Ibn ʿArabî for the hidden saints in *Fut.* vol. 2, p. 32; O.Y., vol. 11, p. 444; also *Fut.* vol. 2, p. 98; O.Y., vol. 12, p. 476; see also *Mawâqiʿ al-nujûm* (Cairo, 1325 A.H.), p. 138. The choice of this word is perhaps inspired by a remark by Bistâmî reported by Qushayrî (*risâla*, Cairo, 1957), p. 118.

41. Let it be remarked that the establishment of correspondence between the *Tajalliyât* and the verses of sura 2 do not always rigorously conform to the arithmetical order, besides the fact that one theophany can refer to more than one verse. Also, certain verses are not taken into consideration. The surest guide is the correlation of ideas and especially of terms.

42. First published in the journal *Études traditionnelles* (Paris), nos. 363–365 (1961), this translation was edited posthumously and published as *Le Livre de l'extinction dans la contemplation* (Paris, 1984), with an extremely rich introduction and notes. It is to this edition that we are referring. The Arabic text appeared in Hyderabad in 1948 in the series of *Rasâʾil Ibn Al-ʿArabî*, vol. 1, no. 1.

43. Ibn ʿArabî, *Le Livre de l'extinction*, pp. 9, 47–48.

44. Ibn ʿArabî states expressly in the *Kitâb al-fanâ fî l-mushâhada* that he is going to treat the subject more at length in the *fasl al-manâzil* (p. 48 in the French text, pp. 8–9 in the Arabic). Concerning this *manzil*, see also chap. 369, *wasl* no. 17, *Fut.* vol. 3, p. 395; chap. 559 (under no. 295, and not 286, as it should be), *Fut.* vol. 4, p. 388; Ibn ʿArabî, *Dîwân*, p. 174; Ibn ʿArabî, *Ishârât al-qurʾân*, p. 37. In all these texts there are identical or very similar expressions that underscore the relationship, but whose different uses admirably illustrate the way in which one theme (that of *Lam yakun*, about which we will soon speak) is dealt with in several different accounts.

45. *Fut.* vol. 3, p. 118. M. Valsân translates *munâzala* by "divine condescendence."

46. Let it be remembered that 78 is also the total number of times that the *hurûf nûrâniyya* (the "luminous letters") occur in the Qurʾân, counting their repetitions.

47. *Fut.* vol. 2, p. 567; *Kitâb al-shâhid* (Hyderabad, 1948), p. 1.

48. Ibn ʿArabî, *Kitâb al-tarâjim* (Hyderabad, 1948), p. 4. We have also used, as a cross-reference, the MS. Fâtih 5322, f. 47–53. We have not been able to consult the commentary on this treatise mentioned by O. Yahia, RG 737.

49. Ibn ʿArabî, *Kitâb al-tarâjim*, pp. 1–2.

50. Chaps. 315–83.

51. We limit ourselves to the case of the *Kitâb al-tarâjim* and the *Kitâb al-shâhid* in the interest of clarity. The "networks" whose paths we trace here are actually much more complex.

52. *Fut.* vol. 3, pp. 567–68.

53. *Kitâb al-shâhid*, p. 17, line 4.

54. *Fut.* vol. 3, pp. 110–15.

55. The theme common to these three texts is that of the debasement (*dhilla*) of the saint in this world. The word itself or the verbal forms of the same root appear in these three texts. See *Fut.* vol. 4, pp. 16–17; *Kitâb al-shâhid*, p. 11; *Kitâb al-tarâjim*, p. 50.

56. The title of this chapter (*Fut.* vol. 4, pp. 17–18), as that of all the chapters of the *fasl al-munâzalât*, is presented in the form of divine monologue. The corresponding chapters are found in the *Kitâb al-shâhid*, pp. 11–12; and in the *Kitâb al-tarâjim*, p. 51.

57. *Fut.* vol. 3, pp. 313–21.

58. *Fut.* vol. 2, p. 126; O.Y., vol. 13, pp. 141–42. On the acquisition of the "names" or the "divine characters" see especially *Fut.* vol. 2, p. 595, 602; vol. 3, p. 148.

59. *Fut.* vol. 3, p. 94.

60. *Al-isfâr 'an natâ'ij al-asfâr* (Hyderabad, 1948), p. 17.

61. *Fut.* vol. 4, p. 50. On Qur'ân 41:53, see, among others, *Fut.* vol. 2, p. 16; O.Y., vol. 11, p. 343; *Fut.* vol. 2, p. 151; O.Y., vol. 13, pp. 356–57. Cf. also in Chodkiewicz, *Sceau des saints*, pp. 97–98, our commentaries on a passage of chap. 36 of the *Futûhât*.

62. *Fut.* vol. 1, p. 48; O.Y., vol. 1, p. 219. The relationship between the contents of the *Futûhât* and the accomplishment of *tawâf* is addressed at the end of the initial doxology (*Fut.* vol. 1, p. 10; O.Y., vol. 1, p. 73).

63. *Fut.* vol. 1, p. 50; O.Y., vol. 1, pp. 224–25.

64. See *Fut.* vol. 2, p. 493 (where Ibn 'Arabî establishes a relationship between these six names and the six directions in space). In *Fut.* vol. 2, p. 134; O.Y., vol. 13, pp. 238–39, the seven names are placed into symbolic correspondence with the verses of the *Fâtiha*.

65. *Fut.* vol. 2, p. 469.

66. *Fut.* vol. 2, p. 469.

67. *Fut.* vol. 3, p. 283.

Chapter 5

1. *Ishârat al-qur'ân*, p. 35.

2. See above, chap. 4 and chap. 4, note 49.

3. *Fut.*, 4, p. 49.

4. *Tanazzulât*, p. 45. The "two names" mentioned are *rabb*, Lord, and *'abd*, servant, as is explained by a verse from p. 41 ("Would that I knew who is subject to legal obligation when there is only God alone present, and no one other than him") and two verses from p. 42—which express the same paradox ("If you say "it is the servant [who is subject to obligation], he is nonexistent" [literally, "dead"]; and if you say that it is the Lord, whence would come the obligation?").

5. *Fut.* vol. 3, p. 271.

6. *Mawâqi'al-nujûm* (Cairo, 1325 A.H.), p. 4.

7. *Hilyat al-abdal*, p. 8. Ibn 'Arabî then added the chapter about the works of the heart (see the partial translation of this chapter by M. Valsân: "La demeure du coeur de l'invocateur," *Études traditionnelles*, num. 389–90 (1965).

8. *Fut.* I., p. 334; O.Y., vol. 5, p. 156; see also *Fut.* vol. 4, p. 263.

9. The *manzil* of sura 56, which this verse belongs to, is the one that chapter 328 of the *Futûhât* describes. It is called *manzil al-musâbaqa* ("abode of precedence": an allusion to verse 10, where the elect, the "People of the Right," are *preceded* by the "Close Ones," those who have reached the *maqâm al-qurba*). It is part of the "temporal abodes" (*manâzil al-duhûr*) that correspond to the suras beginning with *idhâ*, "when."

10. Bukhârî, *tafsîr*, s. 31; *imân*, 37.

11. *Mawâqi' al-nujûm*, pp. 50–178. The central theme of the *Mawâqi'al-nujûm* is briefly summarized in *Fut.* vol. 4, p. 169 (ch. 526).

12. Bukhârî, *tawâdu'*. On the interpretation of this hadith, often cited by Ibn 'Arabî, see, e.g., *Fut.* vol. 1, p. 406; O.Y., vol. 6, pp. 165–66; vol. 2, p. 68; vol. 4, pp. 20, 24, 30.

13. Asín Palacios translated or summarized the essential of this part of the work in *El islam cristianizado* (Madrid, 1931), pp. 397–428. His tendency to Christianize Ibn 'Arabî's language is, as usual, somewhat disturbing. The French version of his book, *L'Islam christianisé* (Paris, 1982), which is generally quite mediocre, presents the additional inconvenience of having dropped the square brackets which, in the Spanish edition, clearly separated Ibn 'Arabî's quotes from Asín's summaries or commentaries. (Pp. 269–316 of the French edition contains the summary cited.) On the correspondence between the acts of parts of the body and divine graces (and also the "doors to paradise") see also *Fut.*, vol. 4, p. 169.

14. The *manâzil* mentioned in the *Mawâqi' al-nujûm* (not enumerated here) all have, as does this one, their equivalent in the "abodes" of the fourth section of the *Futûhât*. We have decided to not cross-reference, so as to not complicate things. In this passage Ibn 'Arabî mentions that he has written a special treatise on the subject of the"pact with the Pole." O. Yahia (RG 487) has identified no manuscript of this treatise. It might be supposed that the essential was taken up again in chap. 336.

15. We are using the edition, published in Cairo in 1961, with the title *Latâ'if al-asrâr*. The edition is based on three manuscripts, one writ-

ten in Nâbulusî's hand. Another edition, titled *Al-tanazzulât al-mawsiliyya*, was published in 1986, also in Cairo. Our copy has been misplaced and we were thus unable to compare it with the preceding edition. It is to be noted that the *Ishârât al-qur'ân*, to which we have referred numerous times, are described by Ibn 'Arabî as a complement to the *Tanazzulât*, thus emphasizing the Qur'ânic inspiration of these last works.

16. Ibn 'Arabî, *Tanazzulât*, pp. 35–36. In his introduction, the beginning of which we have just cited, Ibn 'Arabî announces 54 chapters. The editors preferred to adopt a division in six parts.

17. Bukhârî, *mawâqit*, 8.

18. Abû Dâwûd, *salât*, 145.

19. Ibn 'Arabî recalls *à propos* of this (*Tanazzulât*, p. 55) that the number 5 "protects itself and protects all things" (as we pointed out in chap. 2 and chap. 2, note 36).

20. Ibn 'Arabî, *Tanazzulât*, p. 55.

21. Chap. 69, *Fut.* vol. 1, pp. 386–544; O.Y., vol. 6, p. 45, to vol. 8, p. 183.

22. Ibn 'Arabî, *Tanazzulât*, p. 54.

23. *Fut.* vol. 4, p. 486

24. A similar remark is found in Ibn 'Arabî, *Kitâb al-'Abâdila*, p. 87. Literally speaking, celestial water is rainwater, terrestrial water being that from springs. But it is actually the interior disposition of the being that determines the degree of purity produced by the performance of ablution.

25. Ibn 'Arabî, *Tanazzulât*, p. 63.

26. Ibn 'Arabî, *Tanazzulât*, p. 63.

27. Ibn 'Arabî, *Tanazzulât*, p. 84.

28. Ibn 'Arabî, *Tanazzulât*, pp. 90–91.

29. Ibn 'Arabî, *Tanazzulât*, p. 92.

30. Ibn 'Arabî, *Tanazzulât*, p. 93.

31. Ibn 'Arabî, *Tanazzulât*, p. 94.

32. Ibn 'Arabî, *Tanazzulât*, p. 61.

33. Ibn Hanbal, vol. 2, 460.

34. Ibn ʿArabî, *Tanazzulât*, p. 95.

35. Ibn ʿArabî, *Tanazzulât*, pp. 98–100.

36. Ibn ʿArabî, *Tanazzulât*, p. 103. Identification of prayer as a *miʿrâj* is not, for the sufis, a simple metaphor; it has technical consequences, a characteristic illustration of which is found in a short epistle (attributed, certainly incorrectly, to ʿAbd al-Karîm al-Jîlî, but written much later than his time) published in Cairo (n.d.) with the title *Al-isfâr al-gharîb natijat al-safar al-qarîb*. It is explicitly inspired by Ibn ʿArabî's thought.

37. Muslim, *salât*, 62–63. The passage on *rukûʿ* is found in *Tanazzulât*, pp. 100–102. See also *Fut.* vol. 1, pp. 437–38; O.Y., vol. 6, pp. 370f.

38. Bukhâri, *tahajjud*, 15; *tawhîd*, 35 for the first hadith ("the divine descent in the last third of the night") and Muslim, *dhikr*, 20–21–22 for the second ("he who approaches Me by an armslength").

39. Ibn ʿArabî, *Tanazzulât*, p. 102.

40. Ibn ʿArabî, *Tanazzulât*, pp. 104–105.

41. *Fut.* vol. 1, pp. 433–34; O.Y., vol. 6, pp. 347–49.

42. In order to simplify the explanation, we are not dealing here with the distinction to be made between the intermediate *jalsa*, which do not entail the recitation of the *tashahhud*, and those that, after the performance of two *rakʿa* and at the end of the prayer, are accompanied by this recitation. On *julûs* and *tashahhud*, besides the *Tanazzulât*, pp. 108–109, cf. *Fut.* vol. 1, p. 427; O.Y., vol. 6, pp. 310f.

43. *Tanazzulât*, p. 110. Cf. *Fut.* vol. 1, p. 441; O.Y., vol. 6, pp. 336f.

44. *Fut.* vol. 3, pp. 127–28.

45. *Fut.* vol. 4, p. 24.

46. Ibn Hanbal, vol. 6, 256.

47. The term *nawâfil* is properly applied only to supererogatory acts that have one of the obligatory works as model and as "principle" (*asl*). Cf. *Fut.* vol. 1, p. 203; on their compensatory role, *Fut.* vol. 2, p. 268.

48. *Fut.* vol. 4, p. 24. On the *qurb al-farâʾid* and the *qurb al-nawâfil*, see also *Fut.* vol. 2, pp. 166–68, and vol. 2, p. 559; vol. 3, p. 67; vol. 4, p. 449; Ibn ʿArabî, *Kitâb al-ʿAbâdila*, p. 54.

49. *Fut.*, pp. 43–44; O.Y., vol. 12, pp. 81–86. See also *Fut.* vol. 3, p. 222, where Ibn ʿArabî writes: "Know that God has sittings with his ser-

vants equal to the number of acts which he has prescribed to them." The word *majâlis* is there to be understood in its broader sense and not in the specific sense (*majâlis al-hadîth*) that it has here.

50. This prayer, which is the first of the day, is also the one that was instituted the first; this explains why Ibn 'Arabî mentions it at the beginning of the list. It must be clarified that the number of *jalsa* here includes the short *jalsat al-istirâha* which comes at the moment where the person in prayer rises from prostration before returning to the vertical position.

51. Response to question 6, *Fut.* vol. 2, p. 44; O.Y., vol. 12, pp. 87–89.

52. In the response to question 8, for example, the traditional phrase of *du'â* to be recited in the *jalsa* is found word for word at the beginning of the text; and at the end of the text, there is a significant allusion to the astronomical determination of the times for prayer. As for the distinction the Ibn 'Arabî introduces (*Fut.* vol. 2, p. 44; O.Y., vol. 12, p. 83) between his own point of view and that of Tirmidhî (for which there are twelve extra *majâlis* "because he takes into consideration the [physical] nature of man"), let us briefly say that it is based on the fact that Adam's body was created by "the two hands" of God (while the spirit proceeds from a unique insufflation). To the *witr*, an odd-numbered prayer, is then added the *shaf'*, where the *rak'a* are of an even number.

53. *Fut.* vol. 2, p. 47; O.Y., vol. 12, p. 105–106.

54. *Fut.* vol. 2, p. 47; O.Y., vol. 12, pp. 108–11.

55. *Fut.* vol. 2, p. 48; O.Y., vol. 12, pp. 113–19.

56. *Fut.* vol. 2, pp. 99–100; O.Y., vol. 12, pp. 483–90.

57. *Fut.* vol. 2, p. 100; O.Y., vol. 12, pp. 490–95.

58. *Fut.* vol. 2, pp. 101–102; O.Y., vol. 12, pp. 500–507. On "prostration of the heart," see in particular *Fut.* vol. 3, pp. 302–308.

59. Muslim, *birr*, 136; Ibn Mâjah, *zuhd*, 16.

60. *Fut.* vol. 2, pp. 103–104; O.Y., vol. 12, pp. 508–20.

61. *Fut.* vol. 2, p. 103; O.Y., vol. 12, p. 514.

62. *Fut.* vol. 2, p. 105; O.Y., vol. 12, pp. 522–25.

63. *Fut.* vol. 2, p. 107; O.Y., vol. 12, pp. 538–44.

64. Dârimî, *wudû*, 3. Cf. Bukhârî, *wudû*, 3, where it is said that those who observe the rules of ablution "will have shining foreheads on the Resurrection Day."

65. *Fut.* vol. 2, pp. 108–109; O.Y., vol. 12, pp. 545–61.

66. *Fut.* vol. 2, pp. 125–28; O.Y., vol. 13, pp. 140–51.

67. Here Ibn ʿArabî recalls that he has already dealt with this subject in chapter 69, on prayer (*Fut.* vol. 1, p. 427; O.Y., vol. 6, pp. 310f.).

68. The word *tahiyya*, which has the meaning of "salutation," also has that of "vivification," which is essential to understanding this verse.

69. *Fut.* vol. 2, p. 88; O.Y., vol. 12, p. 408 (question 78).

70. *Fut.* vol. 2, p. 97; O.Y., vol. 12, p. 437 (question 86).

71. ʿAbd al-Karîm al-Jîlî, *Al-isfâr ʿan risâlat al-anwâr* (Damascus, 1929), p. 274. Cf., also, the *Nasîm al-Sahar*, p. 30, where Jîlî states that it is in ceaselessly observing his own form in the science of God that the *ʿabd* achieves contemplation of Divine Perfection. On the *Risâlat al-anwâr* itself, see our analysis in Chodkiewicz, *Sceau des saints*, chap. 10.

72. *Fut.* vol. 2, p. 122; O.Y., vol. 13, p. 111 (question 138).

73. *Fut.* vol. 3, p. 41. On *ʿubûda* and related ideas see *Fut.* vol. 2, pp. 213–16; vol. 3, pp. 18, 224.

74. Christian "exemplarism" (which has its sources in St. Augustine, St. Anselm of Canterbury, and, more clearly, in John Scotus Erigena) is inseparable from trinitary theology: it is in the Word that creatures have their "eternal exemplar" (Cf. Suso, *Œuvres complètes*, "Livre de la vérité", chap. 3, trans. J. Ancelet-Hustache [Paris, 1977]). Our borrowing from the vocabulary of the Rhineland mystics is certainly not to imply that their doctrine is identical to Ibn ʿArabî's.

75. *Fut.* vol. 4, p. 312; vol. 3, p. 255.

76. *Fut.* vol. 4, p. 316.

77. *Fut.* vol. 2, p. 587.

78. Contrary to usage, we translate *dahr* here by *eternity* rather than by *time*. For Ibn ʿArabî, *al-dahr* is a divine name, which excludes the possibility of its assimilation into a duration (cf. *Fut.* vol. 2, p. 201; vol. 3, pp. 201–202; vol. 4, pp. 175, 265). Cf. Jurjânî, *Taʿrîfât* (Cairo, 1938), p. 94: "*Al-dahr huwa l-ân al-dâʾim…wa bihi yattahid al-azal wa l-abad.*" On the inclusion of *Al-dahr* in the list of divine names, see Gimaret, *Noms divins en islam*, pp. 186–87 (see chap. 4, note 20). For all commentators, the interrogative particle *hal* should be interpreted in this verse as having the same meaning as *qad*.

79. *Fut.* vol. 3, p. 315. Concerning Ibn ʿArabî's interpretation of Qurʾân 76:1, see also *Fut.* vol. 2, pp. 201; vol. 4, p. 167, 340.

80. The authenticity of this hadith is more than controversial. But Ibn ʿArabî—after many other spiritual masters—validates it in virtue of an "unveiling" (*kashf*). On this validation (or invalidation, as the case may be) of prophetic traditions, see *Fut.* vol. 1, p. 150; O.Y., vol. 2, p. 358.

81. Ibn ʿArabî, who gives different interpretations of it according to the context, cites it on a number of occasions: *Fut.* vol. 2, pp. 298, 472, 508; vol. 3, pp. 44, 73, 101, 275, 289, 301, 536; vol. 4, p. 245; *Fus.* vol. 1, pp. 81, 122, 125, 145, etc. On the subject of the priority of knowledge of the self over the knowledge of the Lord, see *Fut.* vol. 3, p. 378: "Our knowledge of him comes after our knowledge of ourselves."

82. Concerning this saying, of which there are several variations reported, cf. Suyûtî, *Al-durr al-manthûr* (Beirut, 1314 A.H.), vol. 6, p. 297; Râzî, *Tafsîr*, vol. 30, p. 235.

83. *Fut.* vol. 1, p. 710; O.Y., X, p. 359; *Fut.* vol. 3, p. 3. For Rûzbehân Baqlî (*ʿArâʾis al-bayân*, vol. 2, p. 352), the interpretation of Qurʾân 76:1 is in accord with Ibn ʿArabî's doctrine.

84. *Fut.* vol. 1, p. 48 (verse); O.Y., vol. 1, p. 217. In the *Kitâb al-ʿAbâdila*, p. 113, Ibn ʿArabî, alluding to the rock of Moses (Qurʾân 2:60) and to Qurʾân 2:74, states "Rocks are the places of secrets and the springs of life."

85. *Ishârât al-qurʾân*, p. 37; see also Ibn ʿArabî, *Dîwân*, p. 174.

86. For references to this hadith, see note 10.

87. See M. Valsân's translation referenced in chap. 4, note 42, pp. 48–50. ʿAbd al-Karîm al-Jîlî gives the *in lam takun tarâhu* in his *Kitâb al-nuqta* (Cairo, n.d.), pp. 54–55, an interpretation based on the same caesura.

88. See *EI²*, s.v. *ʿibâdât*, G. Bousquet's article.

89. Ibn Hishâm, *Sîra nabawiyya* (Cairo, 1955), vol. 1, p. 238. This validation of the Muhammadan revelation by a representative of the Christian tradition is, from an Islamic point of view, neither the first nor the only one: there are also those of the monk Bahîra, of the *Najâshî* (the king of the Abyssinians), and of Salmân al-Fârisî, to whom a priest taught the signs by which the awaited prophet would be recognized.

90. Ibn ʿArabî, *Rûh al-quds*, p. 48 (no. 1); Ibn ʿArabî, *Tarjumân al-ashwâq*, p. 71 (commentary on the third verse of poem no. 18); *Fut.* vol. 3,

p. 395 (this last reference is to the section from chap. 369 that completes chap. 286, where the *manzil* of sura *Al-bayinna* is described; the citation is thus expressly connected with the theme of *Lam yakun*). In Ibn al-'Arîf's *Mahâsin al-majâlis*, ed. Asin Palacios [Paris, 1933], p. 97) there is another version of the wording cited by Ibn 'Arabî. On the problem of attribution that we mentioned, see the article by B. Halff, "Le Mahâsin al-majâlis...et l'œuvre du soufi hanbalite Al-Ansârî," REI, XXXIX, 2, p, 1971.

91. Ibn 'Arabî, *Kitâb al-'Abâdila*, p. 43. The term translated as "acts of supererogation" here is not *nawâfil* but *sunan*, which actually refers to the acts of supererogation instituted by the Prophet.

92. These are the verses already cited in note 4 of this chapter. See also verses, of identical meaning, appearing in *Fut.* vol. 4, p. 41.

93. On this recurring idea in Ibn 'Arabî's writings, see, e.g., *Fut.* vol. 3, pp. 72, 286, 316, 364, 503; vol. 4, pp. 212, etc.

94. *Fus.* vol. 1, p. 90.

95. *Lisân al-'arab*, vol. 14, p. 466b.

96. *Fus.* vol. 1, p. 225. See also *Fut.* vol. 3, p. 378.

97. *Fut.* vol. 4, p. 275.

98. *Fus.* vol. 3, p. 225.

99. This is an allusion to the verse *laysa ka-mithlihi shay'un* (Qur'ân 42:11), Ibn 'Arabî's double interpretation of which we summarized in chapter 2.

100. Ibn 'Arabî, *Tanazzulât*, p. 26. Our translation deviates slightly from the literal, to facilitate the reading of this quite dense text.

101. *Ijâz al-bayân*, p. 30; *Fut.* vol. 1, p. 417; O.Y., vol. 6, p. 245.

102. *Fut.* vol. 2, p. 136; O.Y., vol. 13, pp. 250–51 (see above, chap. 2).

103. *Fut.* vol. 1, p. 389; O.Y., vol. 6, p. 63. On the related idea of "perpetual invocation" (*dhikr dâ'im*) see especially *Fut.* vol. 3, pp. 222–23, 417; vol. 4, p. 184.

104. See above, chap. 4 and chap. 4, note 28. We are dealing here with what Ibn 'Arabî's school calls *"al-farq al-thânî,"* the "second separation" (cf. above, chap. 4). On this theme of "descendent realization," often brought up by Ibn 'Arabî, in particular in chapter 45 of the *Futûhât*, see Chodkiewicz, *Sceau des saints*, chap. 10.

ABOUT THE AUTHOR

Professor Michel Chodkiewicz is director of studies at the Ecole des hautes études en sciences sociales in Paris. The majority of his works have been dedicated to Ibn ʿArabî and his followers.

By the same author:

Emir ʿAbd al-Kader: Ecrits spirituels, editor and translator (Editions du Seuil, 1982).

Awhad al-Dîn Balyânî: Epître sur l'Unicité absolue, editor and translator (Les Deux Océans, 1982).

Le Sceau des Saints, prophétie et sainteté dans la doctrine d'Ibn Arabî (Gallimard, 1986). An English translation of this work is in preparation.

Les Illuminations de la Mecque, selected texts from the *Futûhât Makkiyya,* edited and translated with the collaboration of W. Chittick, C. Chodkiewicz, D. Gril, and J. Morris (Sindbad, 1988).

INDEX OF NAMES AND TECHNICAL TERMS

INDEX OF QUR'ANIC CITATIONS*

*If the number of the sura is not followed by a verse number, the reference is to the sura as a whole.